THE REFERENCE SHELF (*Continued*)

Volume XIV. $3.60

Volume XIII. $3.60

THE REFERENCE SHELF

Vol. 17   No. 7

POSTWAR
WAGE STABILIZATION

Compiled by
JULIA E. JOHNSEN

THE H. W. WILSON COMPANY
NEW YORK   1945

PREFACE

Throughout the more critical years of World War II a prominent factor in the internal economy of the nation has been the government effort to maintain stabilization. Most noteworthy among the controls set up, in relation to their popular effect, has been the Federal regulation of prices and wages. These controls, the major aim of which has been to check impending inflation, with all its disastrous connotations, have been widely acknowledged to have contributed to a marked extent to the well-being of the nation. At the same time there has been an appreciable amount of criticism and opposition. With the near approach of a postwar economy, with increasing pressure for extending or removing government regulations, the importance of a re-examination and revaluation of these economic controls becomes of moment.

The present wage stabilization movement is closely associated with government price control in origin and in common reaction and effect. It was discussed during the consideration of the Emergency Price Control Act of January 1942. In the Act of October 2, 1942, amending that law, wages were definitely brought into the anti-inflationary program under broad and strong statutory control. The National War Labor Board has been responsible primarily for the administration of wage regulation, but the actions of various other government agencies, including the Executive, have served to modify and complicate the total results and effects.

Organized labor soon protested the inequalities and inequities of having wages under more or less rigid government control, with the increasing lag of wages behind the rising costs of living. Its contentions for fairer wages and for the liberalization or abrogation of the formula applied to wage adjustments have gone through various phases. More immediately, indirect benefits have been increasingly sought, and advanced wages that might offset, in the postwar period, losses because of shorter hours and other changes. A guaranteed annual wage has also become an objective of the Congress of Industrial Organizations, and a study of this proposal was ordered just recently by the late President Roosevelt.

The conviction exists among many that wage controls cannot safely be relinquished in the immediate future, but should be continued after the close of the war, at least until normal production and economic balance are again assured and inflation no longer threatens. Countering this conviction is a strong movement for the restoration, with the least delay, of the fullest possible measure of "free enterprise," with wages once more under the control of the labor-employer groups immediately concerned. Some look to flexibility and freedom to secure the right to push up wages, others seek the same conditions of freedom to hold down undue rises, and to re-establish practical adjustments in line with industrial needs, expansion and profits.

Economic effects are woven deeply into the lives of peoples and of nations, and carry to the far ends of the earth. Whether government controls in a total war effort are a measure of the need for like controls in peace remains for the future to decide. The right relationship of economic factors rests on a profound and pervasive hope, a hope for an orderly, constructive, and better way of life, a way that will react not only to the higher welfare of individuals, but of mankind.

The question of wage stabilization has been examined with respect to some of the leading aspects at stake. For greater timeliness, and since earlier material on wages has been covered in two previous numbers of the Reference Shelf, *Wages and Prices,* April 1942 and *Wage Stabilization and Inflation,* May 1943, this book covers mostly the more recent material. It has been the aim to represent without bias, in discussions and in bibliography, varied and diverse views.

The compiler acknowledges gratefully copyright permissions and other courtesies that have facilitated the preparation of this book.

JULIA E. JOHNSEN

April 26, 1945

CONTENTS

GENERAL DISCUSSION

A STABLE ECONOMY FOR THE POSTWAR WORLD [1]

It is an arresting fact, and a disturbing commentary on our institutions, that our economic system has worked better during the war than it did in the preceding years. It has worked better in that more has been produced. It has worked better in that distribution has been more equitable and more economical. Industrial production stands 125 per cent above the 1939 level. Income has been more widely spread. Distribution of food has been more healthful. We now have a more equitable tax system.

Despite the fact that individual incomes have more than doubled for the nation as a whole, we have avoided a runaway spiral of prices. As a result of price control, we have reduced our personal debts and have accumulated personal savings at an unheard-of rate. Our concern now is with how our economic, political, and social systems are going to function during the postwar transition and in the peacetime that will follow. We are anxious, of course, to be rid of wartime controls and we feel the cumulative strain of several years of government orders and regulations that have been irritating at the best and maddening at the worst. Most of us have accepted these controls as necessary, but in our hearts we do not like them.

After the Armistice on November 11, 1918, the major controls were lifted almost overnight. Opinion was unanimous that prices would move downward and that maximum prices were entirely academic. Removal of price control was begun by the War Industries Board two days after the signing of the Armistice. By the end of January it had removed all restrictions on the prices of coke and coal. The Food Administration began liquidation in mid-December 1918. Between January 10 and February 22, 1919, licensing requirements were withdrawn, thus

[1] By Don D. Humphrey, Chief, Price Analysis and Review Branch, Office of Price Administration, Washington, D.C. *National Conference of Social Work, Proceedings.* 1944. p. 59-66. Columbia University Press. New York.

automatically canceling all food regulations. There was a general desire to abolish, not only price controls, but all government regulations as rapidly as possible. Even a modest program suggested by the Secretary of War, Newton D. Baker, under which the army would have been demobilized in accordance with occupational employment opportunities, was ignored in the general impatience to get men out of the army. By April 1919, almost two million men had been demobilized. At the same time, the operations of war plants were abruptly reduced by the cancellation of contracts. Neither the Federal Government nor the state and local governments had planned any compensating public works programs to cushion the transitional shock. Purchasing power created by the war was rapidly cut off. Prices began to fall.

In the following year four million men were demobilized, government expenditures were cut from an annual rate of about twenty-two billion dollars to about five billion dollars. Between two and three million men were discharged from the production of war goods. Nevertheless, the bottom did not drop out of the market. Consumer buying continued. Automobile output and employment in furniture manufacturing, both of which had been sharply curtailed during the war, began to rise before the end of 1918. In the manufacture of clothing and textiles, employment rose, as did the output of all nondurable goods. After the spring of 1919, in fact, total employment increased.

Wholesale prices, which reached a low three months after the Armistice, began a rise which continued rapidly until May 1920. In fifteen months all wholesale prices increased by 87 per cent, the peak being 55 per cent higher than the levels prevailing in the month before the Armistice.

The cost of living rose rapidly. In sixteen months the index rose by 29 per cent. In the same short space of time, retail food prices rose 34 per cent, reaching a level of 126 per cent above that of July 1914, the last prewar month. Retail clothing prices also rose continuously, and by June 1920, the clothing index was triple that of the July 1914 level. At the time of the Armistice it had been double that level. Sugar, which sold for five cents a pound when the war broke out in 1914 and for eleven cents a pound when the war ended in 1918, reached twenty-seven cents a pound in 1920. Bituminous coal, which sold at $5.50 a ton in 1914 and $8.00 a ton in 1918, reached $12.50 in 1920.

The postwar inflation caused such popular indignation that in August 1919, the President sent a message to Congress. As a result, food controls were revived and, in fact, were extended even beyond their wartime scope. These efforts to re-establish controls constituted an admission that they had been dropped too hastily. But it was too late, and the attempt to reintroduce price regulation proved to be futile.

These experiences, someone has suggested, ought to be carefully put together and labeled "How Not to Do It."

Now there are some who say that we have ogres in the Federal Government who want to control merely for the sake of controlling. It is the opposite extreme, I think, that we need to guard against, namely, the danger of lifting controls merely for the sake of lifting them.

Why has our economy worked better during the war? First, there has been no problem of markets. We needed more goods of every description, and the enormous volume of war production meant that wages were put into the pockets of workers although there was not a corresponding supply of goods on which their money could be spent.

Secondly, there have been controls which prevented the expansion of production from being hampered by speculation and artificial shortages. There have been controls which prevented hoarding of goods. While these controls have operated most imperfectly, we have obtained a vast increase in output together with a drastic change in its composition and character, as for example, in the shift from the manufacture of automobiles to the production of tanks.

Thirdly, is the spirit of agreement regarding the basic job to be done. Patriotism covers part of it. We have operated under a forced draft that would not have been possible under normal conditions. But beyond that, I believe that we have done so well because the government was generally supported by all groups in the community. Moreover, we felt assured that whatever needed to be done would be done, and because of this assurance, business and labor and agriculture were willing to produce.

In this, I find the key to our postwar needs. If we want to make our economy work as well during the peace as it has during the war, it can be done by means of this same attitude. Despite the large backlog of unfilled demand for consumer goods, and despite the vast accumulation of personal savings, one senses everywhere an uncertainty regarding the turn of events at the war's end. Collapse has followed every war in the past, and we are naturally anxious lest history repeat itself. Uncertainty and fear can cause consumers and businessmen alike to withhold their orders, "to see what happens first." If a postwar collapse is to be avoided, we must first banish the fear of collapse. Only the government can provide such assurance. The firmer the commitment that the government stands ready to sustain a stable economy at high levels of production and employment, the more effective and far-reaching the guarantee, the less will be the positive action which the government will be called upon to take in order to make good its commitment. The more effective the guarantee—the more widely it is accepted—the greater will be the confidnce in the economic outlook and the more certainly will the backlog of demand be translated into orders in the market.

The Federal Government is now buying war goods at an annual rate of $75,000,000,000 which is greater than the total national income before the war. What will happen when this demand is withdrawn and when, in addition, six or eight million soldiers return, looking for jobs?

Today the labor market is geared to a forty-eight-hour work week, with time-and-a-half for all hours in excess of forty. The first effect of any general easing of the manpower situation will be an elimination of overtime. Moving from a forty-eight-hour to a forty-hour week will entail a cut of just under 25 per cent in weekly wages.

At the same time, reconversion will shift employment from the war industries back to civilian industries. Quite apart from the matter of overtime, this means a reduction in earnings, because it is in the war industries that the highest wages are being paid. Even if total employment is maintained at present peak levels and even if wage rates remain unchanged, these two factors alone will reduce the annual purchasing power of wage earners by fifteen or twenty billion dollars. If employment drops 10 per cent and wage rates are lowered 10 per cent, that will take another $15,000,000,000 out of our consumer demand. Thus we are confronted with an estimate of thirty to thirty-five billion dollars that will not go into pay envelopes. Can the economy take such a blow?

These adjustments will be difficult. But no one should doubt our ability to make them successfully, provided that the national buying power can be sustained and markets found for all the goods we can produce.

Can we find those markets? First, there is an enormous backlog of demand for millions of automobiles, vacuum cleaners, refrigerators, house furnishings, and other durable goods. We shall come out of the war with over one hundred billion dollars of wartime savings with which to purchase them.

Secondly, there is a vast backlog of business investment requirements. Stocks will have to be replenished, obsolete and worn equipment will have to be replaced, many plants will have to be expanded to fit increased civilian requirements. Business will have liquid reserves accumulated during the war amounting to more than twenty-five billion dollars.

Thirdly, there is a great backlog of regular public construction, local, state, and Federal. In recent years many necessary projects have had to be suspended for lack of manpower and materials; even essential repairs and replacements have been postponed.

Fourthly, full advantage must be taken of the export market. Europe and Asia will need vast quantities of goods of every character and description, and ours will be the only industrial economy which will not have suffered the ravages of war. I have no doubt that the greatest single contribution that we can make to world prosperity and peace will be to maintain full employment at home. By doing this we shall be serving, not only ourselves, but the cause of international stability as well.

Finally, there are vast markets which have never been tapped. There are still millions of our farmers who do not have electricity, who still lack modern improvements and conveniences of every description. Before the war there were tens of millions of city dwellers who were living below the level of proper nutrition, who lacked the money to buy decent houses or to wear decent clothing. Although our production of automobiles, house furnishings, and equipment was large, it was still far below the actual requirements of our citizens. Moreover, as a nation we have unfilled needs for more schools and colleges, for more hospitals, for more parks, for modern highways and bridges— in fact, for the development of the complete, modern, social, economic civilization with benefits for all which we, of all nations, are so fully capable of building.

Taken together, these demands can more than fill the void that will be left when government war expenditures are tapered off. They can keep our economy running indefinitely at peak capacity. But we must remember that these are only potential demands. Whether they will materialize in actual orders will depend, first of all, upon how effectively we plan the job of unwinding our wartime economy. If, when the war is over, we fail to take full and immediate advantage of our export opportunities, if we are not prepared with a program of public works when it is needed, business activity will slow down. If that happens, employment, pay rolls, and prices will begin to fall, and the vast potential demand will dry up.

Men who have lost their jobs may draw from the family savings to buy bread and to pay rent. But will they buy a new refrigerator and a new car? And will they make a first payment on a new home? If we permit the level of employment to drop, most of the hundred billion dollars of wartime savings will stay in the banks.

What is true of consumers is also true of businessmen. Businessmen do not invest on a falling market. If prices are dropping, there will not be much restocking and there will not be much replacing of equipment. To a large extent the $25,-000,000,000 of reserves that business has accumulated will remain right where they are—in reserve.

In other words, if we permit the economy to sag immediately after the war, we face the menace of deflation feeding upon itself. There is a school of economists who believe that deflation is necessary to our economic health. Prices and wages, they say, must be cut back before we can go ahead. This view is comparable in economics to the blood-letting stage in the development of medicine. Prices were farther out of balance at the end of the deflation in 1932 than they were at the beginning of 1929. I do not accept the old dogma that we must go through the wringer of liquidation and bankruptcy after a few years of prosperity. Balance is not achieved by cumulative movements whereby wages are reduced because prices are reduced and prices, in turn, are further cut because wages are cut. We need no general deflation. Quite the contrary: high wages must be maintained. It was the high wages achieved during World War I that accounted in a large measure for the prosperity of the twenties, and it was the failure to raise wages or adjust prices in the late twenties that contributed to the collapse. I distinguish, of course, between the reduction in prices to match technological reductions in cost and cyclical or postwar deflation. We must have low profit margins per unit and efficient production for mass markets.

The greatest obstacle to maintain the high level of performance that our economy has proved itself capable of is distrust of government. The steel workers, who see the threat of a return to the irregular work of prewar years, demand a guaranteed annual wage. Farmers, fearing a collapse, demand support prices. Business demands the liquidation of the vast industrial empire that the government now owns in a manner that will interfere least with private enterprise.

It will be generally agreed that only the Federal Government can provide the requisite guarantee that our people want. Yet the distrust of government lies deeply imbedded in our history. Most of us have been familiar since childhood with the cartoons that represented the politician as a fat bureaucrat with graft bulging from his pockets. This was understandable. We were a new nation, and even a generation ago the periodic breakdown of the economy could be tolerated. There was a time when most of our city workers were not more than a generation from the farm, and when depression hit and the plant closed, the individual could return to the family farm and there find a living.

Although we wish to cling to the old tradition, the fact is that we have adopted the industrial system. Our economy has grown infinitely more complex. We are no longer individually self-sufficient; we are dependent upon outside markets. Industrial workers can no longer retreat to the family farm. In fact, the farmer of today is almost completely dependent upon the markets provided by the industrial workers. Moreover, our leading markets have become international ones. We still like to indulge in the pleasant, romantic idea of retiring to a few acres to make a living and to find security; but we know that the industrial system is here to stay. Mass production is too efficient for us to give it up. This necessarily means that, for most of us, the kind of living we make and the kind of security that we find will be in the big industrial cities. We shall find a reasonable security and make a good living only if we have the imagination and courage to make the industrial system serve us as well in peace as it does in war. And this requires a reexamination of our attitude toward government.

We can no longer tolerate the breakdowns and the wholesale bankruptcies that periodically beset us in the past. Therefore, the function of government in a highly organized industrial society must be to sustain the level of national income at all times in order to insure that markets are available for all that can be produced under conditions where everyone who can and wants to work has a job. It will be difficult enough adjustment for our soldiers to come home to jobs and to security; for them to return to unemployment and insecurity would be intolerable.

The central function of the postwar government will not be to regulate the economy, as has been necessary during the war, but to provide the framework within which free enterprise can regularly produce as bountifully in peace as it has in war. We accepted a generation ago the control of credit by the Federal Reserve Board; we now need to put fiscal policy on a similar footing.

When, for any reason, the flow of private investment and consumption expenditures diminish, the government can, by decreasing its taxes and increasing its expenditures, offset that decline. On the other hand, when the flow of private expenditures increases to a point which threatens inflation, through increased taxes and decreased government expenditures, the economy can be kept on an even keel. This is an extremely powerful device. By determining the time and the rate at which it releases purchasing power into the markets through its expenditures, the government can maintain an even flow of purchasing power at levels sufficient to provide markets for all we can produce.

I believe that we shall have less government and a healthier, more vigorous free enterprise by planning and agreeing in advance upon a program of government action rather than by waiting for disaster and then resorting to makeshifts. Any suggestion that government action will be too little and too late will confirm the fear of collapse and unloose the forces of deflation. If we are unprepared to accept enough government in time, we invariably end with too much. If we are reluctant to grant the government enough power to meet its essential obligations, the unsolved overtake us, and in the ensuring crisis, we are obliged to go far beyond what would have been necessary if we had taken steps sooner. Our experience in the thirties yields a significant lesson. Because we did not promptly require the government to assume responsibility for stemming the growing depression in 1930, the complete collapse of our economy in 1932 left us with no alternative but for the government to move in much further in order to put our economy back on the road to recovery.

If we want to avoid too much government after the war, we must recognize in advance the proper functions of government and we must agree on the policies and on the appropriate organization to discharge those functions efficiently and democratically. We can avoid the controls that will surely be demanded after a collapse by planning now to avoid that collapse. Fear, which is half the cause of collapse, can be banished by being firm in our commitments and by seeing to it that they are neither too little nor too late.

WAGE REGULATION IN POSTWAR AMERICA [2]

In prewar days, direct governmental regulation of wages was primarily limited to the establishment of minimum hourly wages to assist in eliminating substandard conditions of living. The National Recovery Act did, for a short time, extensively regulate labor costs in some industries but the results were neither effective nor promising. There were also governmental programs to protect standard wage-scales from the forces of unregulated competition such as in the Davis-Bacon Act for the building trades and in the Guffey Act for the coal industry. The basic governmental regulation affecting wage policies, however, was indirect. Reference is to the encouragement of collective bargaining under the National Labor Relations Act. This Act also recognized collective bargaining as the institution best adapted for the determination of wage policies whenever the employees are organized into unions of their own choosing.

Wage regulation in prewar America primarily consisted, therefore, of (1) the encouragement of collective bargaining; (2) the specification of minimum hourly rates to correct substandards of living; and (3) specific regulations to meet the particular problems of certain industries.

The national wage policies of a peacetime economy were not adapted, of course, to the mobilization of national resources for war. The war economy of the past two years was dominated by scarcities, not only of civilian goods but, more important, of life-saving military supplies. Cost considerations were therefore of secondary interest, either to the nation fighting a war for its existence or to producers who had a virtually guaranteed demand for all goods they could turn out. Vast increases in purchasing power occurred while production expanded although the supply of many important consumers goods was curtailed or entirely shut off. Manpower shortages resulted not only from the creation of an armed force and because of the difficulties of shifting employees to new areas and to new industries but also from the increased demand for war materials.

[2] By George W. Taylor, National War Labor Board. *American Economic Review*. 34:sup.181-92. March 1944.

Great concern was expressed about the widening gap between purchasing power and the supply of consumer goods. Programs effectively to control the growth of this gap have not generally been developed as respects either taxation or savings. The pent-up force of unused purchasing power has, nevertheless, not erupted. It may well have done so if there had been a pell-mell race between wages and prices. This could easily have created a demand for goods not merely to meet individual needs but to provide some measure of security. An inflationary movement of this sort would have jeopardized the maximum production of war goods and resulted in a haphazard distribution of available consumer goods. Not the least important consequences of a pell-mell race between wages and prices would have been in a staggering increase in the cost of the war to be bequeathed to future generations.

Such considerations led this country not only into extensive regulation of wages but into the widespread regulation of all phases of our economic life. There were no guides based upon experience. There was only a determination to do everything necessary to win a war against brutal enemies and at the same time to take every intelligent step to minimize inflationary tendencies.

The year of 1943 was filled with great events and historical moments. One of the great facts of 1943 is that inflationary forces were held in check.

The wartime economic policies center about the program to stabilize all prices and all wages. Initially formulated by the President on April 27, 1942, a part of the stabilization program was later adopted by Congress in the Act of October 2, 1942. Appraisals of the results of the stabilization plans vary with one's definition of stabilization and with the measures of the relative changes in wages and in prices which are used. A detailed discussion of these particular questions cannot now be undertaken. It is pertinent to the purpose of this paper, however, to review the program of wage regulation as carried out in wartime America because of its significance to postwar policy questions.

In the development of a national wage stabilization program, work was undertaken in a virtually uncharted field. Our knowledge of wages, of the forces behind their fluctuation, and of their intricate interrelationships, is really not every extensive. It had long been assumed in many quarters, for example, that there was something quite fundamental in saying that "within non-competing groups, all other things being equal, wages tend to be equal." One does not work very long in setting wage rates, however, before contacting strong forces which act to create disparities between wages even within interchangeable groups of employees. The forces which press toward disequality are evidently more potent than those which tend toward equality since, at any time, the dominant characteristic of industrial wage structures is a great and wide diversity of wages. Perhaps this is because "all other things" are seldom and perhaps never equal.

Wage regulation on any widespread scale must center largely about differences in wage rates and the determination of a myriad of complex rate relationships. In a surprisingly large number of instances, action taken to equalize related rates serves not to stabilize the rates at all but only to generate an insistent demand for the "restoration of historical differences." This force is often particularly strong even as between interchangeable groups of employees and during wartime when there is no unemployment.

Stabilization does not mean the equalizing of rates. Nor can it mean that all wage-rate relationships would be "frozen." Some changes in such relationships are necessary to account for changed economic conditions and to use certain wage disparities as an allocator of manpower. Wage regulation is not a simple matter even in wartime when there are also programs for extensive regulation of prices, production schedules, manpower movement, profits and salaries. The complexities of the problem increased naturally when it became necessary to restrict both the process of collective bargaining over wages and the wage determinations customarily made by employers. Use could not be made, therefore, of the established procedures for setting wages.

Collective bargaining, nevertheless, has been materially strengthened as a democratic institution during the first two years of war. The maintenance-of-membership clauses, evolved by the War Labor Board, not only settled the serious question of union status for the period of war, but insured that unions and collective bargaining would be preserved despite the serious threats to their existence that arose with the war and with economic regulation. Comprehensive labor agreements have been developed in many plants and industries where only casual and doubtful arrangements previously prevailed. Wage-rate schedules have been embodied in agreements, often for the first time. Grievance procedures to take care of the day-to-day problems of industrial relations are slowly but surely being made more adequate. Arbitration has been widely adopted and commonly accepted as a proper means of settling many disputes. These developments, and many more which might be mentioned, are building collective bargaining into a well-developed institution despite the restrictions imposed by wartime regulations upon wage changes. It is also of moment to recall that all the terms of collective agreements, except for wages, are subject to being worked out by bargaining between the parties themselves. There is, therefore, a not inconsiderable area in which unrestricted collective bargaining is being undertaken.

It is to be hoped that collective bargaining will be an institution sufficiently strong to carry a major part of the postwar industrial relations program. If this is so, extensive wage regulation may be unnecessary in postwar years.

It is now necessary to consider the fundamental details of the wage-regulation program which has been developed as a phase of the economic stabilization program in wartime.

Some forces, acting to bring about wage changes, have such a widespread and permeating effect that they may be compared to ground swells which powerfully move general levels upward or downward. In recent years, these forces have frequently resulted in uniform "across-the-board" increases to all the units in an industry or throughout large groups of industries. They have been in response to increased costs of living, increased profits, decreasing reserves of manpower or to organization for collective bargaining processes.

Other forces often necessitate particular wage changes within the general level. They may be compared to crosscurrents or to surface movements. At any general level of wages, crosscurrents exert frequent pressures for a change in the relationship between the wages paid by plant A and plant B. There are also surface movements acting to change the relationship between the rates paid within a plant to occupation X and to occupation Y. A lack of balance between the wage rates of two particular plants in an industry will persist even after ground-swell pressures have resulted in a general wage increase to all the plants in the industry. Similarly, a real intraplant inequality between occupational groups remains even after a general "across-the-board" wage increase has been provided to every employee in the plant.

As the existing wage stabilization program has evolved, it has been essential to provide not only for a limitation upon changes in the general level of wages, but also to provide a basis for making necessary changes in interplant and intraplant wage-rate relationships. A simple stabilization program would be wholly inadequate if it failed to provide for the various types of wage adjustments which are constantly being made at one point or another in the national wage structure.

The Little Steel formula, related to general wage increases, and the wage bracket program, related to interplant differentials, are the basic parts of the present stabilization program. Changes in intraplant wage relationships may also be approved, as long as production costs are not appreciably increased, on the basis of job analysis or by comparison with prevailing relationships between jobs in other plants. It has also been recognized that grossly inequitable rates should be corrected, even in wartime, and provision is made for the approval of increases in wage rates necessary to correct substandards of living. . . .

Interplant Wage Relationships. Variations in wage rates between different plants frequently represent an established and a stabilized relationship. Even these variations may be subject to change from time to time, however, as changes occur in the causative factors, such as ability to pay, area wage levels, and the local labor market. These are the crosscurrents affecting wage relationships.

A comprehensive wage stabilization program in this time of war has to provide not only for necessary adjustments of interplant rate relationships in order to maximize productive efficiency, but also for adjustments within the existing general level of wages if inflationary tendencies are to be controlled. There would obviously be a slow but steady rise in the general level of wages if rates between plants were first equalized and then further adjusted to restore historical differences. On the other hand, relatively low wage rates which nevertheless drew sufficient manpower to a certain plant when there was a readily available labor supply may be entirely obsolete at a time of manpower shortages. If such a plant is to be counted upon to supply war goods, its wages must be brought into a closer alignment with the great majority of plants in its area.

Prior to April 8, 1943, when Executive Order No. 9328 was issued, the National War Labor Board was free to adjust interplant rate relationships through the exercise of its judgment based upon data concerning (a) the relationship between the wage rates paid in various plants of the same company; (b) the relationship between wages paid by companies in the same industry regardless of area; and (c) the relationship between plants in the same labor market area regardless of industry. The weight given to each factor in particular cases obviously could not be precisely evaluated. The problem before the Board was to differentiate between those "sound and tested" rate differentials which should not be changed even in wartime and the disparities which had to be minimized in order to create a balanced rate relationship. Attention to such matters in time of war, moreover, had to take cognizance of two all-pervading factors: the relationships between wage rates paid by individual companies in particular labor market areas, irrespective of industry, became increasingly important as manpower problems mounted at a time of guaranteed demand for all products; there are indications that variations in wage rates between plants in the same industry, as well as in the same area, tend to widen when ample manpower reserves are readily available but to narrow in a period of manpower shortages.

The principal effect of Executive Order No. 9328 was the withdrawal of the authority of the War Labor Board to approve further corrections of interplant inequalities. The May 12, 1943,

clarifying order of the Director of Economic Stabilization, however, again recognized the necessity for wage adjustments in
interplant relationships. Under that order they were limited to
a minimum, however, and had to be determined in accordance
with an objective standard rather than through the exercise of
judgment. In the first place, interplant wage adjustments were
virtually restricted to rate relationships by industries within particular areas and, secondly, they were to be made by reference
to so-called "established brackets of sound and tested rates for
occupational groups in each area."

The various Regional War Labor Boards were called upon
to specify for particular occupations in each industry, and in each
labor market area, a range of wage rates encompassing all the
various rates being paid which were deemed to be "sound and
tested." This compilation has been almost completed. All
existing wage rates within the brackets are to be maintained.
Only those rates which are below the minimum of the bracket
are subject to change for the adjustment of interplant relationships and then to a point not above the minimum of the bracket.
In actual operation, the minimum of the bracket rates are approximately 10 per cent below the average wage paid in an area
for a particular type of work. In general, therefore, interplant
wage relationships can now be changed only as respects occupational wages which are 10 per cent or more below the average
wage paid in the area and then only to within 10 per cent of
the average wage. The brackets of sound and tested rates, which
are considered as stabilized rates, embrace the large majority of
rates being paid. Provision was made for changing rates to a
point above the minimum of the bracket only in rare and unusual
cases where a greater change in interplant relationships was clearly necessary for the successful prosecution of the war.

Intraplant Wage Relationships. At any general level of
wages, and even though there may be no question of interplant
relationships, problems frequently arise concerning the intraplant relation between the rates paid for occupation X as compared with occupation Y. The absence of a proper internal rate
alignment may often be more destructive of employee morale
than interplant differences. One of the most surprising findings

incident to the wartime regulation of wages is that large segments of American industry have neglected the establishment of job classifications and rate schedules designed to insure a reasonably balanced internal wage-rate structure.

The minute aspects of intraplant wage relationships cannot be worked out by government regulation if local conditions, which are compelling, are to be taken into account. Executive Order No. 9328 permits the reclassification of jobs to bring about a proper internal rate relationship, as long as there is no resultant "appreciable increase" in the costs of production. The War Labor Board, through its General Orders, has encouraged the installation and refinement of job classifications and rate schedules by management and through collective bargaining. It has been found necessary in particular instances, however, for the Board actually to specify detailed classification and rate schedules in order to resolve a labor dispute which threatens to interfere with the successful prosecution of the war. No government agency should undertake to work out management problems of this sort on any extensive scale. It goes almost without saying that the numerous and intricate intraplant rate relationships can best be developed by those familiar with the jobs and with the people in each plant. Collective bargaining, using the results of job studies, is the process for considering intraplant wage relationships whenever employees are organized into unions.

Substandards of Living. The correction of substandards of living has always been a justifiable reason for wage increases under the wartime stabilization program. The Fair Labor Standards Act presently requires a minimum wage of 30 cents per hour although virtually all industries in interstate commerce are now subject to a 40 cents per hour minimum wage because of action taken by industry committees under that Act. The War Labor Board has no power to order any minimum wage for general application, but it will approve voluntary wage increases up to 50 cents per hour to correct substandards of living and in so doing it will make the minimum adjustments in interrelated job classifications which are necessary to maintain productive efficiency.

The tremendous growth and change in the composition of national production, in response to the demands of war, has resulted in significant departures from prewar standards of employment, wage rates, hours of work, total earnings, and living costs. Wartime wage policies center about stabilization to minimize inflation while allowing sufficient flexibility to adjust wage-rate relationships in the interest of maximum production. The major problems of the transition to a postwar economy will be generally similar in nature. They may be concerned, however, either with the avoidance of a rapid and cumulative inflation or of a sweeping and cumulative deflation. The creation of new relationships in the national wage structure will be particularly urgent as adjustments are sought, not only to liquidate the restrictions imposed during the war, but also in response to the new set of economic conditions which will be faced.

Shortened work weeks will bring proportionately greater decreases in weekly take-home since overtime pay will be lost. Basic wage rates have been maintained, however, more closely to prewar levels than either average hourly rates or take-home wages. It may be anticipated that, by and large, there will be no drastic changes in straight-time hourly rates. At any event, such a prospect appears to be likely unless there develops a ground-swell movement in the cost of living. Even should there be no fundamental change in the general level of wage rates, intercompany and intraplant rate relationships will almost inevitably be subject to extensive readjustment as competitive relationships again come into operation. These necessary adjustments will not be amenable to general over-all regulation but will require a series of programs worked out for individual situations. They should be based upon the economics of particular industries and upon the status of individual companies.

One can certainly not anticipate how government regulation could possibly be effective in making the postwar wage adjustments which will be necessary, even if there is no general movement of wages, at a time when the right to strike will again be freely exercisable and when, it is hoped, there will be a marked relaxation of governmental regulation of price, production, and consumption. And underlying every postwar problem is the question: How can employment be maintained? No one can now forecast the effect of this question upon wage-rate policy.

The inevitable maladjustments and pressures in the postwar years will undoubtedly give rise to numerous demands for governmental regulation of wages. There may be problems so acute, moreover, as to necessitate some governmental regulations. Before jumping to any hasty conclusions about such questions, it is well to recall that, in peacetime America, the national labor policy which was finally evolved recognized collective bargaining as the institution charged with determining the principal questions of wages. Wartime regulations have interfered in many ways with the normal use of collective bargaining but they have also developed it as a useful institution in many other ways. It has a vital function to perform in postwar years. To a large extent, the degree of governmental wage regulation which will be demanded, and perhaps which will be necessary in postwar years, rests largely upon the efficacy of collective bargaining.

Many of those who want to see the postwar wage problem met primarily by collective bargaining rather than by government regulation, are motivated partially by a realization that extensive wage regulation may well mean an extensive regulation of all phases of our economic life. One of the most urgent aspects of postwar regulation of wages is the need now to develop collective bargaining relationships so that they can assume heavy postwar burdens. This emphasis upon collective bargaining is not only in line with America's prewar labor policy but is prompted by a realization of the complexities of the problems involved in working out wage relationships. Most of them can best be worked out by the parties directly affected. Wartime regulations have, however, made clear the importance of wage-rate differentials between various plants in the same industry or the same area. It is concluded, therefore, that the blueprinting of the postwar job of collective bargaining should not preclude careful attention to the possibilities of industry-wide collective bargaining in determining interplant relationships. In addition, if it is to attain the fundamental position assigned to it in prewar years, collective bargaining must be developed with full consideration to the ways of achieving high and secure wages to employees, reasonable profits to employers, and relatively low costs to consumers.

The importance assigned to the role of collective bargaining in meeting the postwar wage problem is based upon a conviction that wartime regulation does not point the way to a peacetime pattern. If collective bargaining is developed as the foundation of postwar labor relations, then governmental wage regulation will most likely follow the pattern of the prewar years rather than that of the war years. This would indicate the need of attention to minimum wage legislation designed to correct substandards of living and the likelihood of requests for specific legislation to meet the economic problems of particular industries. One cannot now visualize what lies ahead in these directions. One can now, however, note the possible use of the tripartite agency as an effective mechanism in dealing with such matters.

The tripartite agency to deal with economic matters, and particularly with wage questions, is gradually evolving as one of the effective instruments of government. Its use—a logical extension of collective bargaining—presupposes that detailed questions of industrial economics can best be resolved through discussion of those directly representative of the conflicting interests of those concerned. The procedure was first attempted, on any large scale, in the committees which developed industry codes under the National Recovery Administration. The results were not very salutary, to say the least, but some experience with a new procedure had been attained. The next significant use of the tripartite machinery was in the so-called "industry committees" which determined the minimum wages for particular industries under the Fair Labor Standards Act. The results of this second use of the tripartite mechanism were quite encouraging. Then the National War Labor Board was established with a tripartite composition, and, in my judgment, the efficacy of such a type of organization became fully evident. The stresses and strains of the moment should not be permitted to obscure the strength of the War Labor Board, derived from its tripartite composition, in developing a well-rounded and workable program under adverse conditions. Its method has been to charge representatives of industry, labor, and the public with equal responsibility, not only for settling controversies and evolving policies, but for carrying out the conclusions reached by the majority. The tripartite process embodies the essence of our democratic wisdom. On the record, there are strong reasons for believing that in the tripartite board there is gradually evolving a new type of administrative arm of government which can be of inestimable value in resolving wage questions—and perhaps economic questions in general—under a general policy established by the legislative branch. Its usefulness should not be overlooked when a program for postwar wage policy is under consideration.

The suggested program for treating postwar wage problems is primarily one under which government regulation on any large scale is quite unnecessary. There are not many who still believe there can be or should be a return to the unilateral determination of wages by employers as a standard practice. A choice must be made, therefore, between dependence for wage determination in postwar years upon collective bargaining or government regulation. There are real difficulties involved in making collective bargaining work. This is, however, the task which lies ahead as we strive to preserve and to protect economic democracy. With an effective collective bargaining system, and perhaps a fuller use of the tripartite administrative body in developing the government regulations considered to be essential in limited areas, the mechanism is available to resolve postwar wage questions in a manner appropriate to a democracy.

PROBLEMS OF WAGE POLICY AFTER THE WAR [3]

What problems of wages and hours will confront the nation after the war, and what should be done about them? Should wages and working hours be permitted to move freely in response to whatever market influences exist, or should the nation have a wage policy and an hour policy which would limit their movements? If the latter, what should the policy be, how

[3] By Sumner H. Slichter, Lamont University Professor, Harvard University. *Academy of Political Science. Proceedings.* 21, no.1:64-88. May 1944. Reprinted from "The Problems of War and the Transition to Peace." Columbia University. New York.

should it be related to price policy, how should it be made, and how should it be implemented? Should the present War Labor Board be kept, and, if so, what mandate and authority should it have? Attempts to reach conclusions about these questions should take account of five principal possibilities:

1. That the wage level after the war will be too high in relation to the price level for a satisfactory level of employment;

2. That the wage level will be so low in relation to the price level that the demand for labor exceeds the supply;

3. That the wage structure will be badly distorted in relation to the patterns of labor demand and labor supply after the war;

4. That the country will be confronted with the danger of severe deflation after the war;

5. That the country will be confronted with the danger of severe inflation after the war.

The controls of wages and the controls of prices have operated more or less independently. Hence one should not be surprised to find labor costs after the war substantially higher or lower in relation to prices than before the war. It is extremely difficult to judge whether labor costs on the whole have risen or fallen in relation to prices. The best measure of the price of labor is straight-time hourly earnings, corrected for shifts between low-paying and high-paying industries. In 35 industries—20 manufacturing and 15 nonmanufacturing—covering about 60 per cent of the civilian employees of the country, straight-time hourly earnings (corrected for shifts) have risen about 30 per cent, from 64.2 cents in 1939 to 83.3 cents in January 1944. In the same period the wholesale prices of finished goods rose about 25 per cent; raw materials, about 60 per cent; farm products, about 87 per cent. Corporate profits after taxes are low in relation to the volume of business done. In 1943, they were 50 per cent above 1926, although corporate sales were about double the sales of 1926. Corporate profits *before* taxes, however, were considerably higher per dollar of sales in 1943 than in the twenties. Hence substantial reductions in corporate income taxes after the war might make present cost-price relationships yield quite a satisfactory return. Furthermore, labor costs are abnormally high, because of the large proportion of "green" workers, of high labor turnover and absenteeism, and of large payments for penalty overtime. In 1943, for example, the wage bill for penalty overtime was $3 billion. Finally, half of the output of American industry is sold to the government at prices not reflected in the price indexes. All of these abnormalities make it impossible to judge whether costs would warrant a drop or compel a rise in prices after the war. All in all, however, it looks as if the war has not greatly disturbed the relationship between labor costs and the prices at which finished goods are being sold.

Suppose it turns out that wages in most industries are too high relative to prices to make full employment possible. Should the nation adopt the public policy of reducing wages or should it adopt the policy of raising prices? The practical obstacles to reducing wages on a broad scale are obvious and formidable. Furthermore, the immediate effects of wage reductions upon the volume of spending need not be favorable, or, if favorable, then they may be favorable only in slight degree. These observations lead to the tentative conclusion that if wartime controls leave wages too high in relation to prices, public policy should aim in the main to raise prices rather than to reduce wages. This conclusion, however, requires important qualifications. The price level might be too low relative to wages, but too high relative to foreign price levels—as was the case in Britain during the twenties. Furthermore, the accomplishment of a satisfactory wage-price relationship through a rise in prices faces two opposite types of difficulties. On the one hand, wages which are too high relative to prices would under most circumstances reduce the response of the economy to stimulants. On the other hand, if the war has built up large quantities of liquid assets in the hands of individuals and business concerns, it may be difficult to raise prices without touching off a disorderly and uncontrollable rise.

What if wages after the war are "too low" relative to prices, too low in the sense that the quantity of labor demanded exceeds the available supply of labor? Should the desired relationship between wages and prices be created by raising wages, by lowering prices, or by doing both? The answer to this question must depend upon circumstances. Again the relationship of the domestic price level to foreign price levels must be taken into account. So also must the possibility that general increases in wages would encourage a large-scale conversion of liquid assets into goods and thus precipitate a disorderly rise of prices and an ultimate collapse.

A great upheaval such as the war may be expected to produce large changes in the wage structure, in the wage differentials between regions, cities, plants, occupations, industries. The war has done this—considerably more than the published figures reveal but considerably less, I believe, than one might expect. The following is a brief summary of the principal changes:

1. *Between regions.* Changes between regions appear to have been small. The wage level on the Pacific Coast, higher than the rest of the country before the war, appears on the whole to have increased slightly relative to the rest of the country except the South. Wages in the South appear to have risen relative to the North and East.

2. *Between small towns and large cities.* Satisfactory evidence is lacking, but there has apparently been little relative change in hourly earnings between small towns and large places. Wages of farm labor rose about 120 per cent between July 1939 and January 1944. This leads one to expect a fairly substantial rise in wages in many small towns. Men who are well informed on trends in the labor market believe that, in the early days of the war effort, wages in the large cities rose faster than wages in the small towns, but that during the last year or year and a half the small towns have been catching up. The use of fairly broad areas in applying brackets by the Regional War Labor Boards has tended to raise rates in small towns more than in large cities. This is true, for example, in the New England metal trades. In the automotive parts industry of the Middle West, small towns of under 25,000 in Michigan have been brought closer to Detroit, which, in June 1939, had the highest straight-time hourly earnings. A special study recently made by the United States Bureau

of Labor Statistics for presentation to a committee of Congress shows that the median rise in straight-time hourly earnings of white-collar workers in twelve nonwar towns of 20,000 or less in widely scattered states between January 1941 and December 1943 was about 20 per cent. The rise from 1939 to the end of 1943 would undoubtedly have been somewhat greater.

3. *Between common labor, semi-skilled and skilled labor.* Common labor is generally believed to have gained greater percentage increases, but smaller absolute increases than skilled labor. Satisfactory data, however, are lacking, and the safest conclusion is probably that there has been little change in relationships.

4. *Pieceworkers in comparison with timeworkers.* This is one of the most important changes of all. In many plants the earnings of pieceworkers are from one-fourth to one-half above the earnings of timeworkers who previously received the same amount. Some pieceworkers are earning three or four times as much as timeworkers who were formerly their equals. The earnings of pieceworkers have risen partly because runs of work are abnormally long and change-overs less frequent than usual but in the main because offsetting changes in rates have not been made as working conditions have improved.

5. *Union wages in comparison with nonunion.* Information on this point is lacking. In the first World War nonunion wages went up faster than union wages. This proved to be an important advantage to many unions after the war, because they were able to obtain increases when nonunion workers were accepting reductions. It is probable that there is little difference in the rise between the two groups of wages since 1939.

6. *In relation to employment increases.* When industries with large increases in employment are compared with industries with small increases in employment, no differences in the behavior of wages appear. It is likely, however, that a different result would follow if the comparisons were between cities with large increases in employment and cities with small increases in employment. Among twenty-five cities in Wisconsin for which the Industrial Commission has gathered information, the largest percentage increases in straight-time hourly earnings (unfor-

tunately not corrected for shifts between industries) are generally associated with the largest percentage increases in employment, but exceptions are numerous.

7. *Between industries.* Among thirty-four industries (twenty manufacturing and fourteen nonmanufacturing) the increase in straight-time hourly earnings between 1939 and January 1944 varied from 14.1 per cent in street railways to 54.9 per cent in lumber and timber. In absolute terms the increase in straight-time hourly earnings ranged from 10.1 cents in street railways to 36.8 cents in the manufacture of transportation equipment (except automobiles). The rise in straight-time hourly earnings was below 15 cents an hour in five cases and above 25 cents in four cases. In percentages it was below 20 per cent in three cases and above 40 per cent in eight cases. Since war production is concentrated largely (although not entirely) in the durable goods industries, one might expect that the rise in wages would be greater in those industries than in the nondurable goods industries, and this is true. The difference, however, is surprisingly small. In the durable goods industries wages rose 38.5 per cent between 1939 and January 1944, and in the nondurable, 36.7 per cent. In general, the war has produced the largest absolute increases in industries where wages were high before the war and the smallest absolute increases in industries where wages were lowest before the war.

8. *Between high-wage and low-wage plants and companies within the same industry.* Information is again scanty and inadequate, but the largest *percentage* increases appear to have occurred among the low-wage plants. Whether the largest *absolute* increases have occurred in the small plants is doubtful.

All of these comparisons seem to indicate that the war has produced relatively small effects upon the wage structure. Nevertheless, the effects have been far greater than the comparisons indicate. The reason is that comparisons of changes between regions, large and small cities, different plants and industries, group together plants and occupations with large increases and plants and occupations with small increases. If one could segregate the particular plants where the changes have been greatest and those in which they have been smallest, one would find that the spread is very considerable. Are these various changes in wage relationships produced by the war to be regarded as increasing or reducing distortions in the wage structure?

A distortion may be defined as a relationship between wage rates which is not justified by the pattern of the demand for labor and the supply of labor and which, therefore, attaches an excessive number of men to a plant, industry, or locality or which causes a persistent number of vacant jobs. Consequently, whether distortions are increasing or decreasing will depend not only upon what the war does to wages, but also upon what it does to the pattern of the demand for labor and to the supply of labor. The war is giving men new skills, it is changing the geographical distribution of labor, and it is altering the preferences of men concerning the occupations and places in which they work. It may well be that the net effect of the war will be to reduce distortions in the wage structure. Nevertheless, some more or less serious distortions are to be expected. Among them are:

1. *Between the Pacific Coast and the rest of the country.* The war will increase the proportion of people who would like to live on the Coast. Consequently, other things being equal, wages on the Coast should be lower relative to wages in the rest of the country than they were in 1939. The war, however, has tended to raise wages on the Coast more than in the country as a whole.

2. *Between cities.* A few war centers will have virtually priced themselves out of competition. Seattle, for example, may have trouble in getting wages down to a competitive level.

3. *Between pieceworkers and timeworkers.* Much of the advantage of pieceworkers will disappear, because many rates which now yield high earnings will not be used after war goods are no longer made, and because the smaller lots in which civilian goods are made will require more frequent job changes. Pieceworkers are attempting in some plants to get peacetime rates adjusted to yield wartime earnings. To the extent that this happens it is likely to perpetuate distortions.

4. *Between the metal trades and heavy industries and other trades and industries.* The war will increase the proportion of

workers who are skilled in the metal trades and in the heavy industries and who would like to continue to make their living in these occupations and industries. Other things being equal, therefore, wages in the metal trades and heavy industries should be lower relative to wages in general after the war than they were before the war. But the war will bequeath to the country relatively high wages in a considerable part of the metal trades.

5. *Between individual plants.* A few plants in each industry are likely to have priced themselves pretty largely out of competition. These plants may not be particularly numerous, but possibly nearly 5 per cent of the manufacturing population may be employed in them. Machine tool plants or airplane plants which wish to keep operating by taking subcontracts for electrical equipment or automotive parts may find the employment which they are able to give greatly limited by their wage scales.

Should the community do nothing about distortions or should it seek to remove them? Failure to remove them would mean some maldistribution of resources and some unemployment— "wage distortion unemployment," it might be called. The aftermath of the last war provides many examples of costly wage distortion unemployment. The history of the Chicago men's clothing industry and the history of the bituminous coal industry are well-known and conspicuous illustrations, but many others might be cited.

Distortions may be reduced either by cutting the wages which are high or by raising the wages which are low. Each method is likely to be used. Everyone will agree, I believe, that much less conflict and bitterness will be engendered by raising wages which are low than by reducing wages which are high. Removing distortions by raising low wages, however, would require considerable increases in the general wage level, probably by as much as 15 to 25 per cent and possibly even more, because widespread wage increases might cause some rise even in the peak rates. This would require some rise in the price level. There are, of course, some places where large increases in prices would not be necessary, but they are likely to be few. The reduction in war taxes on business might save enterprises about $8 billion a year. This might on the face of it seem to allow a rise of about 10 per cent in the wage level without an increase in prices. The distribution of war profits and war business taxes has been very uneven. Both profits before taxes and tax payments have been concentrated in a few war plants and industries—many of them plants and industries in which the price of labor has risen more than the average. Hence, off-setting the drop in taxes by increases in wages would aggravate distortions in the wage structure rather than remove them. In some industries technological progress may make possible wage adjustments which will improve the balance in the wage structure and yet will not compel increases in prices, but these opportunities will be limited.

Would it be worth while to incur a rise in perhaps four fifths or more of all wage rates and in most nonagricultural prices in order to remove distortions affecting the wages of probably not more than one fifth of the work force—distortions which would not produce more than a million unemployed and probably not that many? Of course, a rise in wages and prices would have to be spread over a period of roughly three to five years, or it would touch off speculative buying and eventual collapse. Many persons—perhaps most persons—would find this method of removing wage distortions objectionable. Suppose, however, that a rise in prices occurs anyway or that it is desirable on other grounds, such as to improve the country's international economic position by making it easier for other nations to earn dollars. Should a general rise in prices occur after the war, it would afford an opportunity to reduce distortions in the wage structure and this opportunity should not be missed.

In connection with the problem of distortions in the wage structure it is appropriate to discuss the proposal that wage rates after the war be increased in order to offset reductions in weekly working hours. One reason why the war has created so few distortions in the wage structure is that the Labor Board has wisely refused to deny wage increase on the ground that weekly earnings in the particular plant have gone up. Were wage rates in various plants now raised to maintain weekly earnings, the distortions which have thus far been excluded from the wage structure would be introduced with a vengeance. Plant by plant figures are not available, but the discrepancies which would be introduced may be illustrated by comparisons between industries. Suppose, for example, rates were increased to maintain present weekly earnings under a 40-hour week. In four industries (apparel, anthracite coal, retail trade, and building construction) no upward adjustment would, on the average, be required. In the machinery industry, however, the average rise would be 37.6 cents per hour, or 37.8 per cent; in the street railway industry, 33.5 cents, or 41.0 per cent; in transportation (except automobiles), 30.5 cents, or 26.7 per cent. The median rise required would be 12.8 cents, or 16.4 per cent. In many instances the greatest increases would go to the plants or industries which have already had the greatest advances.

Are wage controls needed to protect the country against deflation? Many people fear that the drop in federal expenditures from over $90 billion to $25 billion a year within the space of several years after the war may precipitate severe deflation and unemployment. What wage policy is indicated by this danger? Would it help to prevent deflation to give assurances that the general level of wages would remain unchanged? If a precipitous fall in prices started, would it help to arrest that fall to hold wages unchanged or to reduce them as prices dropped? The answer to these questions depends upon circumstances. If cost-price relationships were unfavorable or if the country's price level was too high relative to the price levels of other countries, assurances against wage reductions might simply aggravate the contraction of employment. Were a precipitous fall in prices to occur, recovery of employment might be helped by fairly widespread reductions in wages, particularly if reductions were made in high-cost plants and if they were made after raw materials had fallen too far and were rising. The combination of rising raw material prices and falling wages seems to be favorable to a reduction in liquidity preference. There appears to be little likelihood, however, that the country will face the problem of severe deflation or that it will be confronted with the necessity of reducing its price level relative to the price levels of other countries.

Of more practical importance is the question of whether the price of labor should be increased after the war to prevent a drop in payrolls. If wages remain substantially unchanged, the transition to a peacetime economy will see a drop in payrolls of $15 billion to $20 billion. Would such a drop in payrolls be seriously deflationary and, if so, would it be helpful to prevent it by raising the price of labor? An accompanying drop in prices would not necessarily be deflationary because it would be largely offset by drops in costs—the withdrawal of many workers who are not worth their wages and the abandonment of penalty over-time. Nevertheless, enterprises would undoubtedly plan larger production programs immediately after the transition and thus would give more employment if they anticipated a slowly rising price level rather than a slowly falling one. Hence wage policy after the war should not prevent wages from rising to some extent for the purpose of limiting the *drop* in payrolls and for producing a *slow* rise in prices. This would be an important modification in the objectives of wage policy which is now de-signed to limit the *increase* in payrolls.

Are wage controls needed to protect the country against a postwar inflation? Between the Armistice and the middle of 1920, there was a rise of roughly 14 cents in the hourly earn-ings of factory workers—nearly as much as in the preceding four years. The cost of living rose 22 per cent and wholesale prices by 23 per cent. Compensation of employees increased from $32.3 billion in 1918 to $35.4 billion in 1919 and to $42.3 billion in 1921. If wage rates had not increased after 1918, how-ever, there would apparently have been a decrease instead of an increase in payrolls and the postwar inflation would soon have collapsed. Both the accumulation of needs and the accumulation of liquid assets in the hands of individuals and business enter-prises are far greater in relation to productive capacity than in 1918. Hence, is not the danger of a postwar boom (and later collapse) far greater today than it was in 1918?

There are two dangers: (1) that individuals and enterprises will start a rise in prices by spending their huge liquid resources too rapidly; (2) that increases in wages will force such rapid increases in prices as to touch off conversion of liquid assets into goods, thus bringing still further increases in prices. The danger will reach its peak when the shift to civilian production is almost, but not entirely, complete—when the fears of transition unemployment are pretty well over, when the demand for labor is high, but when the flow of consumers' goods is still restricted. Wage policy cannot directly deal with the first of these dangers, but it can do much about the second. Wage demands will be numerous, partly because many unsettled wage issues have accumulated during the war, and partly because many unions will have gone two or three years without an increase and will be looking for an issue. Wage demands will be particularly numerous and insistent if the relief needs of Europe are permitted to push up still further the price of food. Hence the prevention of increases in food prices will be of crucial importance. Possibly the opposition of employers to large wage increases might be sufficient to prevent a dangerously rapid rise in wages—as rapid as occurred in 1919 or 1920. Nevertheless, one cannot be sure, and, with an enormous deferred demand waiting to be met, it would be folly for the country not to have a national wage policy and an agency to implement it at least until the most impatient part of the accumulated demand has been satisfied. This indicates the retention of the War Labor Board for a year or more after the end of hostilities.

The retention of the War Labor Board for a year or so after the war would raise important questions concerning (1) its jurisdiction, (2) the criteria it should use in deciding cases, and (3) the sanctions behind its decisions.

1. *The jurisdiction of the Board.* During the transition to civilian production many concerns will be bringing out new products to which existing wage scales will not completely apply, and will be opening up new departments and new plants. Experience after the First World War indicates that business births will reach a record-breaking high within two years after the demobilization of the armed forces—perhaps as many as 300,000 or more a year. Most of these concerns will not come under the jurisdiction of the Board because they will have less than eight employees, but the case load of the Board will be extremely heavy. To prevent unsettled cases from creating unemployment, it would be desirable to exempt from the Board's jurisdiction concerns with twenty-five employees or less and voluntary wage increases which involve no advance in prices.

The Board would then be limited to hearing dispute cases and nondispute cases where price relief is needed.

2. *The criteria employed in setting wages.* The present statute requires the President to maintain the wage rates of September 15, 1942, except as changes may be required (1) to correct gross inequities; (2) to remove substandard wages; and (3) to aid in the effective prosecution of the war. Obviously new criteria would be needed. It would no longer make sense to attempt to hold wages rigorously to the level of a given date—particularly one as early as September 1942. Furthermore, it would be unwise to repress the bargaining and organizing activities of the unions so drastically. Such an attempt would produce an increasing number of strikes, either authorized or unauthorized, and a revolt against the wage policy. On the other hand, the Board should not be *required* to raise the price of labor sufficiently so that straight-time hourly earnings rise in proportion with the cost of living. Such a rule would prevent the Board from introducing balance into the wage structure—it would compel increases even in peak rates which are likely to create "wage distortion unemployment." Of course, an attempt to compensate for rises in the cost of living by wage increases would be self-defeating to some extent, because in many instances it would compel price increases which in turn eventually produce further wage increases. This spiral effect would vary from industry to industry. Since a central purpose of public wage and price policy will be to avoid precipitating a huge conversion of cash and other liquid assets into goods, the Board must be given the responsibility of keeping the spiral effect of wage increases down to a safe rate—that is, a rate which does not precipitate a rush from liquid assets into goods.

3. *The sanctions behind the decisions of the Labor Board.* Although employers are required to obey the orders of the Labor Board, unions may strike against these orders. It would not be wise to make strikes illegal—even in time of war the country has been unwilling to do this. A real understanding between the government and trade unions that strikes will not be countenanced against decisions of the Labor Board until the danger of a disorderly rise in prices is over would be an enormous contribution to stability. It would not be an easy agree-

ment for unions to make because strikes may be forced upon them by employers. Such an agreement would presumably involve an undertaking by the unions to discipline members or local officials who foster strikes against the Board—another difficult responsibility especially for new unions. It would have to be implemented by maintenance of membership clauses. At any rate, since employers are compelled to obey the orders of the Board, they are entitled to protection against strikes which have the purpose of compelling them to violate the law. This means that aiding or abetting strikes against the Board's decisions by picket lines, boycotts, or payment of strike benefits should be prohibited and that workers should not be permitted to retain wages paid in violation of the Board's orders.

Whether or not direct wage controls will be retained for a year or two after the war must be regarded as exceedingly doubtful. Unwise and even reckless as would be their immediate abolition, it would not necessarily be disastrous. Other important controls will remain. The most promising of these will be large and prompt increases in production—and production, I believe, will rise much sooner and faster after the war than is generally supposed. A substantial budget surplus might be planned for the period of impatient demand. Attractive bargains in annuities might be offered holders of cash and war savings bonds.

Even if the War Labor Board is retained for a year or two, it should not be kept indefinitely. It restricts too drastically the ordinary organizing and bargaining activities of labor organizations. The country, however, cannot escape facing the long-run problem of whether or not it should have a national wage policy and, if so, how it should be formulated and implemented. With a regular budget after the war from $20 billion to $25 billion a year, the nation must steadily have a high level of employment. Must not the nation, therefore, have an employment policy? And if the nation has an employment policy, must it not have a wage policy? Does not the necessity of maintaining a high level of employment greatly increase the national interest both in the structure of wages and in the response of wages to changes in the demand for labor? The wages of well over half of the workers after the war will be set by collective bargaining,

A too prompt response of wages to changes in the demand for labor would cause changes in demand to produce mainly wage effects rather than employment effects—thus seriously limiting the increase in jobs. And the wage structure created by collective bargaining will reflect the bargaining power of different groups of workers and employers—it will be high where the workers have great bargaining power and low where the employers are relatively strong. This method of setting wages is bound to create more or less "wage distortion unemployment"—that is, unemployment which reflects the different attractiveness of wage bargains in different industries and occupations.

All of these considerations indicate a national wage policy. But, except in times of great emergency, the country is not used to thinking in terms of national interests. Indeed, the wage policy which would emerge in time of peace would probably not be truly national. Rather the making of the policy would be taken over by this, that, or the other special interest, just as special groups took over the making of the tariff. The foundation for a national wage policy must be a lively sense of national interest by all members of the community and willingness to go quite far in putting national interests above special interests. The best operation of collective bargaining requires such a national wage policy, but the most that one can hope for in the immediate future is that the public will become gradually interested in the relationship between wages and employment, and that a scholarly and discriminating literature on the economics of wages will gradually grow up to influence public opinion and to guide arbitrators. Let us hope that this will be one of the legacies of the war.

WAGES AND WAGE CONTROLS [4]

Wages and wage controls, price controls, and rationing are all closely bound together. Wage controls will be considered first because what happens to wages may go far to decide what will be possible in the field of price control. Under the Amer-

[4] By John Maurice Clark, Professor of Economics, Columbia University. *In his* Demobilization of Wartime Controls. McGraw-Hill Book Company. New York. 1944. p. 144-7.

ican system any attempt to control wages, even in time of war and still more in time of peace, faces peculiar difficulties. It is easier to set floors than ceilings on wages; but even floors cannot be set without regard to their effect on the volume of employment or the possibility of continued operation of the industry in question. In fact, Philip Murray and W. H. Davis would probably agree that it is peculiarly true of wage policy that what is ideally desirable must give way to what is feasible.

When the fighting ends, organized labor's anti-strike agreement will naturally end with it. This will reduce the power of the War Labor Board to enforce ceilings on wages during the next six months after the war, the limit of its present statutory authority. The wartime institutions of wage conrol might become ineffective and might be promptly disbanded. How revolutionary this would be would depend on market pressures prevailing at that time.

Wages would continue to be adjusted by collective bargaining, with conciliation and mediation in case of disputes and with public or quasi-public umpiring in case mediation fails. Moreover, there is already in existence a set of wage floors, formulated under the provisions of the Fair Labor Standards Act, which has raised the pay of many of the lowest-paid labor groups. Collective bargaining and the forces of supply and demand modify one another, and one important unsettled question is how far the war has changed this balance and increased the power of strong unions to disregard the forces of supply and demand in their wage bargains. This may decide whether wage rates, if freed of War Labor Board controls, would tend to move up or down.

On this whole question predictions differ, but some things are fairly clear, and as to others there would be fair agreement on the zone within which the results are likely to fall. The five dimensions of wages are basic rates, average hourly earnings, average weekly earnings, total pay rolls, and the wage cost of production per unit of product. Assuming that basic rates in the first instance are unchanged, average hourly earnings will be lowered by a reduction in overtime both before and after the armistice. Average weekly earnings will be reduced more, and total pay rolls still more, by the inevitable transitional reduction of employment. As to basic rates, it seems safe to predict that some of those most inflated by the war, in industries like ship-building or airplane building, will come down. They were special incentive rates to attract abnormally large numbers into these trades in a hurry, and to compensate for transportation difficulties in getting to the war job, inadequate living facilities and any other difficulties and disadvantages.

Furthermore, it seems fairly certain that there will be a tendency, possibly prompt but more likely gradual, toward restoring something more like prewar relations among different trades and industries, where the war has violently disturbed these relationships. White-collar workers and others who have had no wage increases, or increases that were much less than the increase in the cost of living, will, over a span of five years or so, either make headway toward catching up with the war-inflated trades, or else hold where they are while the war-inflated trades come down. This is a desirable tendency, but it is likely to be obstructed, especially since it implies that the position of comparatively unorganized occupations will be improved, relative to the position of organized trades. Nevertheless, it is likely to show considerable force in the long run.

But in which direction will the adjustment be made? As soon as the armistice is signed, there will undoubtedly be a strong move to scrap wage controls, including the Little Steel formula if it survives that long, and to make demands for basic rates that will come as near as possible to affording wartime real weekly earnings. Something more may be added on the ground that the official cost-of-living index does not show the full amount of the increase.

The presence of many unemployed workers will, of course, not be favorable to success in pushing these demands; but experts disagree as to how substantial a difference this will make. One simple view is that wage rates will not rise when there is con-siderable unemployment, unless some authority steps in to push them up, as the government did under the National Industrial Recovery Act in 1933. Those who reason in this way, and who want wages sustained, naturally look toward a continuation of wage controls which would regulate upward rather than downward.

Others discount the depressing effect of postwar unemployment on wage rates on the ground that the unprecedented strengthening of the bargaining position of organized labor, which has taken place in recent years, has tended to insulate wage rates fairly completely from the effect of an excess supply of labor. Where a tight contract exists, even if there are qualified workers willing to work for less than contract rates, the employer is not in a position to take advantage of their willingness as a lever to reduce the contract rates. How much effect this will have can naturally not be predicted surely in advance; but it seems clear that certain factors in the bargaining position of organized labor are stronger than ever before and that they tend toward protecting wages against the effect of an excessive supply.

Perhaps the best surmise is that the prevailing general level of hourly wage rates will not go down, but that some of the more extremely inflated ones will. If corporate taxes are reduced, this may make room for some wage increases without necessitating higher prices. Within these limits, wage increases should be so distributed as to improve the equity of the wage structure. Mere yielding to the most powerful demands might have the opposite effect. It seems certain that there will be need for some strong influence working for a consistent and equitable national wage structure.

If the cost of living continues to rise for a time after the end of the fighting, then an inflationary wage-price spiral might continue or be speeded up by the relaxation of controls, and it is conceivable that this might happen even in the face of a certain amount of unemployment. This being the case, there would seem to be some need of wage-stabilizing controls after the war, available to prevent a possible wage-cost inflation. On the other hand, if a strong tendency to wage-deflation develops, the War Labor Board might well act to moderate it and prevent a serious collapse of buying power. For all these purposes there is need for continuance, both of the War Labor Board's formal powers and of its de facto influence.

There may be pressure to promote work-sharing, and some forms of it might be sound emergency measures. The most obvious form, and the one surest to be advocated, is to reduce the standard working week to thirty-five hours or less, charging time-and-a-half for anything beyond. There is little question this would be a mistake, chiefly because experience indicates that it would not remain an emergency measure, but would persist as a limit on future productivity. . . .

On the whole, unemployment may be more likely to lead to further output-limiting rules on the part of labor than to the acceptance of lower rates of wages; and this would contribute toward price inflation of the wage-cost variety. The best way to guard against a serious increase of output-limiting rules would be: (1) to plan for increased employment in a way that is definite enough to afford the workers fair assurance of jobs, once the brief transitional unemployment of the retooling period is over, and (2) to assure them of fair maintenance in the meantime.

WAGES: SQUARING THE VICIOUS CIRCLE [5]

Purposely or blindly, wage stabilization helps to determine the war use of 51 million wage workers in field and factory and forest, on railroads and in mines. It can pad or pare pay-envelope cash. It has to do with the perils pointed up by Edward O'Neal, head of the American Farm Bureau Federation: "There must be a price incentive for food production just the same as for industrial production. Inflation? We seem to be headed for it." Wage stabilization, moreover, is a pivot for the *Realpolitik* of the United States labor movement, American Federation of Labor, Congress of Industrial Organizations, Railroad Brotherhoods. And it cuts across the personal aims and political aspirations of John L. Lewis, now in his twenty-third year as president of the United Mine Workers. Wage stabilization, in short, is a necessary if many-edged instrument for fusing scattered parts of the national economy into a single-minded war operation.

[5] *Fortune*. 27:79-81+. May 1943. Copyright Time, Inc.

The agencies that seek to stabilize wages consistently run into trouble. In the National War Labor Board management and labor clash with each other and with the government. War Production Board's Shipbuilding Stabilization Committee, with its industry-wide approach to wages, challenges the case-by-case methods pursued by the War Labor Board. Both agencies try to keep workers reasonably content with their pay while preventing wage demands from blowing off inflation controls. The record of such efforts and the problems they raise are the subject of this article.

Wage stabilization is not a freeze. It has rather the consistency of a thick, heavy tar which, while hardening, can still be spread out to cover some extra patch of surface. The purpose: (1) to prevent the kind of wage rise that augments the cost of war weapons and punctures the price ceilings placed upon basic civilian items; (2) to curtail competitive bidding (a result of excess spending ability) for the dwindling amount of nonmilitary commodities; (3) to stop scamping or pirating of workers away from one employer to another by baiting the hook with big-money promises; (4) to provide labor with living essentials that insure diet, health, and other standards sufficient to maintain the tangible of high, regular output, and to maintain somewhere around par the intangible of morale.

To achieve this elastic if not elusive objective is primarily the task of the War Labor Board. It is a tripartite agency of twelve members: four representing management, four the public, and two each the American Federation of Labor and Congress of Industrial Organizations. It was set up by Executive Order No. 9017 (on January 12, 1942) to "finally determine" any labor-management controversy that could not be otherwise resolved and that in the Board's judgment would hamper the national drive toward full martial might.

The Board's tumultuous dealings with wage stabilization fall into two periods. From January to October, 1942, the Board frequently acted to stiffen the United States wage structure. But it only did this incidentally to settling industrial disputes. From last October [1942] up to the present, the Board has been operating with an enlarged scope and more positive authority. Executive Order No. 9250, delegated to the War Labor Board the entire job of stabilizing wages and salaries in all industries for all employees.

But W.L.B. wouldn't be a legitimate member of the Administration's family of agencies if it had retained its original all-embracing power in the stabilization field. First it exempted from its control all establishments with eight or less persons on their payrolls. To the Bureau of Internal Revenue in the Treasury Department eventually went jurisdiction over salaries above $5,000 a year, along with those of executive, professional, and supervisory employees not represented by a recognized labor organization. However, because the bureau's rulings affect relatively few people, their impact upon the economy, politics aside, is negligible.

The War Labor Board's scope was further diminished when in November 1942, Stabilization Director James F. Byrnes transferred to the Secretary of Agriculture the function of stabilizing farm wages, which had risen 76 per cent above their prewar level to a scarcely munificent $2.76 a day, without board, for 2,500,000 farm laborers. After looking at this chore, Secretary Wickard declared, "The principal problem in agriculture is to allow wages to rise so as to attract enough labor to achieve farm production goals." The department's method of grappling with this situation has been to ignore it. Up to the appointment of Chester C. Davis as food administrator, the department held tenaciously to the hope that the uneven, uncontrolled ascent of wages from farm to farm and section to section would somehow allure and direct an adequate amount of labor to critical crop areas. That expectation has not been fulfilled.

The third exception to the War Labor Board's authority, but still subject to its review, is Department of Labor's Wage Adjustment Board for building-trades workers on government projects. Some 1,250,000 shipyard workers are similarly detached from W.L.B. Their wages are passed on by W.P.B.'s Shipbuilding Stabilization Committee, which, since it provides the most widely debated contrast to the War Labor Board regimen, will be discussed in detail later.

Finally the President last February removed by Executive Order No. 9299 some 1,400,000 railroad and airline employees from the jurisdiction of both the War Labor Board and the Bureau of Internal Revenue, assigning to the National Railway Labor Panel the duty of stabilizing their wages and salaries. The creation of this panel some months before, in response to requests by the unions, and in return for their pledge to relinquish the right to strike for the duration, had modified the National Mediation Board's mechanism for resolving trans-portation disputes. The panel system permits the unions to ask for the appointment of tripartite fact-finding boards, composed of panel members, before controversies become critical. The chairman of the panel can approve any wage or salary changes that in his opinion accord with over-all stabilization policy. If in doubt, he selects a special board of three from the panel to study and resolve the issue. Recently in Chicago a board of this character has been taking testimony in the demand of 900,000 nonoperating railroad workers for a 30 per cent hike in wages.

Despite this subcontracting of bits and pieces of stabiliza-tion to other agencies, the War Labor Board's remaining area of activity seems formidable enough. Together with its twelve regional subdivisions the Board, under the terms of its most recent charter, is obliged to prevent United States wage rates from reaching altitudes above the plane of September 15, 1942, "unless such increase is necessary to correct maladjustments, or inequalities, to eliminate substandards of living, to correct gross inequities, or to aid in the effective prosecution of the war." Naturally, the Board sought at once to nail down the meaning of "maladjustments" and the other four exceptions to the general rule. For guidance it turned back to the major decisions of its first period. It especially looked upon the face of its Little Steel formula, announced in midsummer 1942, and found it very good.

In January 1942, the Steel Workers Organizing Committee and the four Little Steel corporations (Bethlehem, Republic, Youngstown Sheet & Tube, and Inland) had become deadlocked in negotiations. The union's demand was a pay boost of 12.5

cents an hour, or a dollar a day, along with the checkoff and union shop. Department of Labor conciliators tried to effect an agreement. Convinced that further discussions would be fruitless, the conciliators so advised Secretary of Labor Perkins, who certified the conflict to the War Labor Board. The Board appointed a fact-finding panel of management, labor, and public representatives to look into the opposing claims, take a record, and report.

The Board quickly saw that Little Steel would be breaking new ground since this was the first major case to fall under certain new directives. In the Price Control Act of January 1942, Congress had instructed the Board and other federal agencies "to work toward a stabilization of prices, fair and equitable wages and cost of production." Moreover, in his message to Congress on April 27, 1942, the President had declared that "to keep the cost of living from spiraling upward, we must stabilize the remuneration received by individuals for their work." He also made it plain that wages in general were to remain at existing scales, leaving room for various adjustments.

The War Labor Board was entrusted with this new job of wage stabilization not because it was particularly prepared for it but because, in its previous performance, it had acquired the cooperation of management and labor alike. From the outset the tripartite Board was organized on the democratic principle that decisions should be made by the groups to be affected. The Board's common-law approach of considering each case on its merits permitted at least a rough and relative justice in a world that was both. But the combination of its tripartite character and its common-law methods became a dubious asset to the Board's new stabilization function. Whenever the Board had to act not as an arbitrator but as one of the government's key administrative agencies, it lacked a clear policy and a single boss.

To be sure, the Board did possess a few scattered guide posts. It knew, for example, that actually there was no such thing as a national wage level. It knew that there were thousands of wage levels, differing from factory to factory, city to city, and constantly in flux; that wage levels are influenced by technology, labor productivity, and management methods, as they are influenced by the movement of capital from North to South, the growth of one industry and the decline of another, by the strength or weakness of unions, by varying regional customs, by the waxing of demand and the waning of supply for certain skills.

Against this background and with this equipment, the Board tackled the perplexities of Little Steel and used the opportunity to proclaim that the time had come to halt the hot race between prices and wages. It was going to evolve a "terminal," on the assumption that the other six goals in the Administration's anti-inflation program would be achieved.

The Board denied the union's demand for a dollar-a-day increase and awarded 44 cents instead. It asserted, first of all, that for several years prior to January 1, 1941, wages and living costs had been pretty much in balance. But early in 1941, continued the Board, both wages and prices started to climb. By May 1942, the month after the President's stabilization message, living costs had risen about 15 per cent. However, during the sixteen-month interval between January 1, 1941, and May 1942, United States labor had won a round of wage gains, matching and often surpassing the upsurge in living costs, and completing a cycle in the wage-price relationship. If during this period, ruled the Board, any group of workers averaged less than a 15 per cent rise in their straight-time rates, their established standards had been impaired. They had suffered a "maladjustment" and could have it rectified. Since workers in Little Steel, between January 1, 1941, and April 1942, had secured various rate increases amounting to an average of almost 12 per cent, the Board ruled that they were entitled to a stabilization factor of an additional 3.2 cents per hour, or the difference between their current income and prevailing living costs.

There was also a consideration in the realm of simple ethics. The Little Steel case had been submitted to the Board prior to the President's stabilization message. While the result was pending (the panel study took over four months, the Board's deliberations two more weeks), the rules had been changed in the middle of the game. The workers in Little Steel might have felt that they could have done better if the Board had not considered itself bound by the President's stabilization edict. The Board therefore added to its 3.2 cents for stabilization purposes, another 2.3 cents an hour as an equity factor—in part justifying this action on the ground that living costs in steel towns were somewhat higher than the national average. It conceded that there was no stringent logic in the choice of the 2.3 cents; that the fraction of a cent specified was taken to provide an over-all rate practical for making up payrolls—all in all, an illustration of the intensely human and pragmatic character of wage adjustments in general.

Finally, the Board warned that labor could count on having its wages keyed to living costs to only a partial extent; that it could not throughout the war anticipate "upward changes in its wage structure which will enable it to keep pace with upward changes in the cost of living."

The Board's award to Little Steel's workers of $2.20 a week or $114.40 a year was a majority, not a unanimous, finding. The four public and four industry members voted for it, but the four labor members dissented sharply. They accused the Board majority of ignoring the facts and substituting "theoretical discourses on putative dangers for consideration of the justice of specific demands." They charged the Board with an academic devotion to the national cost-of-living index, and with failure to take into account the panel's findings that rocketing prices in steel towns had cut the buying power of workers some 13 per cent—a contention that was to herald many more of the same kind from unionists in war-boom communities.

To sterilize the $1 raise asked by the union, the labor advocates urged that the award be made in war bonds, since "money has value even when it must be saved." Yet this was a paradoxical position. For if it was true that steelworkers required extra cash to meet rising retail prices, war bonds, unless immediately redeemed, would be of little use. The Board's public and employer members were not impressed by this "let's have it either way" line of reasoning. What labor did obtain, however, beyond the amount granted, was endorsement of the principle of equal benefits from a pay boost. As union leaders had often pointed out, a flat 10 per cent increase means that the $1-an-hour worker gets a dime, but the 50-cent-an-hour worker, although he needs an increase more, gets only a nickel. The Little Steel decision gave a straight 44-cent raise to all workers involved. To United States unionists this is generally the preferable arithmetic in correcting "maladjustments."

The Board, in seeking to remedy "maladjustments," rarely considers particular occupations or individuals. It rather concentrates upon appropriate groups, whether comprising employees in a bargaining unit, a department, a plant or company, or even in an entire industry. Excluded from its maladjustment deliberations are such tangents as pay in lieu of vacations, merit increases, and promotions from learner to operator. But still remaining to plague the Board are the interchangeable terms of "inequalities and gross inequities," along with "substandards" and the execution of the President's positively cosmic adjuration to "aid in the effective prosecution of the war." Consider each in turn; they are the stuff out of which labor headlines will be made.

There is no single cause more likely to feed a worker's dissatisfaction than the discovery that somebody else, doing the same or virtually the same job, is getting paid more than he is. To measure and remedy such inequalities the Board uses a cluster of precedents, in the same way it invokes Little Steel as the guiding principle for maladjustments.

First of all, the Board has emphasized that mere differences in rates are not de facto inequalities. There are countless legitimate distinctions arising from geographical or other well-established patterns. For example, wages paid in the South have been for generations less than those paid in the North. The Board therefore denied pleas of textile unions to wipe out such long-standing differentials.

In general, there are two types of inequalities—interplant (between firms in the same locality or industry, between branches of the same company, between regions) and intraplant (discriminations in the internal wage setup of any given enterprise). In St. Louis the Board favored an upward revision of scales in a metal-fabricating concern to bring it into line with nineteen other plants in the vicinity performing comparable operations. In the case of the Ford Motor Co., the Board refused to sanction any adjustments on the ground that wages in the converted Detroit automobile industry had already attained an equilibrium that it would be reckless to disturb. But when a carbon company with nine plants in different parts of the country raised pay in eight of them, the Board saw no reason why employees in the ninth plant shouldn't receive the same treatment.

In applying its "equal pay for equal work" doctrine to the internal wage arrangements of engine, electrical-equipment, and ordnance plants, the Board ran into complications stemming from the influx of women. When they perform comparable tasks, decided the Board, they should be paid the same as men. However, it is often impossible for women to do the heavy lifting or other strong-back labor required. Hiring women often entails extra "setup" and "carry-off" men, and supervisory expenses. Thus the Board recommended that such additional unit costs be computed and then deducted pro rata to arrive at an "equivalent" scale for women workers.

With its ingrained suspicion of any thinking that moves from the general to the particular, rather than the other way around, the Board has not sought to define "substandards of living." It has merely ruled on them, in a mood of happy ignorance. In assessing maladjustments, the Board has the gauge of its Little Steel formula. In handling inequalities it has applied horse sense based upon a firm grasp of United States industrial practice and logic. But for the Board, "substandards of living" have no realistic frame of reference other than the laudable hope that even in the lowest brackets real wages will permit health and decency. The Board has stipulated that 78 cents an hour for men and 60 cents for women in a Bayonne, New Jersey, cable plant do not promote substandard living. It came to the same conclusion about waiters and waitresses in San Francisco who receive $3.25 a day, plus meals and tips.

Even in awarding an extra 5 cents an hour to stevedores along the Great Lakes (because their casual, seasonal employment placed them in what the Board called a "substandard" category) the Board didn't relate the meaning of "sub" to any discernible standard. It has rejected any attempt to figure out, in particular communities, a basic budget for meat, spinach, lodgings, and medical care required, say, to keep a man doing heavy manual labor fit and efficient. Yet this physical criterion, or something like it, would seem indispensable to save the Board from having its rulings on substandards degenerate into a series of contradictory expediencies. Necessarily, the question of substandard living is bound up with the utilization of manpower. But the Board has consistently evaded the problem—with one notable exception.

In the late summer of 1942 it became urgently obvious to various war agencies that a special adjustment of low wages was indicated to overcome an acute manpower deficiency in the output of copper, zinc, lead, and other nonferrous metals. During the first seven months of 1942, many mines, mills, and smelters of the nonferrous-metals industry in Utah, Montana, Idaho, the Pacific Northwest, and elsewhere were losing workers more rapidly than they could hire them. The Tacoma, Washington, branch of the American Smelting & Refining Co., which on September 1, 1942, employed 829 workers, recorded from January through July 998 quits and only 505 newcomers, even though it had reduced its age minimum from twenty-one to eighteen. Hence the copper smelter was running at 70 per cent capacity, and its refinery at 80 per cent. It was losing 2,000 tons of copper a month for lack of 300 unskilled laborers.

Similar conditions prevailed throughout the industry, primarily because its wages were lower (and its working conditions more difficult) than in industries competing for the same labor supply. Timbermen in the mines, for example, who make excellent carpenters or shipwrights, were earning from 38 to 55 cents an hour less than their fellow workers in building construction in Salt Lake City, and in San Francisco shipyards. The mine timbermen kept leaving for these and similar jobs as did, for the same reason, other nonferrous-metals workers. To end this growing migration the War Manpower Commission issued its drastic order to freeze in twelve western states nonferrous mine, mill, and smelter labor to its job. At the same time, military exigencies were calling for further expansion of output in this supercritical industry. New workers had to be attracted while existing labor was being forcibly retained. And since appeals to patriotism had not sufficed in the past, the workers, commanded to stay put, had on the other hand to be convinced that they had been fairly dealt with.

When a mass of evidence was submitted by the War Manpower Commission, the War Production Board, the Army, the Navy, the Office of Price Administration, the Labor Department, the nonferrous-metals companies, and the Mine, Mill and Smelter Workers Union (C.I.O.), the Board consented to act. After brief hearings, it granted a 2.5-to-12.5-cent rate increment to 10,000 workers in the industry. But as if to silence the last expiring pangs of conscience for having any truck with manpower considerations, the Board took pains to point out that it had accepted this specific case only because the existence of "an emergency war problem of national significance" dictated its intervention.

To explain the Board's reluctance to accept manpower problems as part of its responsibilities, various spokesmen cite the (theoretical) situation in a labor-shortage city where there are 25,000 jobs in 100 plants but only 20,000 locally available workers. If, says the Board, it permitted a wage increase in any single plant in order to attract more labor from outside, the other local firms would similarly want wage increases for the same purpose, lest their own employees be tempted by higher pay elsewhere in their home town. In other words, the Board would only have played the march for a game of musical chairs.

The Board's manpower attitude contrasts sharply with that of W.P.B.'s Shipbuilding Stabilization Committee. In fact, back in 1940 the committee was established in the old National Defense Advisory Commission largely to abolish chaotic manpower conditions disrupting the shipbuilding industry. At a merry pace employers were scamping skilled labor from their competitors. Along the West Coast calkers and machinists who had been getting $8 or $9 a day were being coaxed away to other jobs by monthly salaries up to $350, plus a bonus and a wink. Workers would hardly settle down to routine in one yard when the magnet of higher rates would pull them to another. Unless this trend that impaired both production and morale was broken, there could be no roof on the costs of ship construction, no check upon the inflationary influence of constantly rising wages.

Hence in November 1940, N.D.A.C. appointed the Shipbuilding Stabilization Committee to bring order into the bedlam. The committee was composed of representatives of shipbuilding management, labor (A.F. of L. Metal Trades and the C.I.O. Marine and Shipbuilding Workers), plus the Maritime Commission, the Navy and War departments. The chairman was taken from N.D.A.C. as the over-all production agency, a practice retained when N.D.A.C. merged into Office of Production Management, and O.P.M. into W.P.B.

As a first step the committee divided the country into its four natural shipbuilding zones: the Pacific, Gulf, and Atlantic coasts, and the Great Lakes. It held conferences in each area to formulate an operating agreement covering eight fundamental points. In three zones it pegged a basic rate of $1.12 an hour ($1.07 in the Gulf) for skilled mechanics who composed 50 per cent of the industry's labor sought after as key men. Instead of trying to set scales for all shipyard workers, the committee assumed that by stabilizing the pay of this group, in all new employment, it would check the most serious migration. The wages of the 30 per cent semiskilled and the 20 per cent unskilled workers were left to employer-employee negotiation. But apprenticeship periods for craftsmen, traditionally averaging three and one-half years, were cut to a year or less. At the same time, the many "trainees" who specialized in only a part of an operation were rapidly upgraded. Both apprentice and trainee, after acquiring enough facility, were allowed the same basic hourly rate, while more expert old-timers kept moving into the top of the grade, or into posts as lead men.

Each zone pact furthermore standardized overtime pay, reduced premiums for second and third shifts, "abolished" strikes and lockouts, set up grievance and arbitration machinery for handling complaints, and fostered more effective training and upgrading programs. All such obligations were to be kept for two years.

The wage-stabilization agreement, as first adopted, contained an escalator clause under which rates were tied to living costs. At the committee's first national conference, however, held in Chicago in the spring of 1942, such automatic adjustment of wages to prices was replaced by a provision for an annual review of the ratio, since both management and the unions wanted government guidance to keep rates in line with the newly announced anti-inflation program.

Today, as a result of wage stabilization and corollaries, scamping in the United States shipyards has been greatly reduced. By the end of 1943 the committee's wage program will have saved the government an estimated $400 million through elimination of Sunday and other extra-hour premiums, and the regularizing of base rates.

The Shipbuilding Stabilization Committee operates on the theory that, in wartime, problems of production, industrial relations, manpower, and wage stabilization are inseparable. As part of W.P.B., the committee concerns itself with production questions, fosters continuous round-the-clock shipyard schedules, surveys the comparative productivity of workers on eight-hour as against ten-hour shifts, day and night. It integrated local collective bargaining into the formulation and application of its industry-wide policy. It used wage stabilization as an effective device for regulating labor supply.

However, since the committee is confined to a single industry, its actions have often unstablized wages in other industries and communities. When a year ago it lifted the basic rate for all four zones to $1.20 an hour, it raised hob with local wage structures. What the committee lacks in dealing with wages is the community-wide flexibility possessed by the War Labor Board.

The War Labor Board, on the other hand, lacks the industry approach. To be sure, in its piecemeal disposition of wage issues it often indirectly promotes industry-wide stabilization, for instance when it made Big Steel's rates accord with those in Little Steel. Yet while the Shipbuilding Stabilization Committee has a single national wage policy, with elbowroom for local initiative in ironing out details, the Board—in giving more and more autonomy to its twelve regional subdivisions—has tended to decentralize not only its administration but also its policy making. Recently, for example, the Curtiss-Wright Corporation submitted to the Board a wage plan to regularize rates for its plants in Buffalo, Columbus, and St. Louis. The Board referred the question to the three regional offices concerned. But from them may come three distinct rulings, partly because the W.L.B. has no clearinghouse through which one regional unit can keep informed as to what the others are doing.

In other respects, too, the Board's routine is widely criticized. Early in March it had a backlog of 16,000 cases clogging its dockets. In fact, labor indignation that swept over the Board because of its recent West Coast air-frame decision was due in part to an eight months' delay. Yet in handling both disputes and stabilization cases, some 70 per cent of the Board's findings have been unanimous, though the wrangling that accompanies the other 30 per cent often conveys the impression that the Board is about to fall apart.

Considering the difficulties of wage stabilization in a country as big as the United States, the Board—within the self-imposed limits of its purposes—has pretty well achieved what it set out to do. The real hurdles, of course, have yet to be taken. During the last quarter of 1942 wage advances, in terms of hourly earnings, were kept to .5 index points (as against 4.7 during the previous comparable period) while living costs went up 2.5 points. It has aided "effective prosecution of the war" less by its lone foray into manpower mobilization than by beveling, at the least, the edges of labor discontent through its handling of maladjustments and inequalities; even though in its treatment of substandards it has avoided exploring the important connection between the vitamin content of a worker's diet and his ability to produce. And by preventing and arresting wage increases it has been a strong guy rope holding down the balloon of inflation. But should the other ropes, such as price control, ravel and break, the balloon will go up, perhaps taking the Board with it.

Certainly the Board's troubles have been multiplied by the continuing rise in living costs and the tardiness of rationing.

Not all the blame can be put on O.P.A., despite its lethargy, its vacillations, and the confusion it has widely generated. Stabilization of wartime economy is inconceivable unless it is generally approached from one, and only one, point of view: maximum production. If, for example, Congress approves government subsidies to the farmers as the necessary profit incentive to increased production, O.P.A. might be able to keep food prices reasonably firm. But if Congress rejects this course and continues to legislate in terms of prices alone, the final barriers to a geometric progression of food prices may be swept away. And since about 40 per cent of the worker's budget goes to the grocer and the butcher, wages would start panting after prices.

Using August 1939, as a base, United States labor income, in terms of weekly "take-home," by January had risen 65 per cent —a figure that reflects constant employment plus a 45 per cent advance in hourly earnings. During the same period (August 1939 to January 1943) living costs have gone up 22 per cent according to the Bureau of Labor Statistics index. But in certain war-boom centers such as Seattle and Savannah they have gone up 4 per cent more than the national average. Even so, United States labor, outside of low-bracket and special inequality groups, retains a sizable margin of safety in the ratio between what it earns and what it buys. Yet prices are still moving up (at least 6 per cent a year by the most optimistic prophecies), while the War Labor Board—notably in its packing-house and air-frame decisions—has clamped down on wages more resolutely than ever before, rendering them the most immobile factor in the war economy.

In February and March of 1943, exigencies of labor politics put to a test W.L.B.'s prestige and cohesion. The A.F. of L. and C.I.O. questioned again the validity and usefulness of the Board's Little Steel formula. This action was partly meant as a warning to the Administration to do something drastic about prices before they got completely out of hand. But obviously the A.F. of L.-C.I.O. protests were also undertaken to offset John L. Lewis's most recent endeavor to capture the headlines.

In his union's biennial negotiations with the soft-coal operators, Mr Lewis began portraying himself as the one labor leader of consequence who has not "sold out" to the Administration and who could therefore place labor's interests above other loyalties. He asked for an increase of nearly $4 a day—$2 as a cost-of-living adjustment, $1.50 to $1.85 as "portal-to-portal" compensation pay. While A.F. of L. and C.I.O. leaders urged the Board to revise its Little Steel formula, they wanted to retain the Board; and when it rejected their request, they proposed to remain under its jurisdiction and to abide by its verdicts. Mr Lewis, however, wanted to destroy the Board as he had destroyed its predecessor, the National Defense Mediation Board, by concentrating against it the random labor dissatisfactions with rising living costs. Failing in this aim, he didn't want the Board to pass on the miners' claims. He yanked his lieutenant, Thomas Kennedy, from W.L.B. to dramatize his strategy of discrediting among labor's rank and file any and all Administration agencies. Looking to 1944, Lewis shares with Big Bill Hutcheson, chieftain of the A.F. of L. carpenters, the leadership of a Republican bloc, now forming in labor circles. The more resentment Lewis can stir up against Administration wage policy, as exemplified by the War Labor Board, the more important he expects to be, personally and politically, when presidential candidates are nominated.

More objective critics of the Board, however, appreciate that its shortcomings mirror the haphazard character of national labor policy and administration. Labor bureaus and divisions are strewn among many Washington agencies; nine have a hand in wage stabilization alone. It would seem elementary enough to centralize both labor policy and administration in some single overall body, in which labor should be fully represented along lines recently recommended by the Truman Committee. Such an agency would be empowered to plan and direct the allocation of all manpower, to mediate and arbitrate, to handle wage stabilization, to do the research and keep the records—to achieve, in short, a unified mustering up of United States human resources.

To be successful, any such agency must be part of a supreme war-mobilization council that would determine and schedule battle-front and home-front needs, and mesh them with courage and common sense. For, as suggested in a high government official's appalling revelation of the obvious: "In the final analysis, you can't make a blueprint for wages unless you've got a blueprint for the whole damned show."

THE OPA, PRICE CONTROL, AND INFLATION [6]

The disastrous effects of inflation, which I take to mean a significant and continuing increase in the price level and in the cost of living, are immediately economic, and ultimately social and political in character. Should inflation escape the leash, war costs will mount at an increasing rate, governmental income will lag behind governmental expenditure even more than at present, and national debt will assume proportions that will paralyze the American economy in the postwar period. Moreover, as inflation proceeds, profiteers and speculating hoarders will gradually take over, and the price structure will get more and more out of balance; and military and civilian production, the effective continuation of which depends upon the predictability of costs and upon the preservation of equilibrium in the national price structure, will be more and more curtailed. Finally, through the establishment of price levels and a price structure which cannot be maintained in the postwar period, inflation will make inevitable a catastrophic postwar economic collapse that will render military demobilization and transition to peace dangerously difficult at best.

Turning to the distributive basis of society, we find that inflation is as destructive of private property and its foundations as is violent revolution. Inflation wipes out large portions of fixed income values and instruments, such as insurance policies, annuities, pensions, military allowances, bonds, and relatively stationary salaries and wages. For example, the inflation that accompanied the First World War erased three fourths of the prewar value of French life insurance portfolios and policy values and virtually all corresponding German values. When inflation blots out these sources of income, it also destroys

[6] By Joseph J. Spengler, Professor of Economics and Business Administration, Duke University; Regional Price Executive for Region 4, O.P.A., 1942-1943. *South Atlantic Quarterly*. 43:111-30. April 1944.

each economic and social class whose income flows from these sources, and it wrecks every educational and charitable institution supported out of such income. Inflation, therefore, will wipe out virtually all private higher educational and charitable institutions in the United States; and it will multiply far beyond the danger point the number of men and families without a stake in the existing society and its continuation in the present form.

Far more serious ultimately than the economic effects of inflation are its social and political consequences, which develop as rising prices open up latent fissures in the body politic. The stakeless men whom it brings into being, when it undermines important elements in the middle class, constitute the stuff out of which the leadership of revolution is made. The multitudes of workers who cannot find employment in consequence of inflation-engendered economic and business collapse provide the mass support for revolutionary movements. The dissipation of stabilizing moral values and customs, which always accompanies inflation, removes an important barrier to social tumult and revolution. In sum, inflation brings in its wake a conjuncture of circumstances and conditions inimical to social stability, uncongenial to peaceful social change, and conducive to interclass war and revolution. Its proponents, the "enemies of price control," as Clare Wilcox points out, "are children playing heedlessly with high explosives," who, if uncurbed, can undermine both the war and the home fronts.

Inflation, therefore, may be described, without much exaggeration, as a destroyer of states and a corrupter of civilizations. Its "pestilent effects" were feared and opposed by the Founding Fathers. Its corrosive influence was responsible for much that was dismal in the history of post-1918 Europe. Its divisive consequences are recognized by the Nazis, who urge Americans by short wave to disregard the President's anti-inflation program.

War, with its insatiable demand for men and materials, weakens when it does not destroy those controls which, in times of peace, serve to hold prices in leash and in proper balance. Had it not been for "the political pressures of war and the makeshift financing methods that always seem to accompany war," concluded the late N. J. Silberling, "almost all the instability in the purchasing power of the dollar would have been eliminated." War strikes at economic and monetary stability from three directions. It creates a condition of universal scarcity, of which special interest groups, if not held firmly in check, take advantage. It fills the land with *dangerous money* when the government waging war lacks the courage to meet the bulk of the expenditures occasioned by war out of revenues obtained through taxation and the exchange of War Bonds for honest-to-goodness savings. It brings into being, when outlays for it are not largely provided through taxation, a vast public debt, from the burden of which important elements in the nation may later seek to escape by supporting inflationary policies.

War gives rise to universal scarcity. An almost unlimited supply of manpower and resources is required to provision and operate the machinery of war; and as men and materials are diverted to the armed forces and to the industries of war to meet these virtually unlimited requirements, the condition of scarcity, initially present in the military portion of the economy, spreads to the civilian portion and so becomes universal. Some conception of the requirements of modern war may be gained from the fact that by the close of 1943 the United Nations spent in preparation for and the conduct of the present war about $450 billions, or more than three times the unprecedented outlay of the Allies on the First World War; or from the fact that our annual war expenditures now exceed by about one seventh the annual income received by individuals in 1940; or from the fact that Federal expenditures now absorb 48 per cent of the gross national product in contrast with less than one third in 1917-18.

The universal scarcity that comes in the wake of war did not develop at once in the United States. Monthly war expenditures rose from a peacetime level of one-half billion dollars in 1941 to $2 1/3 billions in early 1942 and to about $7 billions in mid-1943; in 1944 they will run about $7½ billions per month and comprise 92 per cent of all national governmental expenditures. Much of this increase in expenditure has been met out of our great latent productive power which, in terms of annual gross product, expanded from $119 billions in mid-1941 to $187 billions in 1943. In 1943, 45 per cent of this product was devoted to war, while the physical volume of civilian goods and services was being maintained at the 1941 level. Now, because this latent reserve is virtually exhausted, and therefore civilian output cannot be augmented, the growing pressure of increasing purchasing power against a nonexpanding supply of goods and services is intensifying the consciousness of universal scarcity.

Universal scarcity can give rise to inflation because of the manner in which prices, costs, and the component parts of the economic system are reciprocally interconnected. Every price is a cost to somebody, and every increase in price is an increase in cost to the purchasers of that whose price is increased, whether they consume the item in question or employ it productively; and every purchaser who suffers such an increase in cost, be he wage-earner or producer, seeks to recover it by increasing, in turn, the price of that which he sells; whence it is quite likely, especially in time of universal scarcity, that an initial increase in price will spread until finally it pushes up the very cost of the seller who initiated the increase in price. An initial increase in price, therefore, may, if no obstacles are interposed, set in motion an endless chain of price increases which serve to raise to ever higher levels the average of all prices, but which, in the end, bring little or no net advantage to the vast majority of the participants in the endless price-increasing process. Inflation, therefore, spreads as the drug habit grows, each dose calling for a larger and yet no more effective dose, until finally all semblance of control disappears. . . .

A government, if it would prevent inflation in time of war, must take five steps, First, it must ration all essential goods and services which are in short supply and cannot, therefore, be properly allocated by marketing mechanisms adequate in peacetime. Rationing helps to restrain prices; it protects Lazarus against Dives; it insures that limited supplies are distributed equitably, democratically, and in consistence with the maintenance of health and morale and the effective conduct of war.

Second, when practicable full-employment has been attained, a government must raise half, and preferably more, of its annual expenditures through taxation; and all of the remainder through the exchange of war bonds for the *real* savings of individuals and institutions rather than for inflationary deposits manufactured by banks. If, after taxes and bond sales, there remains a spendable surplus of cash unmatched by goods and services and not otherwise required by the economy, the government must impound that surplus by means of a program of forced bond sales, or neutralize it by inculcating in the population thrift and other attitudes which actuate individuals to hold their excess liquid savings until such time as offsetting goods and services are again available for purchase. If a government succeeds in raising nearly all of its outlays through taxation and the exchange of bonds for *real* savings, and in circumvallating the remaining excess liquid savings, it will have sponged up or sterilized that dangerous money from which issues the upward pressure against prices. If it does not do this, it cannot effectively control prices by other methods.

Third, effective controls must be established over *all* selling prices and over such other costs of production as wages, rents, and profits; and these controls must in no way be subordinated to reformist efforts to correct so-called inequities. This step remains necessary when all excess purchasing power is being absorbed by taxation and bond sales; for even then the insatiable demands of war for the limited supplies of productive factors exercise a tremendous upward pressure on costs; and an upward movement of costs, once it gets under way, will as certainly produce inflation as will the upward pressure of unrestrained demand against unanchored selling prices. This step is all the more imperative when the government is not taking up all excess spending power. Control of virtually all, if not all, prices and costs, rather than only of certain prices and costs, is necessary because when some prices and costs are free of control they not only rise but tend also to pull up controlled prices. For factors of production tend to move into uncontrolled industries, thus intensifying cost pressures in controlled industries, while sellers subject to controls are more likely to press for higher prices when they observe uncontrolled prices moving upward. In like manner, any price increase allowed to correct an inequity merely creates additional inequities and so multiplies the demands for price increases; in time of war there is little room for economic reform.

Fourth, a judicious use of subsidies is necessary to solve at least two problems of price control. First, when additional outputs of given commodities, essential to the war economy, can be supplied only at higher than prevailing costs, the payment of subsidies secures these additional outputs at no increase in the over-all price; thus each dollar of subsidy paid out to increase copper production has saved the government $28 which otherwise it would have had to pay in the form of higher prices. Second, the use of subsidies to hold down agricultural prices prevents pyramiding food price increases which otherwise would result, and thereby keeps down the cost of living to which wage levels have been tied in part by the Little Steel formula. For every dollar spent on subsidies, direct gross savings to consumers and government approximate $2.50. Subsidies thus hold down costs, wages, and prices and save the government and consumers several times their amount. Pooling agreements have a similar effect.

Fifth, since the threat of inflation does not end immediately with the coming of peace, a government must continue its price and fiscal controls for several years after war has ended. Specifically, it must prevent the flow into the market of currency and bank deposits piled up during the war until the market can absorb this cash without inflationary effect; and it must prevent the conversion of government bonds into cash until the economy can accommodate this cash without threat to the level of prices. The postwar price control program will have to be comprehensive and strong in proportion as the government's fiscal policy has been weak, as has ours, during the war.

If these five steps are taken, war will not give rise to inflation. But whether they will be taken is another matter. For inflation can be prevented, when a nation is at war, only if the people composing it are determined, and their elected leaders and representatives are determined, to take these steps; and if there exists a competent bureaucracy whom the nation's leaders stand willing to charge with the task of administering freely and without restraint those powerful instruments of price control which modern economics has forged.

By a bureaucracy competent to administer price controls I mean an assemblage of: (1) economists who understand price relationships and have the courage and moral fiber to resist the pressure of the powerful protagonists of inflation; (2) businessmen who understand business operations and pricing, and are bent upon effectively controlling prices; and (3) lawyers, accountants, statisticians, and administrative specialists. To this assemblage may be added a few men of the shrewdness and acumen peculiar to the professional politician.

Ultimate responsibility for the making of price policies, which affect not only business but every aspect of life, cannot be vested completely in any one of these groups alone. The professional politician is unsuited, for he is too much in the habit of living by greasing the wheel that squeaks the loudest. The businessman frequently finds it difficult to grasp all the elements present in situations, or to rise completely above the line of enterprise with which he has been identified; moreover, he sometimes is actuated by what Adam Smith termed "the propensity to truck, barter, and exchange one thing for another," and therefore to compromise when compromise is not in order. The economist may not be sufficiently conversant with the tricks of various trades. The lawyer is not, as a rule, familiar enough with both the economic principles and the business practices involved; neither is the accountant nor the statistician nor the administrative specialist. Ideally, responsibility for price-policy making may best be vested in small bodies composed equally of economists, of lawyers, and of business specialists familiar with given branches of industry; but all must be determined, come what may, to hold the price line.

That inflation will not be effectively controlled where a competent bureaucracy does not exist is evident in present price trends. Prices have been more or less effectively controlled in the United States, Great Britain, and Canada, which have competent bureaucracies; prices have risen markedly in Latin America and in parts of Europe and Asia which lack well-developed administrative organizations.

Even given a competent bureaucracy, price control will not be effective if the national will to control prices is lacking in the population at large and in the nation's elected leaders; for then the bureaucracy will be denied effective instruments of control, and will be subjected to unprincipled attacks calculated to undermine its morale and reduce its effectiveness. "No one can estimate," declared the President in his January (1944) budget message, what "unfounded disparagement of government employment . . . has cost in impaired morale, employee turn-over, recruitment difficulties, and retardation of essential war work."

Although the United States has been at war more than two years, an all-inclusive and adequate system of inflation controls has not been achieved. Taxation provides too little revenue, wage controls are insufficient, and some prices remain unregulated. Nonetheless, despite these conditions, and despite lack of personnel and weaknesses in the Emergency Price Control Act, the Office of Price Administration has been very successful to date in its efforts to control prices.

Under executive authority, formal price control, begun in the spring of 1941, was extended step by step to cover basic industrial war materials; these controls were re-established on a statutory basis when Congress in January 1942 passed the price control act. Under this act rent control was extended gradually to cover most of the population. In late April 1942 the General Maximum Price Regulation, which froze at the March 1942 peak most prices eligible to control and not otherwise covered, was issued, and at once stopped the upward movement of all prices but those of farm products and other excepted items, together with wages and salaries. On October 2, 1942, following pressure by the President, Congress authorized him to issue a general order stabilizing prices, wages, and salaries affecting the cost of living, at the mid-September 1942 level, with the proviso, among others, that agricultural prices could not be "ceiled" below parity or the pre-September 15, 1942 peak, whichever was higher. On April 8, 1943 the President issued his important hold-the-line order requiring that uncontrolled cost of living items be brought under control, and prohibiting increases in ceiling prices except to the minimum permitted by law. . . .

To large portions of labor, but not to all, the war has brought augmented employment, higher wage rates, and transfer to better paying jobs. Between 1940 and 1943 annual wages and salaries increased $50.8 billions, or 102 per cent. In the same period national income increased 85.5 per cent; entrepreneurial income, 91.7 per cent; corporate profits *after* taxes, 69.2 per cent; dividends and interest, only 6.5 per cent. To wages and salaries went 77.7 per cent of the $65.4 billion increase since 1940, the percentage of total going to wages and salaries rising from 65.1 in 1940 to 70.8 in 1943. Between 1940 and 1943, in the manufacturing industries, which in 1943 accounted for one third of nonagricultural employment, the annual wage rose by $923, or 70.5 per cent. This means, allowing for the 23 per cent increase in living costs, a 38.5 per cent increase in *real* wages; and, allowing also for income tax and social security deductions and for War Bond purchases, a 17.8 per cent increase. Between October 1939 and October 1943 *real* monthly farm wages rose 78 per cent. In mid-1943 *real* wages in mining and quarrying were 25 per cent or more above the late 1940 level. In a number of well-paid and not so well-paid employments (construction, finance, trade, services) *real* wages are somewhat above 1939-40 levels. In a few employments (e.g., some utilities, some clerical occupations, and some branches of transportation) *real* wages are at or slightly below the late 1940 level.

While wages have been controlled, they have not been controlled adequately; in consequence, the dike against inflation has been weakened. The great increase in wage payments has pressed up costs and flooded the economy with excessive and unspendable purchasing power. Until July 1942 the War Labor Board—the principal but not the only agency charged with handling labor and wage disputes—lacked a definite policy. Then it laid down the Little Steel formula, which provided that since the cost of living had risen 15 per cent between January 1, 1941 and May 1942, the "established peacetime standards" of pay would be preserved by a "15 per cent increase in *hourly wage rates* during, or immediately preceding or following this period." At first it gave the benefit of this formula to nearly all who applied, but later, in part because of the restraining influence of the Executive orders of September 1942 and April 1943 it did not allow the benefit of the formula to better paid workers.

This formula is inadequate on a number of grounds. It assumes that in time of war peacetime standards can be preserved, and "inequalities" and "inequities" can be corrected without danger to the whole system of inflation controls. It is inflationary because it construes "peacetime standards" in terms of *hourly rates* and makes too little allowance for hours worked, overtime, and other wage-increasing differentials. It does not incorporate the principle that wage increases commensurate with advances in the cost of living be restricted to very low paid workers at the minimum living level.

The inherent weaknesses of the formula, together with mistakes in the handling of certain wage demands threaten to undermine the whole system of wage control. It is a time-tested axiom of government that in time of war the state must not, under pressure of threats, give in to or appease special groups. It is an equally time-tested axiom that the state, when granting requests, not grant more than is permitted under the formula or principle governing such requests and grants. In late 1943 both axioms were violated. When the Administration stretched the Little Steel formula to grant seven eighths of Mr. John L. Lewis's strike-supported demand for the miners, *The New York Times* (November 5) described the grant as "a notice to other unions that they stand to gain rather than to lose by striking or threatening to strike." Strike threats followed in the railroad and steel industries, and again, as *The New York Times* observed (December 29), "the Administration . . . surrendered to union demands in wartime," and in so doing "undermined the authority" of the boards and administrators appointed to handle such matters and "dealt a damaging . . . blow . . . to wage stabilization policy." In early 1944 the C.I.O. and the A.F. of L., whose membership apparently has averaged about a 37 per cent increase in *real* wages since January 1941, attacked both the Little Steel formula and the Bureau of Labor Statistics cost-of-living index, which has the approval of the highest statistical authority. Had earlier wage policy been firmer and had this formula not suggested that "established peacetime standards" can be preserved in time of war, this attack probably would not have occurred. Wage-control policy is now at the cross-roads. Unless Congress and the President tighten the Little Steel formula appreciably and refuse to capitulate to strike threats, the whole anti-inflationary program will be significantly weakened. . . .

The battle against inflation is not yet won. It is only beginning, for it is but part of the larger struggle between full mobilization and money-making and politics-as-usual. The nation remains divided in opinion and will, for many do not yet realize that even on the home front the only admissible standard of duty is that required of the soldier. To the accentuation of this division a number of factors are contributing: a touch-and-go election is at hand; political opponents of the administration in power sometimes tend to identify price control with that administration instead of with the requirements of a wartime economy; the nation is passing through one of those recurring periods of increasing antagonism to governmental controls as such. In such an atmosphere the advocates of higher prices grow bolder as the forces of inflation gather strength. Witness the mounting volume of dangerous dollars; the opposition to higher taxes, quality standards, subsidies, etc.; the multiplying demands for higher wages and prices; the heavy tribute to black markets (estimated at $1.2 billions annually for food alone). Witness the testimony of the late Raymond Clapper: "Off with price control. . . . That's the game. . . . Pressure groups are running wild . . . every politician is fleeing for his life to fall in with the demand to break up price control. . . ." Witness Mr. Walter Lippmann's appraisal of Congressional reaction to the farm-labor fight over subsidies and price control: "At the climax of this great war . . . it is a sorry spectacle to have the Congress of the United States demeaning itself to this struggle instead of insisting that it be composed. For these lobbyists, to whom they bend their quaking knees, are quarreling about money while men are dying and the world is on fire."

This division in the opinion and will of the public at large is reflected and magnified, as the remarks of Clapper and Mr. Lippmann suggest, in the national legislative and administrative sphere. Legislation relating to price control and taxation is the resultant of many conflicting interests, of which the public good is but one and not always the most important. Most legislators are mindful of Viscount Bryce's dictum that "ten men who care are a match for a hundred who do not"; therefore groups effectively organized, as are some of those seeking higher prices or opposing heavier taxation, can give the appearance of mustering political strength and so shape legislation out of all proportion to their numbers.

The nation is troubled, in short, with the factionalism which James Madison so feared. What *The New York Times* calls "greatness" has not yet completely superseded "small purposes and unworthy motives." It is in this unfriendly atmosphere that the renewal of the price control act, together with other anti-inflation measures, will be considered this spring. It is in order, therefore, for the executive branch of the government to mobilize the *potentially* overpowering force of the prospective victims of inflation, who range from the holders of bonds and insurance to pensioned war veterans and the families of soldiers. It is even more in order for each citizen to impose upon himself, and for each legislator to impose upon himself and the nation, the standard of duty expected of the common soldier.

The steps necessary to prevent inflation and all it entails are few and simple. Taxation must be increased to provide at least $15 billions more revenue. Net war bond sales must be augmented. Wages must be frozen at virtually all present levels. The price control act must be renewed, tightened, and extended several years beyond the war's end. Subsidiary controls such as subsidies must be continued. Legal enforcement of all these controls must be greatly strengthened. Whether these steps will be taken turns upon whether the public weal is put above everything else.

THE POSTWAR PRICE PROBLEM, INFLATION OR DEFLATION? [7]

Postwar is still some time in the future. Nevertheless, if we are to win the peace as well as the war, we must know where we are going when war no longer is the driving force of the economy.

[7] By Marriner S. Eccles, Chairman, Board of Governors, Federal Reserve System. From address before the National Industrial Conference Board, New York, November 16, 1944. *Federal Reserve Bulletin.* 30:1156-62. December 1944.

In less than four years this nation has accomplished a miracle of production. At the same time we have had a remarkable degree of economic stability. All of us have seen the miracle happen—many of you helped greatly to bring it about—although at times some have lost sight of it in criticism of details. The problems have been and still are staggering. Nevertheless, under government direction, program after program has been put through successfully. The vast cooperative achievement of our people—industry, labor, agriculture, and all other groups—was only possible because of government organization of united effort, government planning, government financing, and government settlement of countless conflicts of interest on the economic front. Within this framework, the accomplishments of industry have been tremendous. The over-all results have been magnificent. . . .

The question before this Conference is "Postwar Price Problem—Inflation *or* Deflation?." The question so stated implies that we have a choice between one or the other. But if we have inflation, we shall certainly have deflation following it. Thus we may be faced with having both. However, if we avoid inflation, we shall still face the danger of deflation. If, in the period of transition from war to peace, we fail to maintain wartime price controls and rationing until civilian goods become available in adequate quantities, an inflationary situation may well develop. If, later on, we fail to raise the flow of consumers expenditures greatly above prewar levels, deflation will be inevitable. The danger of inflation in the transition period can surely be met. The danger of deflation presents a vastly more difficult problem. To solve it, will be the main challenge to our postwar economy. . . .

It has been conservatively estimated that in order to have reasonably full employment in the second year after victory, we will need to produce goods and services amounting to 170 billion dollars at 1943 prices. As the labor force and efficiency increase, this figure will have to be revised upward.

Yet, even a 170 billion dollar total reflects a volume of output vastly above that of 1939. In order to visualize what 170 billion dollars of expenditures means, let's divide them as follows: 110 billion dollars in consumers goods and services, 25 billion dollars in plant, equipment, housing, and other new investments, and 35 billion dollars in goods and services supplied by Federal, state, and local governments.

Allowing for price advances since 1939, these figures mean, for example, that as compared with 1939, we will need to have about 40 per cent more in consumers goods and services, 75 per cent more in plant, equipment, housing and other new investment, and more than double the total of public expenditures.

These are challenging figures. They are significant not because they are in any sense a forecast, but because they indicate the general magnitude of the job that lies ahead of us. It is apparent that we must aim high; that we can never go back. If we were to return to 1939 levels of production, from 15 to 20 millions of our postwar labor force would be without jobs, an intolerable situation. Many of those without jobs would be veterans of this war. . . .

A high level of consumers' expenditures is the basic requirement for postwar prosperity. The consumer is the real employer. If he receives adequate income, business has a buyer for its products, and having a buyer for its products, it has jobs for the workers. If the consumer does not buy, the markets for the output of business shrink and total income and employment fall off. . . .

There is no lack of need for everything that we can produce. There are still a great many people in this country whose standard of living is shamefully inadequate. The basic problem is to see that the necessary purchasing power flows into the hands of those who will use it to increase their standard of living. An adequate Social Security program as well as assured employment will do much to induce the spending of current income and thus increase the standard of living.

A high level of consumers' expenditures is not possible without a large volume of wage and salary income. If our economy is to operate at full capacity, average wage and salary incomes must be high enough at normal hours of work to give the people sufficient purchasing power to take the product off the market. When, after the war, hours return to normal and overtime pay is discontinued, total wage and salary income will decline sharply.

If we are to avoid sharply declining prices and loss of markets which discourage production and business expansion, a gradual upward adjustment will be necessary in the wages and salaries of the great mass of comparatively low paid workers. This must be accomplished without increasing prices. Otherwise the desired increase in consumption would be absorbed by a rise in the cost of living.

Increases in productivity should be passed on to the public largely in the form of higher wages and salaries. In those industries in which productivity is increasing much faster than average, prices should be reduced in order to reach larger mass markets. Throughout, prices should be set on the basis of narrow margins per unit of output.

Once a high level of consumer expenditure is assured, the foundation for investment expenditures of business will be laid. Investment expenditures are made in anticipation of consumer demands and are not likely to be made unless business is assured in advance of an adequate market. We hear much about the reluctance of businessmen to take risks and engage in new ventures because of lack of confidence. However, business confidence is an effect and not a cause. It will exist if there are markets to look forward to; it will not exist if markets are lacking.

To assure adequate total purchasing power, it is necessary for business to disburse the funds which it receives from the buyers of its product. Corporate profits that are not used for capital outlays should be passed on to the workers or the owners, and thus returned to the expenditure stream. Depreciation and depletion reserves which accumulate as idle balances similarly constitute a drain on the expenditure stream. Currency deposits and government securities held by businesses other than banks and insurance companies have increased from 24 billions in 1941 to the unprecedented total of nearly 66 billion dollars. They should not continue to increase after the war because, as I have emphasized, business receipts must be respent currently to help sustain full production and employment. . . .

Our economic problems must be worked out at home. There has been, in recent discussion, too much reliance on the stimulus to our domestic prosperity which may result from world trade. International cooperation is essential and international agreements, such as those planned at Bretton Woods, are desirable. Yet, we must not forget that the level of postwar employment in the United States will depend primarily upon the existence of domestic markets for our products. Our first responsibility is full employment at home and achieving it is the most powerful contribution we can make to a prosperous world economy.

In the period ahead, we should keep constantly in mind that this is a 200 billion dollar a year country. We all know by now that we can not gain by fighting over shares of a small total output. In 1932 when many millions were unemployed, corporations as a whole lost nearly 3½ billions and net current income of farm operators amounted to less than 2 billions. In 1943 with full employment, corporations, after tax liabilities of about 15 billions, had net incomes of nearly 9 billion dollars, an all-time high. Similarly, net current income of farm operators amounted to more than 12 billions, likewise an all-time high. There is no profit in goods that are not produced. On the other hand, we all gain from a larger total output.

WHAT ABOUT INCREASING WAGE RATES? [8]

Wage earners, on an average, are enjoying straight-time hourly wages that are about 50 per cent above prewar. If recent proposals go through, these wage rates are to be pushed up to about 55 per cent above that level. There is some indication, too, that United States industry may be told that it can assume the wartime increase in wage rates, plus the increase now in prospect, without raising prices. These increased costs are to come out of profit margins, on the basis of existing plans.

The White House has been told by economists of the Office of Price Administration, of the Commerce Department, and of the Labor Department that industry will be well able to absorb the higher costs in peacetime by getting along with a smaller

[8] By Forrest H. Kirkpatrick and Nancy E. Oberman, Radio Corporation of America, Camden, New Jersey. *Personnel.* 21:224-8. January 1945. American Management Association. New York.

margin of profits and by depending upon increased volume to yield a return for stockholders and managers. Any price increase based on the new wage increase is opposed. The point is made that labor, not ownership or management, should enjoy any fruit of greater capital investment, improved techniques, and heightened production efficiency.

Recent hearings before the War Labor Board on revision of the national wage stabilization code—the Little Steel forumla—showed that organized labor was much concerned about wages after V-E day. The new wage argument has been advanced by those who want the government to break the Little Steel formula to permit a general increase in workers' hourly rates. Employers and government stabilizers are being asked to accept this argument with a view to keeping labor earnings at relatively high levels after the European war ends. The new wage idea is being put forth by a group of economists who also argue that wages no longer need to be stabilized as a safeguard against inflation. They feel that this country may be fighting deflation in the form of reduced worker income after V-E day.

Some economists are insisting that wages be permitted to rise when the German war ends to compensate for the loss of overtime. This kind of argument is also gaining favor with labor leaders, and some American Federation of Labor and Congress of Industrial Organizations officials leaned heavily on such reasoning in the recent hearings before the War Labor Board. In one of these hearings, the A.F. of L. pleaded for a change in wage policy that would scrap the Little Steel formula. In other hearings, C.I.O. unions appealed for wage increases that could not be granted unless the Little Steel formula were revised.

The arguments that have been advanced in favor of a change in the wage stabilization policy are these:

1. Labor's purchasing power, at today's hourly wage levels, is inadequate to sustain full employment and full production after the war. Defeat of Germany will bring a reduction in consumer buying power of $14,000,000,000 to $16,000,000,000, or about 15 per cent of present consumer spending. Such a reduction, the A.F. of L. contends, would precipitate a depression worse than that of the 1930's. If the Little Steel formula

is lifted, industry could adjust wages upward while still making war goods and while converting to civilian production.

A.F.L. believes that the time has come for the government to drop wage controls, not merely modify them, because inflation no longer is a problem. Workers and employers then would be permitted to settle their wage problems by collective bargaining.

2. C.I.O. officials have told the War Labor Board that deflation already has started, that production has fallen off, employment is decreasing, and cuts in earnings are lowering workers' purchasing power. The steel industry, from which the unions demanded a wage increase of 17 cents an hour, is cited in referring to the loss in earnings that workers can expect after the war unless an hourly wage increase is granted.

Philip Murray told the Board that, if the 17-cent wage demand were granted in full, its effect on average hourly earnings would be largely offset when overtime pay and the effects of wartime upgrading disappear. Overtime and upgrading, he said, account for 16 cents of a 17-cent increase.

Since the recent War Labor Board directive order in the steel case, union leaders have apparently accepted the fact that the Little Steel formula will not be revised so long as the German war lasts. This viewpoint is reflected in a growing conviction that if workers' earnings are to be improved further right now, this improvement must be brought about by methods which do not result in sweeping general rises in basic hourly wage rates. The emphasis will now be on "fringe" demands, such as extra pay for night work, discharge pay, paid vacations and sick leave, without reference to the control formula.

The A.F.L. members of the National War Labor Board issued a statement early in December that the Board's approval in principle of dismissal pay in the steel case meant that "all other workers will be able to insulate themselves partially against the shocks of reconversion." This approval and the award of wage differentials for rotating night shifts in steel plants, they declared, were enlargements of W.L.B. policy. They pledged their efforts to have these benefits extended to all other workers.

The views of the A.F.L. members, George Meany and Matthew Woll, were made clear in their written opinion as

Board members in the steel case. Although concurring in the majority's decision on the so-called "fringe" issues in the case, the A.F.L. members criticized the Board's refusal to recommend to the President a change in the Little Steel formula to meet the steel union's demand for a straight increase of 17 cents an hour. They declared that the Board's decision "to demand the issue of dismissal or severance pay to the parties is a distinct departure from its past practice. The Board," they added, "had approved the principle of dismissal pay and committed itself to order such payments should the parties fail to bargain on the issue successfully within sixty days."

Some predictions have been made that the Wage-Hour Division will increase the minimum hourly rate from 40 cents per hour to 65 cents per hour. The unions are now urging this new floor on wages, and the Senate has already passed a resolution expressing its favor of a 65 cents per hour wage minimum. The claims are that an upward revision is necessary now so that maintenance of consumption can be assured during the period of transition from war to peace.

Although labor favors a 40-hour week, great unemployment in postwar may make it wise to reduce this to 30 hours. Some union leaders have already indorsed the principle of a six-hour day and 30-hour week, effective with the end of the war, as a means of spreading employment when jobs become scarce. This would decrease actual earnings considerably below today's levels. From such fears arise the demands for higher wages *now* and the proposals for a "guaranteed annual wage."

Present trends, as evidenced by the steel workers' request for a guaranteed annual wage, seem to indicate that some form of guaranteed wage will enter into postwar wage policies. The War Labor Board, in denying a guaranteed wage to the steel workers, recommended that a presidential committee be appointed to study the whole question of annual wages.

Those are the arguments pressed in Washington recently in favor of a more liberal policy of wage controls. Aligned against these arguments is the contention of industry and another school of government officials, headed by James F. Byrnes, the Director of War Mobilization, who believe that wage and price controls must continue after Germany is defeated because the relationship between wages and prices must be stabilized.

In the past, American labor has scored its greatest gains during the process of readjustment after great wars. The prices of labor have declined from their wartime peaks, but less rapidly than the prices of commodities at retail. During postwar depressions the slighter fall of wage rates, however, has been more than offset by widespread unemployment. But when business picked up again, the slow subsidence of wage rates compared with living costs has brought about a substantial rise in "real wages." Whether this bit of economic history will repeat itself remains to be seen.

The current mood of many American workers reflects dissatisfaction with their lot because of the uncertainties of postwar adjustment. Quite naturally they would like at least to maintain present standards, which they do not consider wholly adequate. Yet they are fearful lest government and corporate policies ignore their desires and needs. But in considering pressure for a general rise in wages, it may be agreed that the vast majority of those mainly engaged in war work are far better off than at any time previously for many years.

In bargaining about wage rates, labor and management will confront as puzzling a combination of common and opposing interests in postwar as in prewar times. In most industries labor charges are the largest item of expense next to materials. So if it seeks to maximize the incomes of its whole membership, which not all unions do, a union has to consider what effect the wage rates it demands will have upon unit costs, unit selling prices, physical volume of sales, and employment.

Both labor and management will want to expand markets, for employment will depend on sales as truly as do profits. The sales of any product depend in turn on keeping its unit price so adjusted to the prices of other goods as to attract buyers. The lower the selling price in relation to other prices, the larger the sales as a rule; but prices must cover costs if sales and employment are to be assured.

Wage rates can be set so high that they lower the incomes of workers by raising prices and reducing sales or by heightening the employer's incentive to install labor-replacing machinery.

Wage rates likewise can be set so low that the members of a union, however fully employed, receive smaller incomes than a more aggressive policy might have brought. To find what rates between the admittedly too low or too high will be most advantageous to labor will tax the shrewdest judgment. And the wage rates most advantageous to the employer are no easier to determine.

Wage rates of American industry during this war have risen far more than wage rates in other major industrial nations. The result of this situation is a higher level of costs in industry and less favorable competitive position in the struggle for foreign markets. There appears to be agreement that, if a broad New Deal is to be avoided, involving postwar control of wages and prices and postwar direction of investments, a hugh outlet for American goods must be opened in markets abroad.

Present wage levels will complicate the problem of finding these markets in competition with industry of lower-wage countries. Competition would tend to force wages down. To protect labor against this pressure of competition, government may turn to many devices, all of which tend toward a super-New Deal. Under a regimented economy it is possible to compel employers to pay any rate of wages that the government decrees, but so long as industry operates on a private basis for profit, high and rigid wage rates would certainly curtail industrial activity in the postwar conversion period and add to the number of unemployed.

Few employers faced by higher operating costs would expand operations. Consequently a high-wage program designed to maintain mass purchasing power would be more likely to reduce the income of the consuming public by throwing men out of work. A flexible wage policy calculated to encourage employers to hire men would be a better safeguard against a possible postwar deflationary spiral than a rigid wage policy or one that actually increased wage rates and labor costs.

Reduction of hours of work and the growth of civilian industry will inevitably cause the trends of wage rates and of hourly and weekly earnings to diverge. If wage rates are held at a constant level, earnings must necessarily fall. Even a modest increase of rates would possibly be accompanied by a decline in earnings. In view of the large proportion of the national income that consists of wage payments, the level of wage rates will be a factor of enormous importance in our postwar national economy. If and when the wage stabilization policy is changed, all elements of our economy will feel the results. Whether the existing policy is to remain in effect or be replaced by new wage proposals is, therefore, a matter to which all industry must give primary attention in planning for the future.

REPORT OF PRESIDENT'S COMMITTEE ON COST OF LIVING [9]

In a memorandum of October 22, 1943, the President directed the War Labor Board to appoint a committee of its members (labor, business, and government) to look into the question of the cost of living and try "to make clear how the [Bureau of Labor Statistics] index figure is arrived at, whether any changes should be made in its component parts, or other improvements." With the President's approval, the War Labor Board appointed a committee of five: William H. Davis, Chairman; Horace B. Horton and George Batt, to represent industry; and George Meany and R. J. Thomas, to represent labor.

On November 17, 1944, the Chairman of the President's Committee submitted his report on changes in the cost of living since January 1941. This report was transmitted with a letter from the industry members of the Committee, comments on the report by Mr. Thomas, and a letter from Mr. Meany, giving "a special report to clarify certain points which the American Federation of Labor feels have not been sufficiently emphasized." The report, the comments, and the background against which the Chairman's conclusions are presented are summarized below.

At its first meeting, on November 8, 1943, the Committee unanimously agreed, on motion of Mr. Meany, that it would investigate the following:

1. What is the cost of living compared to (a) January 1, 1941; (b) May 15, 1942; (c) September 15, 1942?
2. How is the index figure arrived at?

[9] *Monthly Labor Review.* 60:168-84. January 1945.

3. Should there be any changes made in the present method of securing or computing the figures? This is to include method of collecting data and choice of component parts of the index.

4. What, if any, concrete suggestions have we for improving the method of securing figures?

On January 25, 1944, Messrs. Thomas and Meany submitted a report which they recommended for adoption by the Committee as a whole. The report asserted that, by December 1943, the cost of living in the United States had risen at least 43.5 per cent above the level of January 1941, whereas the B.L.S. index figure had risen only 23.4 per cent. The Meany-Thomas report was immediately submitted to the Bureau of Labor Statistics and to the Mills Committee of the American Statistical Association [10] for comment.

At the request of the President's Committee on the Cost of Living, A. F. Hinrichs, Acting Commissioner of Labor Statistics, on February 25, 1944, submitted a comprehensive statement on the Meany-Thomas report. He pointed out, in sum, that the data in that report did not support the claim of a 43.5 per cent rise in the cost of living and that there was conclusive evidence of the error of such a claim.

On March 22, 1944, Mr. Davis received a communication from the Mills Committee saying:

The central criticisms contained in the Meany-Thomas report were before us when we prepared our report. The various tests we made were designed specifically to evaluate these criticisms. After study of the Meany-Thomas report and the Bureau of Labor Statistics' reply thereto, we reaffirm the major conclusions of our report of October 10th, 1943.

The discrepancy of 20 percentage points between the figures of the Bureau of Labor Statistics and of the Meany-Thomas report represented so large a difference that the Chairman thought the President's Committee should not attempt to evaluate

[10] At the request of the Bureau of Labor Statistics, through the Secretary of Labor, Dr. E. A. Goldenweiser, then president of the American Statistical Association, had appointed a committee in May 1943, to review and appraise the cost-of-living index. This committee, consisting of Frederick C. Mills (chairman), E. Wight Bakke, Reavis Cox, Margaret C. Reid, Theodore W. Schultz, and Samuel Stratton, had previously reported, concluding: "First, that within the limitations established for it, the cost-of-living index provides a trustworthy measure of changes in prices paid by consumers for goods and services. Second, that many of the difficulties and doubts which have arisen concerning the index have their origins in attempts to use it uncritically for purposes to which it is not adapted."

it without the aid of technical experts. He therefore, on March 1, 1944, asked Dr. Wesley C. Mitchell, Dr. Simon N. Kuznets, and Dr. Margaret G. Reid to serve as a technical committee, with Dr. Mitchell as chairman. The technical committee was requested to examine the Meany-Thomas report, the Bureau's reply, and all other pertinent data and present an independent opinion; its report was submitted on June 15, 1944.

In the same month Mr. Thomas filed with the President's Committee a document (Living Costs in World War II) published by Philip Murray and himself, and the Bureau of Labor Statistics and the Bureau of Agricultural Economics prepared, at the request of Mr. Davis, a joint analysis of changes in the B.L.S. cost-of-living index and the B.A.E. index of prices paid by farmers for articles used for family living. The B.L.S.-B.A.E. analysis showed that the two indexes, "being unlike in purpose and in the articles represented, are unlike in construction and items covered. It follows that the two indexes should not be expected to be at the same level."

The industry members of the President's Committee had, in the interval, asked the National Industrial Conference Board to analyze the Meany-Thomas report, and its report had been filed with the Committee in April 1944.

The Chairman's report relied on the analysis by the Mitchell Committee for an evaluation of the differences between the changes shown by the B.L.S. index and the Meany-Thomas report. It quoted from the Mitchell report as follows:

The detailed evidence presented in Part III confirms confidence in the accuracy and representativeness of the price changes shown by the B.L.S. index. On the other hand, the evidence submitted by the Meany-Thomas report in support of these charges does not withstand critical examination.

Because we are convinced that some estimates of the greater expenses incurred because of poorer quality are much too high we are willing to contribute our guess. We believe that family expenditures in general have not been pushed up, by deterioration of qualities and price increases for the full range of qualities, more than two or three points beyond the increase indicated by the B.L.S. index. In making this guess, we isolated the items for which reduced quality tends to force the purchase of increased quantity. We took into account the importance of these goods in the total index and the B.L.S. method of pricing, and studied market data on both quality and quantity. And we considered the probable effect of the B.L.S.'s failure to cover the entire range of qualities.

Where the evidence is inconclusive, the committee has attempted an informed guess. All guesses are based on assumptions that have been examined and stated as systematically as has been possible, within the time available to us. The committee has seen fit to include those guesses because it believes that certain other guesses have greatly exaggerated the shortcomings of the index.

If the B.L.S. had obtained strictly accurate reports of all the prices it tries to collect; if it had caught the change in average prices caused by their reduction in bargain sales; if it had priced the qualities bought by families with very low income and the qualities bought by the most prosperous of wage earners as well as those in the middle groups; and if it had made full allowance for increases in expenditures forced on families by quality deterioration that can be offset by buying more goods, its index would probably not be higher than it is now by more than three to four points.

The report summarized the additions to the B.L.S. index, estimated for the Meany-Thomas report and the Mitchell report, as follows:

Analysis of differences between the increases in prices and rents charged large-city workers, as shown by the Bureau of Labor Statistics index and the estimates of the Meany-Thomas report and the Mitchell Committee:

Reasons given for differences:	Increase (percentage points in total index) over B.L.S. index as estimated by—	
	Meany-Thomas report	Mitchell Committee report
Methods of pricing (greater increases in food not priced for index than in foods priced, and in rents of dwellings not priced than in rents of dwellings priced)	7.22	0.30
Disappearance of cheaper consumption items	3.62	0.06 - .11
Decline in special sales	1.35	.44
Increase in underreporting of prices actually charged	.98	.24 - .48
	13.17	1.04 - 1.33
Quality deterioration	6.93	1.46 - 2.69
Total	20.10	2.50 - 4.02

The Chairman's report pointed out, in answer to the basic question the Committee originally agreed to investigate, i. e., the accuracy of the Bureau's index—

1. The accuracy of the B.L.S. index figures for what they are intended to measure is confirmed. They are entitled to the good reputation they have long enjoyed. They constitute a competent measure of price changes for goods customarily purchased by families of wage earners and lower-salaried workers living in large cities. They provide from month to month an acceptable approximation to changes in the cost of living for urban workers. They are good basic figures for use in the formation of fiscal and other governmental policies and for observing the effects of such policies.

2. Under the exceptional market conditions which exist in wartime, and so long as we have a seller's market, allowance should be made for a hidden increase in the cost of living of probably as much as 3 and certainly not more than 4 percentage points, due to quality deterioration, disappearance of cheaper goods, decrease of special sales, and increases in underreporting of prices actually charged. Unlike the price changes recorded by the B.L.S., these items of temporary disadvantage of the buyer in a seller's market are not directly measureable but they have been soundly estimated by the Mitchell Committee.

3. If the index is to be used to represent changes in the cost of living of urban workers in small as well as large cities there should be an upward adjustment of the index figures by not more than one-half of a percentage point. This item is estimated from the results of data from only a few small cities. It, also, reflects wartime conditions. It should be replaced by a figure based on direct observation when the B.L.S. has extended its pricing to a more adequate coverage of small cities.

For all components combined, the B.L.S. cost-of-living index rose approximately 15 per cent from January 15, 1941 to May 15, 1942. It rose about 2 per cent more from May 15 to September 15, 1942. It continued to rise at about the same rate to April 15, 1943, when it amounted to an increase of about 23 per cent. There was some minor fluctuation but no further significant rise in the 12 months from April 15, 1943 to April 15, 1944. The increase up to December 15, 1943 was approximately 23 per cent. It was 25.5 per cent on September 15, 1944.

To this figure, 25.5 per cent, should be added the Mitchell Committee estimate of 3 to 4 percentage points for the hidden increases in a seller's market, and ½ percentage point if the index is to be used to represent changes in the cost of living of urban workers in small as well as large cities.

The final figure for the over-all increase in the cost of living from January 1941 to September 1944 would thus be found to be 29 to 30 per cent.

The report deals briefly with the second question, "How is the index figure arrived at?" and refers those interested in the details to the *Description of Cost of Living Index of Bureau of Labor Statistics* prepared by the Bureau, and to Part II of the Mitchell report.

Regarding the Bureau's methods of collection and computation of data for the index, the report reached the following conclusions:

No substantial criticism of the B.L.S. methods has survived the searching studies presented to this committee. Certain minor ways in which the B.L.S. methods might be improved if it had more ample funds are discussed below. . . .

I agree wholly with the Mitchell Committee that the methods applied by the committee to estimate the hidden increase in living costs in a seller's market are not suitable for use in preparing an official index and should not be adopted by the B.L.S.

The only concrete suggestion made by the Mitchell Committee is that the B.L.S. index might well be given another name. I would approve of that suggestion if the new name could emphasize the fact that the B.L.S. index measures changes in the total cost of a fixed standard of living, not changes in total family expenditures due to changed standards of living.

But something might be done to improve the index. A more extensive sample of small cities would give greater assurance that price was being measured for wage earners and lower-salaried clerical workers in general. The pricing of a somewhat wider range of qualities for some items might make it possible to get a better measure of average price change for these groups of families, within the limitations of the fact that as the number of qualities priced increases so does the difficulty in identifying the quality. Occasional checks might be made of the importance of sales at mark-downs and special discounts not included in the pricing. There is no evidence that these affect the index much, so there would be a question whether the increased accuracy of the index would be worth the additional costs. An expenditure survey would be valuable in bringing expenditure weights in line with present spending patterns.

On the matter of finding identical qualities and minimizing quality deterioration of items in the index, two changes seem to have merit: (i) To have more information on labels, and (ii) to have quality floors for items for which serviceability is important and to allocate materials to manufacturers in such a way that adequate supplies of these are available in the market. But effecting these changes is outside the province of the B.L.S.

These suggestions have all been considered by the B.L.S. Recommendations bearing on them appear in the report of the A.S.A. Committee and the B.L.S. has testified before Congressional Committees concerning the need for and possible ways of providing more adequate data. The controversy which has given rise to the present report indicates their significance.

In the report of the Mills Committee of the American Statistical Association, at pages 403 to 405 inclusive, a number of recommendations were made to the Bureau of Labor Statistics. We are informed that the Bureau has given careful consideration to these recommendations. The Mills Committee recommendations are more specific than the coverage of the above-quoted extracts from the Mitchell Committee report, but they point in the same direction.

We note particularly that both the Mitchell Committee and the Mills Committee recommend further study by the B.L.S. of family expenditures and spending patterns, and the Mills Committee advises (p. 404, *Journal of the American Statistical Association,* December 1943):

"That frequent *small-sample studies of family expenditures and incomes* be conducted, and that once in 5 years a comprehensive study be made to provide data on local differences in income and consumption habits among occupational groups in the United States. Furthermore, that adequate analyses and integration of these studies and existing data be planned and regularly provided for. Since these kinds of studies provide the weights which reflect the changes in consumption habits and are important in keeping the cost-of-living indexes in line with current economic development, it is essential that they be made periodically."

These suggested improvements in the methods and scope of the B.L.S. work would involve, of course, additional expense and therefore additional budget appropriations. It is my opinion that the suggestions should be given careful consideration by all of the Government agencies involved and that action upon them should be left to recommendations of the B.L.S., review by the Bureau of the Budget, and action by the Congress.

The report explained in some detail that the B.L.S. index measures changes in retail prices and rents charged city workers, in terms of a standard market basket, and does not measure changes in total family expenditures. There have been very great changes in family expenditures since early 1941, not only because prices are higher but also because of rising incomes, increased taxation, scarcity of durable and certain other consumer goods, very considerable migration to war centers, and the entrance of some 11,000,000 men into the armed forces.

It is emphasized that the Bureau never has tried, and does not now try, to measure the cost of living in the sense of changes in the total amount of family expenditures. As to this the report stated:

As a matter of fact it seems to me highly important, particularly from the standpoint of those who have to battle for better standards of living in America, that it should be generally understood that the thing measured by the B.L.S. index is the change from time to time in the aggregate cost of a fixed typical family market basket, so that urban workers may know whether their wage dollar has kept its real value in the market. Their interest is in how much goods and services a given amount in the pay envelope will buy. If prices go down but the workers, through their unions, manage to keep wages stable, then they have won an increase in real wages and can improve their standard of living. If prices are held steady and wages go up, again an improved standard of living is made possible. If prices go up, then an equivalent increase in wages must be achieved if the workers' standard of living is to be maintained. If the B.L.S. permitted changes in income to change its index, these people would have no way to measure either the gains or the losses in the value of the dollars for which they work. With a great falling off of real income, and the inevitable reduction of total family expenditure, they might be asked to believe that the "cost of living" had declined as their incomes fell off and that they were really as well off as before.

The industry members of the President's Committee concurred in the main with the general conclusions of the Chairman. Their letter, commenting on the application of the index to wage *rates*, pointed out—

Although minor technical inadequacies, due mainly to wartime conditions, have developed in the B.L.S. cost-of-living index, their aggregate significance is relatively unimportant. While a rough "guess" of their magnitude is possible from time to time, competent technicians, such as those on the Mills Committee and the Mitchell Committee, agree that dependable adjustments cannot be made in the B.L.S. index to compensate for these factors. The Mitchell report stated "We have little advice to offer for improvement in the methods used by the B.L.S." Our studies confirm this conclusion.

The letters from R. J. Thomas of the C.I.O. and George Meany of the A.F. of L. stated that wartime change in the manner of living should be taken into account in fixing wage rates.

Mr. Thomas said that "there is substantial agreement among all concerned [that] retail prices have risen at least 20 to 30 per cent between January 1941 and September 1944. . . . Our studies indicate that the conclusion of the Mitchell Commitee is most conservative. We believe that the factors of quality deterioration, disappearance of cheaper items, decline in special sales, and increase in underreporting of prices actually charged—the factors which, according to the Mitchell Committee, result in an understatement of from 3.5 to 4.5 percentage points—account for a much larger error. The conclusion of the Mitchell Committee must be regarded as a minimum." The letter pointed out that in addition to increased expenditures resulting from higher prices, workers' families have incurred a great variety of extra expenditures because of wartime conditions—migration to war production centers, maintenance of homes in two places, wives working in factories, and increased eating away from home—which are not covered by a price index. It concluded that "the B.L.S. index cannot appropriately be used for wage-adjustment purposes. It is a measure of price changes only; it does not measure the full rise in living costs"—which the Congress of Industrial Organizations places at 44.4 per cent from January 1941 to March 1944.

Mr. Meany's letter also stressed the difference between a price index and an index of changes in the necessary expenditures of the workers, and said:

If the index does not measure these things (changes in the manner of living, eating away from home, the cost of forced purchases in higher-priced stores because of transportation difficulties, increased living costs of migrants), then it does not measure cost of living. Clearly then the index is not and cannot be made a satisfactory indicator of increases in costs of living necessary to adjust wages so that the welfare of the workers can be stabilized.

The letter noted that the section of the Little Steel formula in regard to the correction of substandards of the living has not been carried out, and that "real" wage rates in some trades were lower in 1943 than in 1940. On the basis of the Mitchell Committee's estimate of the increase in living costs, the letter gave figures on "real" wages in cents per hour which show lower figures in 1943 than in 1940 for the building and printing trades, truck drivers, bakery and street-railway workers. It concluded by recommending that the National War Labor Board request the President to issue an Executive order that would allow employers and workers "by mutual agreement to increase wage rates up to the proposed 30 per cent over January 1941," and in cases of dispute to permit the Board "to increase wage rates up to the 30 per cent over January 1941, depending on the particular circumstances found to exist in each case."

WAGE STABILIZATION [11]

The price of labor (wage rates) is the most important price in the economy. Wages and salaries of employees constitute about 65 per cent of the total national income and a still larger percentage of costs of production in the accounting sense. No price-control program can succeed with wages uncontrolled.

Organized labor is seeking to obtain wage-rate increases equal to the rising cost of living. Some firms have agreed to maintain this parity through automatic wage or salary adjustments. At first glance this policy sounds just and reasonable, but further thought reveals that it is not. The drainage of productive resources into war goods production necessarily diminishes the supply of consumers' goods. Curtailment of consumption is an essential sacrifice in an economy devoted to total war. Insofar as labor groups are successful in obtaining increases in money wages sufficient to maintain, in wartime, their customary peacetime standard of living, they are evading their share of this sacrifice. If all groups—labor and nonlabor—were equally successful, there could be no curtailment of consumption and no resources would be released to produce war goods. If labor groups, through successive wage increases, avoid any significant curtailment in consumption, then other members of society must not only bear their own share of the necessary curtailment but must bear the laborer's share also.

Wage increases so adjusted as to fully compensate for rising living costs not only violate justice in wartime, but also set in motion an inflationary spiral. Wages are the chief item in costs

[11] By Edward G. Daniel, Miner Professor of Business Administration, University of Oregon. In his *Federal Finance, Prices and Public Welfare.* p. 23-8. Bureau of Business Research. School of Business Administration. University of Oregon. May 1944.

of production. If labor is successful in obtaining wage increases of this magnitude, then either profits will be seriously reduced or annihilated, and the incentive to production greatly diminished, or price ceilings must be broken. A rise in wages sufficient to fully cover rising living costs causes producers to demand an upward revision of price ceilings to cover increased costs of production; price-control authorities find themselves compelled to revise prices in order to protect output; the higher prices allowed then become the occasion for further wage increases; and this process can go on spirally without end.

Another cause of inflation which works spirally rests upon the relation between wage rates and farm prices. The rise in farm prices has been based upon the parity formula, under which the parity price rises automatically with the rise in price of the industrial products the farmer buys. At the same time, the pressure of labor for higher wages has been based upon the rise in cost of living. Wages and agricultural prices thus interact to create a spiral of inflation.

These spirals are permitted and accentuated through the money and banking mechanism. A successful move by labor to protect itself, under war conditions, from a fall in its customary level of consumption will increase the supply of money in two ways.

First, wage earners insist upon an increase in money wages to offset rising costs of living which are due to *decreased efficiency*. It is common experience that boom periods, even in peacetime but especially in wartime emergencies, are accompanied by a reduction in the output *per unit* of productive resources employed.

In the war emergency, increases in wage rates are unlikely to operate to cause unemployment. Under these conditions wage-rate increases enforced to offset price rises brought about by decreased efficiency must lead to higher costs and hence to larger incomes supported by new money. Private industry meets these higher labor costs, in part at least, by borrowing from banks. The consequent creation of additional bank money operates to raise general prices. If wage earners again demand wage increases to meet this second rise in prices, the whole process is repeated. This process can continue indefinitely. It is independent of the way in which the Federal Treasury obtains its revenue.

Second, the money cost of goods consumed by labor is rising because the Treasury is borrowing from commercial banks. The new money created in this manner results in "deficit-induced" inflation. Labor is admittedly attempting to protect itself from rising prices due to this cause. Rising money wages forces up the prices the Federal Government must pay for war goods in order to give "fair compensation" to producers. This rise in cost to the government of its war supplies causes a larger dollar deficit and, under present Treasury financing, causes the government to borrow still more money from banks, thereby raising prices again. This process too can go on indefinitely. It results from the way in which the Treasury is obtaining its revenue.

At present, both of these causes of an increased supply of money are operating through wage increases. Organized labor is quite successful in preventing a lag of money wages behind rising costs of living. The same basic statistics concerning the relative increases of living costs and wages can be used to show different results by selecting different base periods. Both labor and employers have been skillful in selecting that base period which gives percentage increases most favorable to their arguments. However, on the basis of the statistics of the United States Bureau of Labor, average hourly earnings received by manufacturing workers have risen more than the cost of living in *any representative period* that may be selected since the war began. From October 2, 1942 through September 15, 1943, average hourly earnings increased by 11.3 per cent while the cost of living advanced by only 5.2 per cent.

The unions argue that average hourly earnings do not provide the correct criterion for comparison because this average is raised by premiums for overtime, by differentials for night shifts, by upgrading of workers within plants, and by shifts from low-wage to high-wage industries. This distinction between basic wage rates and average hourly earnings is correct, but the significance of the distinction has been exaggerated. Certainly it is hourly earnings which constitute the money cost of labor to the employer. The premiums paid for overtime and night work are extra costs to the manufacturer.

Other data serve to throw light upon the question of the degree of wage increases and the ability of employers to pay increased wage rates. During the period 1939 through September 1943, the Federal Reserve Board's index of the physical volume of production in manufacturing rose by 145 per cent; the index of numbers of workers employed in manufacturing rose by 70 per cent; and the index of factory payrolls rose by 228 per cent. It can be calculated from these figures that physical output per dollar payroll decreased 25 per cent whereas wages per unit of output increased 34 per cent.

INCOME PAYMENTS TO INDIVIDUALS*

(billions of dollars)

	1939	1940	1941	1942	1943
Total	70.8	76.5	92.2	115.5	141.9
Salaries and wages	45.7	49.8	61.4	79.9	100.6
Direct and other relief	1.1	1.1	1.1	1.1	.9
Social-security benefits and other labor income	1.8	2.0	1.9	2.1	2.8
Dividends and interest	8.9	9.2	9.7	9.3	9.8
Entrepreneurial income, net rents, and royalties	13.4	14.5	18.1	23.1	27.8

*Detail will not necessarily add to totals because of rounding; estimates for 1943 are preliminary. Source: U.S. Department of Commerce.

The same significant rise of wages is reflected by different data from a different source, shown in [above] Table. Whereas entrepreneurial income, rent, and royalties increased in the aggregate by 108 per cent during the years 1930-1943, wages and salaries increased by 120 per cent.

These data lead to the conclusion that the war program, even with its inflation, has not been to the disadvantage of labor so far as *wages* are concerned. Regardless of the validity of this conclusion, it is certain that neither prices nor wages have been stabilized successfully. . . .

The War Labor Board adopted the twofold policy of adjusting wages according to the "Little Steel" formula and of refusing to grant wage increases while workers were on strike. The first significant departure from this policy was made not by the W.L.B. but by the Administration in the adjustment awarded the United Mine Workers Union in November [1943]. The government intervened in the dispute and took over the coal mines. The settlement made departed from previous policy in three respects. First, the government granted the miners an increase of $1.75 per day, which exceeds the increase permissible under the Little Steel formula. Second, in granting this award, the government overruled the W.L.B., which was vested with authority over the case. Third, the award was given while the workers were on strike and was granted to end the strike. In fact, therefore, the government decided in favor of the union and against traditional policy and the W.L.B. The coal case is very significant because it marks the failure to hold the line on wages and prices. The decision meant victory for the strikers, and served as an incentive to further strikes and as a precedent for later decisions.

The threatened railroad strike of December 30 was averted by the President himself, who took over the railroads and awarded an increase in pay beyond the Little Steel formula. Again the W.L.B. was overridden and the strike, though only a threatened one, was successful as a weapon.

The voiding of established policy in these two major cases has stimulated other unions to invoke the strike weapon. The steel workers stopped work while new wage contracts were being negotiated because the W.L.B. voted against making any increases in wages retroactive to the expiration of the old contract. The W.L.B. then reversed its decision, and the increases in wages will be retroactive even though steel prices cannot be. The cost of the strike to the war effort was 170,000 tons of steel.

The auto, aluminum, and textile workers have demanded wage increases. These are C.I.O. unions. The rival A.F.L. unions feel compelled to achieve equal or greater success. It has become a scramble for wage increases, and no union can afford to be left without a comfortable share of the bonanza. Any union leader failing to get wage increases for his members probably would be abandoned for some leader who could. Recently the A.F.L. petitioned W.L.B. to persuade President Roosevelt to "modify realistically" the Little Steel formula. The W.L.B. rejected the petition on March 16, 1944 on the grounds that the Senate Banking Committee was to investigate the whole stabilization program, and that wage stabilization was a question to be decided by Congress and not by the President. . . .

To date, wage stabilization has failed. The record shows conflicting authority, overthrow of established practice, and a loss of prestige and influence of government agencies entrusted with the problem. The W.L.B. decisions have become subject to appeal to higher authority, subject to the pressure of unions through political channels, and subject to the strike weapon.

Failure of wage stabilization has brought failure of price stabilization. If the chief price and the chief item of cost in the economy remains unstabilized, further inflation must and will take place. The upward pressure of wage increases on prices, combined with continued additions to the money stream through commercial-bank lending, will force O.P.A. to grant further price increases. Price-wage-cost stabilization and Federal finance present an integrated problem; and the whole policy and mechanism of price control needs revision.

COMPLIANCE WITH WAGE STABILIZATION [12]

In support of wage and salary stabilization, sanctions have been invoked which are more heroic than any that have been adduced to enforce any other comparable public policy since the days of the Stuart Kings of England. Any single payment of compensation, which is at more or less than the lawful rate, is declared to be a crime, punishable by a one thousand dollar fine or a year in prison or both; and the total amount of such payment—not merely the unlawful increase—by administrative regulation, is denied allowance as a business expense for tax purposes, for price determination, or for reimbursement under government contract.

Most automatic and universal of these effects is obviously that of tax disallowance. Not the least among the hazards involved is that what is the lawful rate for a job, and indeed

[12] By Robert Littler, Law firm of Littler, Coakley and Lauritzen, San Francisco. Controller. 13:16-18. January 1945.

what is a job, may be matters upon which there might be honest difference of opinion. Federal administration being what it is, often the employer cannot secure in advance an official ruling as to what is the lawful rate. So the enterprise is compelled to pay at its peril, with full knowledge that if the guess is too high or too low, there may be trouble.

To maintain a perfect record of compliance is almost impossible. Many specific decisions to be made in salary and wage policy must depend upon what one assumes will be the ultimate policy of enforcement. In the twilight zone of propriety, the legality of a proposed rate may depend upon whether stabilization rules are to be given a loose construction or a strict construction. On this subject there are at least three schools of thought.

There is the "catch me if you can" school, the adherents of which are proceeding to do as they please upon the assumption that after the emergency is over all will be forgiven. We can at least admire the courage of these men, though they are not entitled to a high mark for prudence.

Then there is a large group of employers who assume that if they make a gentle attempt to comply, and do not get too far off the reservation, nothing exceedingly bad is going to happen to them. This may prove to be right, and it is a comforting balm with which to assuage the uncertainties of stabilization; but, if it proves wrong, then swift will be the retribution.

The last approach, and in my opinion the most sagacious, is that the law will be enforced as it is written. It seems hardly conceivable that a policy so solemnly avowed and diligently pursued will be cast into the ash can upon the first relaxation of the crisis. Those businesses which have spent large sums and great exertions to bring themselves within the rules will not look with complaisance upon forgiveness to those who have been more careless or have deliberately cheated. The government cannot afford to forget the whole thing, and there is nothing in our history to indicate that it will.

Practical politics indicates the same conclusion. As the war nears its end, there will be many government servants who will be looking for work and great necessity for increasing the public revenue. At the same time tax rates, they say, are to be reduced.

In this alloy of circumstance, it seems only prudent to expect that agents will be retained and hired to audit payrolls, to pick up such revenues as can be produced from those who appear to have evaded their full share of the inconveniences of the struggle against inflation.

Therefore, to assume that the Federal Government is not going to check up on compliance, at the appropriate time, is an ostrich philosophy. Just what audit will be made, at what time, in what detail, and by whom, is anyone's guess. Even those presently in charge of the administration of stabilization do not know.

Up to the present, so far as I can ascertain, compliance efforts have largely been limited to instances of complaint by third parties of intentional violations, to cases of voluntary confession, and to circumstances of inadvertent disclosure incidental to applications for increases. Positive enforcement efforts have been few and inconsiderable. This limitation has been dictated by the manpower shortage. Income tax audits seem generally to have been very cursory; although I do know a few which have uncovered violations. But this is no guarantee for the future.

It may be appropriate to cast a running glance at exactly what the enforcement rules are and where they originated. Because of the universal impact of tax consequences, we may as well concentrate upon that.

Section 23 of the Internal Revenue Code provides that *"In computing net income there shall be allowed as deductions . . . . all the ordinary and necessary expenses . . . . in carrying on any trade or business, including a reasonable allowance for salaries or other compensation for personal services. . . . ."*

The Wage Stabilization Act of October 2, 1942 (more properly entitled the "Act to Amend the Emergency Price Control Act of 1942") provides, *"The President shall prescribe the extent to which any wage or salary payment made in contravention of such regulations shall be disregarded by the . . . . governmental agencies in determining the costs or expenses of any employer for the purpose of any other law or regulation."*

Executive Order 9250 of October 3, 1942 purported to exercise these powers and to delegate particularization of the rules to the Economic Stabilization Director. On the subject no substantial change was made in Executive Order 9328 of April 8, 1943.

By his directive of October 27, 1942, the Economic Stabilization Director provided that,

If any wage or salary payment is made in contravention of the Act . . . . the entire amount of such payment shall be disregarded by the Executive Department and all other agencies of the Government in determining the costs or expenses of any employer for the purpose of any law or regulation . . . . or for the purpose of calculating deductions under the revenue laws of the United States, or for the purpose of determining costs or expenses of any contract made by or on behalf of the United States. . . . . In the case of wages or salaries increased in contravention of the Act or regulations, rulings or orders promulgated thereunder, the amount to be disregarded is the amount of the wage or salary paid or accrued and not merely an amount representing an increase in such wage or salary.

The War Labor Board has adopted no formal orders repeating these provisions, but Treasury's salary regulations restate them (T.D. 5186; amended by T.D. 5294; now issued as T.D. 5295) and Regulations 111, Income Tax, have been modified to embody the penalty (Sec. 29.23 (a)-16).

Among constitutional lawyers, there has been some debate over the validity of the directive insofar as it requires disregard of the lawful as well as unlawful amount of the wage or salary payment. Among the reasons suggested for invalidity are: (1) that the penalty does not fit the crime (*Ex parte Young,* 209 U. S. 123); (2) that an additional tax must be imposed by Congress and not by the President and no statutory guide is furnished for Presidential action (*U. S. v. Schechter,* 295 U. S. 495); (3) that the phraseology of the original statute ("any . . . . payment made in contravention . . . .") should be construed only as overpayment; and (4) that Sec. 23 (a) of the Internal Revenue Code remains unamended and therefore where a wage or salary is reasonable in amount, that amount is not made unreasonable by the addition to it of an improper amount.

But he would be a bold man indeed who attempted to prophesy with precision what the present Supreme Court will do with these questions. Not before in our history have we had a court majority so willing and so blithe in its disregard of settled constitutional principles. The only thing certain about this Court is its uncertainty.

The Economic Stabilization Director has also ordered that with respect to compensation subject to the control of the War Labor Board, *"The Board shall . . . . have authority to determine whether any . . . . payments . . . . are made in contravention of the Act. Any such determinations . . . . shall be conclusive upon all Executive Departments and agencies of the Government . . . . (and) it shall be final and shall not be subject to review by The Tax Court of the United States or by any court in any civil proceedings."* There is a parallel delegation to the Commissioner of Internal Revenue covering salaries subject to Treasury jurisdiction.

It is unnecessary here to hesitate upon the constitutional implications of this authority, even insofar as it undertakes to freeze out the Tax Court from consideration of tax deductions. The questions and philosophies are the same as those involved in the constitutionality of the main penalty provisions. . . .

These things I think are self evident: that if we are to avoid inflation we must stabilize prices; that if we are to stabilize wages we must have rules; that if we are to have rules governing compensation of millions of employees in thousands of enterprises, under all varieties of terms and circumstances, it is to be expected that there will be inconvenience and even injustice. It does seem to many that the inherent difficulties of the policy have been somewhat augmented through an administration of the law which has failed of perfection by a distressingly wide margin. Still and all, with a background of men in uniform who now offer their lives in forfeit upon the altar of war, it is not seemly for us at home to complain that compliance with wage stabilization is an insupportable hardship.

THE PROBLEM OF OUR AMERICAN SOCIETY [13]

Briefly stated, here is the central problem of our future: How can we see to it that our economy will provide jobs for

[13] From article by Martin C. Kyne, International Executive Vice President of the United Retail, Wholesale and Department Store Employees of America, C.I.O.; and the Editors of *The Commonweal*. *Commonweal*. 41:54-8. November 3, 1944.

all who need jobs, so that an available abundance will replace the scarcity under which a large portion of our people historically have suffered? To do this means to keep the national income at a high and steady level (between 150 and 200 billions) and to ensure that it shall be distributed broadly enough to provide demand for what the nation produces.

If we can solve this problem, we shall not have solved all problems; but if we cannot solve it, most of the more specific social problems will remain unsolved. A decent housing program is impossible unless people have money to pay for it. Nothing in peacetime more greatly contributes to juvenile delinquency than lack of opportunity to work. National solvency, and the security of the vast savings invested by the American people in war bonds, depends upon the maintenance of a high national income; otherwise the government will be unable to bear the burden of its vast indebtedness. An adequate and proper diet for the American people is directly dependent on adequate jobs. Relations between whites and Negroes will deteriorate even further if a scarcity of jobs perpetuates economic discrimination.

And our much-vaunted way of life, our political institutions, our freedoms will melt away under the searing effects of the protracted depression which will be the inevitable result of large-scale unemployment. If we cannot learn to manage our economy for the benefit of the people as a whole within the democratic process, some other process will take its place, and that other process will inevitably be statist or totalitarian. For the war has shown men and women that it is possible for America to operate at full speed, for everyone to have a job, for the national income to reach new record highs. To do so required governmental interference with the normal course of private enterprise. If, when this interference lessens, private enterprise goes back to its old ways, the popular mind is likely to jump to the extreme conclusion; it will go beyond desiring reasonable government regulation and decide that only by means of an all-powerful state can our great natural wealth and energy be harnessed to the welfare of the entire community. This proposition we deny; but its attractive power will be overwhelming if our economy fails to do its job, especially in view of the presence in the population of twelve million discharged service men, habituated to discipline and security. . . .

What means . . . are available to us as we seek to maintain in peacetime the level of production achieved in war, and as we seek gradually to expand it to meet the growth of our population? As has been said, the basic need is the achievement of an economy in which no considerable section of our people is required to live at a level below what our society generally views as a decently comfortable minimum. Otherwise the concepts of the dignity of the human person and of democracy in general are meaningless.

Since this condition is basic, the common good—the public interest—requires that any activity which potentially may prevent the achievement of this condition shall be subject to restraint by the municipal, state or federal governments. Now with few exceptions (postal, telephone, telegraph, railway, etc., services) privately owned monopoly in any form tends to contract production by fixing prices at disproportionately high levels. The price of aluminum, for example, has remained substantially the same for several years, regardless of changes in the cost of production, which have diminished steadily. Thus because of artificially high prices aluminum is not available for use in many products where it could be used to advantage. Likewise certain trade unions, by strictly limiting their membership, have achieved artificially high wage rates. This has been especially true in the building trades. And the result has been to place a serious brake on building activity for which there would otherwise be a ready demand. Hence monopoly cannot be tolerated except where necessity requires it, and in such cases it had best be operated either directly by the government or by means of a public corporation, in order to safeguard the public interest. In any case monopoly must be effectively regulated by the Federal government; and the patent system must be thoroughly overhauled.

Hoarded currency likewise tends to contract production. Any device of taxation and fiscal policy which will make such hoarding unattractive is therefore essential. A tax policy which acts as an incentive to investment, and particularly to equity investment (common stocks as distinguished from bonds, debentures, preferred stocks with fixed dividend rates) in new enterprise is highly desirable.

The traditional capitalist and American attitude toward labor as a mere commodity, to be bought in the open market—which induces powerful interests actually to favor unemployment, because unemployment depresses the labor market—must be modified. A systematic educational campaign, building up moral sanctions, and the enactment of minimum wage laws of universal application, coupled with the establishment of unemployment relief standards truly adequate to cushion dislocations, can help to change our traditional attitude. We must remember that existing minimum wage legislation does not cover whole classes of workers—agricultural labor, domestic help, etc.—and that present unemployment relief varies greatly from state to state and is in most states not only niggardly but disproportionately low in view of the funds actually available in state unemployment relief reserves. . . .

Essential to any over-all solution of the problem of our American society is the acceptance of planning on a national scale. The more such planning can be done by private groups —trade associations, farm organizations, labor unions, large industries, local authorities—the better, subject always to the planning process not degenerating into disguised monopoly. The proper function of state and Federal Government is to integrate and correlate what should principally be done by private initiative. But if private initiative refuses to plan for itself, or to plan with proper regard for the general welfare, a far more direct and active form of government planning is inevitable. Thus the activities of such private agencies as the Committee for Economic Development are praiseworthy in principle, but so far have been largely verbal and hortatory. Furthermore they totally lack formal integration or correlation with government, and have mistakenly been based on the assumption that the job can be effectively done without government's playing any part in it.

When we speak of planning, we mean merely an extension and integration of a procedure with which American business is already familiar. Thus, for example, the American Telephone and Telegraph Company has long had a department whose task it is to determine future needs for telephones, taking into account population trends, business developments, etc., so that its subsidiary manufacturing concern, Western Electric, would not over-expand its facilities and yet would not fail to produce equipment when it was needed. So also some of the automobile manufacturers have conducted elaborate surveys to determine potential markets and supply them efficiently. By planning, then, we mean an attempt to bring production and potential demand as close together as possible throughout the whole of our economy, and thus to stabilize some of the factors which in the past have fluctuated the most violently—leading to booms and depressions. Up to this point private enterprise can do substantially all the work and make all the decisions. But in order that potential demand may be equalled by effective demand, government at this point in the process must intervene and adjust minimum wage rates, unemployment compensation rates and taxes.

Side by side with planning of this type there is a secondary variety of planning designed to raise the over-all standard of living of specific geographical areas. This planning can be done by such private agencies as the great endowed foundations, by municipal government, state government, joint action by two or more states, and finally by the Federal Government. The foundations can do a great deal to further the cooperative movement, to study the problems of housing and medical care, etc. Municipal government can implement housing programs. State government can often play a useful role in extending electrification. Joint action by two or more states can produce such useful enterprises as the Port of New York Authority. The Federal Government can create T.V.A.'s—as it is proposed that it should now do in the Missouri Valley, the experiment in the Valley of the Tennessee having been so successful. The execution of such plans should not be viewed as mere public works, serving a pump-priming function in the face of depression. There should of course be a shelf of such public works (court houses, post offices, super highways, libraries, etc.) developed and ready to be carried out, but the kind of enterprise we have in mind here should be a continuous feature of our economy, to be put under way as rapidly as resources and circumstances allow, since in the long run they will serve to increase effective national demand and supply sorely needed expansive factors.

These, then, are some of the means available to us to solve our great problem. No short article—indeed no individual or group of individuals—could possibly provide a blueprint guaranteed to bring success. But we are confident that success can be achieved if it is truly desired and if the public will think the problem through.

Many of the lines of approach we have suggested are the sort of thing to which thoughtless persons apply labels. There is only one important thing for all of us to do if we are to avoid the tragedy which would spring from another major depression. That is not to be misled by the application of epithets. Study proposals for what they are—not for what someone else calls them. For only by thinking clearly and freshly can we even approximate a decent world to live in.

EXCERPTS

Constant change and adjustment of prices and costs are inherent in a free, dynamic and changing economic society. Rigidity in part or all of the system tends to build up pressures and frictions which result in underutilization of resources. The purpose of a free pricing system is to make possible this constant adjustment. Higher or lower prices are desirable expressions of underlying changing conditions if the competitive motive is given proper opportunity.

The highest wages in conformity with the prevailing productivity of an economy are an indispensable incentive for industrial progress. If the wage level drops below that optimum, it will result in lowered consumption and reduced economic activity. If, by political pressure or other artificial force, the wage level is pushed beyond that optimum it results in increased unemployment and, therefore, again in reduced economic activity to the detriment of both labor and capital. That is why a flexible wage policy as well as a flexible price policy, designed to maintain employment and production, are in the best interest of labor itself.—*Economic Policy: Means and Ends. (Post-War Readjustments Bulletin no. 13) Chamber of Commerce of the United States. Washington, D.C. 1944. p. 11-12.*

From the point of view of the New Zealand Federation of Labor, the fact that changes in rates of pay are to be automatic, when justified by variations in the cost of living, stands out as a fundamental gain. Heretofore workers have endeavored, without complete success, to secure adjustments in wages by argument before the Court of Arbitration. The last 5 per cent wage increase was ordered by the court in August 1940. Efforts made by the Federation, late in 1941, to obtain a general wage increase to compensate for the rise in the cost of living were unsuccessful. Thus, the automatic method of adjustment "represents a considerable advance in the endeavors being made to protect, in time of war, the standard of living of the workers."

Under the terms of the economic stabilization plan, the Arbitration Court has one concern, namely the level of retail prices as shown by the wartime price index. If that index records a 5 per cent rise, the court must increase all rates of wages. Moreover, the Federation pointed out, the order will relate to the actual rates of wages being paid, and not to arbitration-award wages, and it must grant as nearly as possible the full increase recorded by the index.—*Monthly Labor Review. Ag. '43. p. 254.*

In discussing economic stabilization, the report emphasizes the necessity for continuing price, wage and rationing controls after V-E day. So far, economic stabilization has kept the cost of living from rising excessively. In World War I it rose 62 per cent in fifty-two months, whereas in this war it has gone up only 29 per cent in sixty-six months.

The recommendation in the January report that Congress grant the War Labor Board statutory power to make its decisions enforceable is renewed.

The report states that the Director of Economic Stabilization and the Price Administrator have developed a program which is designed, after Germany is defeated, to keep prices in check; to keep consumer buying power under control; to keep corporation earnings under control; to hold wages in check, and at the same time, to establish prices on newly manufactured goods so as to facilitate reconversion.

The Office of War Mobilization and Reconversion has asked that a special study be made to determine those industries in which hourly wage rates have increased substantially less than the cost of living and hence any sharp decline in hours worked per week would lower the standard of living. The purpose of this study is to determine the adjustments which can be made in these industries in the framework of stabilization policies.— *From Text of the Official Summary of Report by James F. Byrnes, Director of War Mobilization and Reconversion, to the President and Congress. New York Times. Ap. 1, '45. p. 28.*

For some years past this country has been living, producing and fighting under a planned economy. Without some form of anti-inflation policy, it is hard to tell what our domestic economic condition would have been. Inflation has been retarded but not stopped. Ask a mortgage specialist in any bank if his appraisals even approach the prices at which farm lands or urban homes are being currently sold. Yes, we now have inflation. To control it, it was necessary to ration goods, stabilize wages and salaries, and place ceiling prices on goods. Modern day war calls for economic controls. These controls may be with us for an indefinite time after the war is over. The Wage and Salary Stabilization Law is a vital part of our anti-inflation program. This law was an emergency measure and the citizens of this nation have some reason and hope that it will expire within a reasonable time. The confusion that has surrounded it since its enactment may diminish, but that seems unlikely. Each point of the law at controversy may eventually rest with the Supreme Court. If that is necessary, it will be years before we have a definite law. . . .

Some have attacked wage stabilization controls as another step away from free private enterprise. And there appears some merit in this conclusion—particularly since we already have government guaranteed loans in nearly all classes of business, a high percentage of bank assets in government bonds, government guaranteed deposits and government bank examinations.

However, even those, in their intense desire to help hasten a victorious peace, usually prefer to consider it as just another necessary and temporary evil—a necessary adjunct to price control of commodities during an extremely unnatural period, which they hope can be safely terminated at an early time.—*Ray T. Bigelow, Member, National Association of Bank Auditors and Comptrollers, Committee on Laws and Regulations Affecting Personnel. National Auditgram. F. '45. p. 24.*

Business and industrial leaders appear unaware of the fact that laissez faire and free enterprise are no longer the shibboleths of our civilization. In part, private enterprise abdicated; in part, it failed to enter fields that had to be cultivated, hence were left to government; in part, it sold its birthright for monopoly and price maintenance, forgetful of social responsibility and public service. Even the First World War placed the system of free enterprise in almost total eclipse while the system of unregulated private enterprise went out years earlier.

This is not the result of malicious intent or of impertinent governmental interference; it is one of the world-wide forces set in motion largely by our consistent abuse and misapplication of scientific knowledge. We face a world of closely regulated economic life and of bargaining between labor and capital, between agriculture and industry, between government and business, and between nations and blocs of nations.

Government interference with business is no new thing. It forms part of our essential American tradition, brought into being at the request or demand of free enterprise. . . .

Private enterprise has increasingly sought security in stabilizing and controlling itself through government aid. Now the masses no longer trust it, but naturally look to government. Each war in which we have engaged has left the nation its heritage of increased government action. That is because war places emphasis squarely upon the functional production of the goods and equipment required for the specific job, not upon profits or anything else. War releases hobbled technology and science, though for destructive ends. During war, government controls industry through its purchases and maintains capacity production with full employment. ...

No enterprise or institution can be better than those who operate it. The government has usually been forced to undertake projects that were too unprofitable or too difficult for private enterprise. Yet we have usually judged private enterprise by its best examples and the government by its worst. Today, the conception that the government is a mere regulatory, policing, and taxing agency, is antiquated. It has been rendered obsolete by scientific progress and the results thereof. In modern technological society government is the nation's common instrument for the expansion of its social and economic welfare in those spheres wherein individuals and private enterprise cannot achieve equally effective results. We should cease quibbling and recognize this basic fact once for all.—*T. Swann Harding, Information Specialist, United States Department of Agriculture. Free World. Ap. '43. p. 323-6.*

President Roosevelt ordered an official study made of the possibility of extending throughout American industry a guaranteed annual wage—"one of the main aspirations of American workers."

The study will be made by the advisory board to the Office of War Mobilization, composed of labor, management, agriculture and government representatives, and on which President William Green represents the A.F.L.

The President acted upon request of the National War Labor Board which said that increasing interest in a guaranteed annual wage "is part of the search for continuity of employment which is, perhaps, the most vital economic and social objective in our times."

Several A.F.L. unions have succeeded in instituting annual wage plans in a few industries but management, in most cases, has been extremely reluctant to undertake the responsibility of guaranteeing employment and wages over periods even of one year.

The Bureau of Labor Statistics of the Department of Labor made public a survey which indicates that the annual wage idea, while growing, has made little headway against management opposition.

The report showed that approximately 42,500 workers are covered by guaranteed employment or annual wages. Most of the workers receiving the guaranteed wage are employed in consumers goods, service and distributive industries B.L.S. declared.

"Although there are a few outstanding examples in manufacturing companies of considerable size, the total number of employees in manufacturing industries who are covered by agreements providing guaranteed employment is very small, about 12,500," the report disclosed.

"Broadly, the plans provided in current employer-union agreements are of two kinds," B.L.S. revealed, "those guaranteeing employment and those guaranteeing annual wages. The employment-guarantee plans specify the number of weeks or hours of work to be provided employees each year without specifying the amount of earnings to be received. In other words, what is guaranteed is a year's job with the total annual earnings left a variable. Under annual wage plans, the employee is guaranteed a weekly income throughout the year regardless of daily or seasonal fluctuations in employment. Actually, the distinction between guaranteed employment and annual wage plans is one of emphasis only, for if the employer cannot furnish sufficient work to fulfill the contract, wages must be paid for the balance of the time guaranteed."

About 6,500 union contracts in manufacturing industries were examined, and B.L.S. found that 132 had some form of guaranteed employment or annual wage plan covering 142 companies. Eighty-eight of these companies, employing about 5,850 workers, now guarantee a full year's employment or wages, the remaining 54 companies, employing about 6,500 workers, provide guarantees of less than one year.

"Most of the guarantee provisions," said B.L.S., "have qualifications which allow cancellation or modification under specified circumstances and which extend the guarantee to only a limited number of employes."—*American Federation of Labor Weekly News Service. Mr. 27, '45.*

Wage rates of American industry during this war have risen far more than wage rates in other major industrial nations. The result of this situation is a higher level of costs in industry and a less favorable competitive position in the struggle for foreign markets. There appears to be agreement that, if a broad New Deal is to be avoided, involving postwar control of wages and prices and postwar direction of investment, then a huge outlet for American goods must be opened in markets abroad. Present wage levels will complicate the problem of finding these markets in competition with industry of lower-wage countries. Competition would tend to force wages down. To protect labor against this pressure of competition, Government may turn to many devices, all of which tend toward a New Deal.

The simple answer of Congress to problems growing from a high United States level of prices and costs is to give its formal legislative approval to the idea of "dumping" surplus goods abroad. Dumping means that American taxpayers subsidize a lower price of American goods for the benefit of people of other lands while these same American taxpayers at home enjoy a higher price level for the same goods. But dumping encourages retaliation on the part of competing nations. If engaged in, it means that this country will not go along with plans for postwar currency stabilization and for postwar cooperation in restoring freer world trade. Freer trade is a prelude to avoidance of a postwar New Deal. Dumping will be sold to voters as a means of forcing other nations into agreement with United States. Actually, however, nations today have too many weapons to use in control of trade to be concerned greatly by a threat of United States dumping.

Now, turn to the matter of profits. With costs increased by government-induced wage levels, industry is told that these increased costs must be taken out in the form of narrower margins of profit, not in higher prices. To enforce this dictum, however, Government must continue price controls into postwar, which involves a New Deal type of postwar control. Yet, if price controls are removed and prices do move higher, as they naturally would in many cases, a postwar price inflation might be touched off in a period of unprecedented supplies of liquid savings. This liquid supply of savings in individual hands by 1946 probably will total $109,000,000,000, a sum of money that cannot be ignored.

Denial to industry of the right to reflect cost increases in prices would lower profit margins and would act as a deterrent to large-scale new investment and to venturing. In that case, Government would have an excuse to move in with plans to provide jobs for all and to make use of war plants that might be standing idle. There then would be a revival of "production-for-use" plans of the early New Deal days.

All of this is designed to give you a glance at some of the economic dynamite that is lying around Washington in this period. Some of it is potent enough to blow the lid from any plans to get back to "normal" after the war. Most of it points in the direction of a postwar New Deal.—*Reprinted from the United States News, an independent weekly magazine published at Washington. O. 6, '44. p. 14.*

Since the nation's involvement in this war, public opinion seems to have formed somewhat slowly and grudgingly in favor of price and wage stabilization. The involvement may be said to date from the early summer of 1940, when the first phases of the "national defense program" were undertaken. Until Pearl Harbor, seventeen months later, the country was technically at peace and almost all peacetime rights were preserved, such as the right to bargain collectively and the right to strike. In this period the increasing orders of the government for munitions and the induction of men for selective service exerted strong upward influences upon wages. There was an increasing demand for trained workers and a diminishing supply. . . .

During 1941 economists clearly pointed out the dangers of inflation created by the expansion of income payments. The Office of Price Administration also issued warnings on this score. The National Defense Mediation Board, on the other hand, took no stand on wage stabilization. To have done so probably would have been suicidal, since both managements and unions were not disposed at the time to accept wage controls not authorized by act of Congress. The Mediation Board, conceived its major task to be the settlement of strikes. It settled many, however, by urging that wage demands be granted and that the cost be passed on in higher prices to the public.

The year 1941 thus presented a major contradiction: economically the nation was being mobilized for war; legally it was at peace. Public opinion could not therefore be strongly influenced in favor of wage and price controls. Yet the need for such controls was increasing with every passing month. In the first place, the unevenness of gain from the war effort was threatening national unity. The people in the munitions and food industries and the farmers were thriving; other groups, particularly the white-collar workers and the men in the armed services, were not so prosperous. Undue interest was being centered upon the distribution of money incomes. Dissatisfaction and contests on this question were interfering with production and morale. Secondly, the upsurge of wages and prices was increasing the cost of the war. The growth of the public debt and the increases in rates of taxation began to arouse concern. Commentators pointed out that the taxes would fall heavily upon investors, and would limit their ability to finance jobs and business operations in the postwar period. Thirdly, it was said that inflation would interfere with reemployment after the initial postwar boom by creating general distrust of the then attained levels of wages and prices. Thus, when restoration of private enterprise on a normal basis would be critically needed, inflated prices and wages would discourage long-term investment buying of buildings and machinery, and even short-term buying of materials. It would prevent the employment of the labor necessary to produce those things. Furthermore, the inflationary process would distort many value relationships. Wherever it would result in narrowing unduly or eliminating the profit margins between unit costs and unit selling prices it would destroy the motive for private enterprise to expand or even continue operations. The more distortions created during the war in cost-price relationships, the more difficulty was feared in regaining economic balance and full employment in the postwar period after the boom caused by pent up demands will have spent itself. For these reasons wage, price, and profit stabilization in this war is in the public interest.

Immediately after the bombing of Pearl Harbor, the major contradiction of 1941 was corrected: we then were both economically and legally at war. Individuals realized that private rights would have to be restricted in the public interest. Organized labor, for example, promptly relinquished the right to strike and agreed to refer disputes for settlement to a board to be established by the President.—*John W. Riegel, Director, Bureau of Industrial Relations, University of Michigan. "Wage Stabilization and Adjustment Policies of the National War Labor Board." University of Michigan Press. Ann Arbor. 1943. p. 95-7.*

We in management and labor firmly believe that the end of this war will bring the unfolding of a new era based upon a vastly expanding economy and unlimited opportunities for every American.

This peacetime goal can only be attained through the united effort of all our people. Today, we are united in national defense. Tomorrow, we must be united in the national interest.

Management-labor unity, so effective in boosting war production to unprecedented heights, must be continued in the postwar. To this end, we dedicate our joint efforts for a practical partnership within the framework of this code of principles:

1. Increased prosperity for all involves the highest degree of production and employment at wages assuring a steadily advancing standard of living. Improved productive efficiency and technological advancement must, therefore, be constantly encouraged.

2. The rights of private property and free choice of action, under a system of private competitive capitalism, must continue to be the foundation of our nation's peaceful and prosperous expanding economy. Free competition and free men are the strength of our free society.

3. The inherent right and responsibility of management to direct the operations of an enterprise shall be recognized and preserved. So that enterprise may develop and expand and earn a reasonable profit, management must be free from unnecessary governmental interference or burdensome restrictions.

4. The fundamental rights of labor to organize and to engage in collective bargaining with management shall be recognized and preserved, free from legislative enactments which would interfere with or discourage these objectives. The process of collective bargaining between labor and management shall be encouraged and promoted. Through the consummation of collective bargaining agreements, differences between management and labor shall be disposed of between the parties through peaceful means, thereby discouraging avoidable strife through strikes and lockouts.

5. The independence and dignity of the individual and the enjoyment of his democratic rights are inherent in our free American society. Our purpose is to cooperate in building an economic system for the nation which will protect the individual against the hazards of unemployment, old-age and physical impairments, beyond his control.

6. An expanding economy at home requires a vastly increased foreign trade. Arrangements must therefore be perfected to afford the devastated or undeveloped nations reasonable assistance to encourage the rebuilding and development of sound economic systems. International trade cannot expand through subsidized competition among the nations for diminishing markets but can be achieved only through expanding world markets and the elimination of any arbitrary and unreasonable barriers.

7. An enduring peace must be secured. This calls for the establishment of an international security organization, with full participation by all the United Nations, capable of preventing aggression and assuring lasting peace.

Management and labor both agree that their primary duty is to win complete victory over Nazism and Japanese militarism. They also agree that they have a common joint duty, in cooperation with other elements of our national life and with government, to prepare and work for a prosperous and sustained peace.

In this spirit they agree to set up a national committee, composed of representatives of business and labor organizations. This committee will seek to promote an understanding and sympathetic acceptance of this code of principles and will propose such national policies as will advance the best interests of our nation.— *Text of Labor-Management Charter adopted March 28, 1945 by William Green, President of the American Federation of Labor, Eric Johnston, President of the United States Chamber of Commerce, and Philip Murray, President of the Congress of Industrial Organizations. American Federation of Labor Weekly News Service. Ap. 3, '45.*

It is not often that a price index, a tool of statisticians, becomes an object of political debate. With the announcement of the now-famous Little Steel formula, in July 1942, the *Index of the Cost of Living of Wage Earners and Lower-Salaried Workers in Large Cities*, compiled by the Bureau of Labor Statistics, came into the focus of national attention. Known for years to a comparatively restricted circle, the B.L.S. index suddenly became a topic of widespread and sometimes acrimonious popular discussion. It was not long before the debate was carried to the technical level. The index was subjected to a series of appraisals, critical analyses, reviews, and defenses. Important private, semi-official, and official experts and committees considered in the most minute detail the B.L.S. index, the technical problems underlying its compilation, and the problem of adapting it to wartime conditions.

Briefly, the chronology of this technical debate is as follows:

May 1943: At the request of Secretary of Labor Frances Perkins and the Bureau of Labor Statistics, the President of the American Statistical Association appointed a special committee to review and appraise the B.L.S. index. This committee consisted of Frederick C. Mills, chairman, E. Wight Bakke, Reavis Cox, Margaret G. Reid, Theodore W. Schultz, and Samuel Stratton. On the technical staff were Dorothy S. Brady and Solomon Fabricant.

October 11 1943: The findings of the Special Committee of the American Statistical Association were released, concluding generally that the B.L.S. index provides a "trustworthy measure." (Published in *Journal of the American Statistical Association*, December 1943: "An Appraisal of the U. S. Bureau of Labor Statistics Cost of Living Index." An appendix to this report, containing statistical evidence and technical recommendations, was published in the same journal in March 1944.)

November 5, 1943: President Roosevelt appointed a tripartite committee of National War Labor Board members to investigate the cost of living and explain what the term means. The President's Committee on the Cost of Living consisted of William H. Davis, public representative, chairman, George Meany and R. J. Thomas, labor representatives, and H. B. Horton and George K. Batt, industry representatives.

January 25, 1944: Labor-members Meany and Thomas, of the President's Committee on the Cost of Living, issued a report, and recommended it to the Committee as a whole for submission to the President. Based on their own analysis, they asserted that the cost of living had risen 43.5 per cent from January, 1941, to December, 1943. (*Cost of Living*, by George Meany and R. J. Thomas, 1944.)

February 25, 1944: A. F. Hinrichs, Acting Commissioner of Labor Statistics, submitted a "Review and Appraisal" of the Meany-Thomas report, as requested by William H. Davis, chairman of the President's Committee on the Cost of Living. This report admitted that B.L.S. index was not perfect, but defended it against the Meany-Thomas criticisms, and reiterated the B.L.S. figure of a 23.5 per cent increase between January 1941, and December 1943. (*The Cost of Living Index of the Bureau of Labor Statistics*, Pts. I, II; Pt. III, Appendix. United States Department of Labor, Bureau of Labor Statistics. 1944.)

March 1, 1944: William H. Davis, chairman of the President's Committee on the Cost of Living, appointed a Technical Committee to examine the Meany-Thomas report, the B.L.S. reply, and other pertinent data. This Technical Committee consisted of Wesley C. Mitchell, chairman, Simon Kuznets, and Margaret G. Reid. Its staff consisted of Solomon Fabricant, Everett E. Hagen, George H. Hildebrand, Jr., Lloyd A. Metzler, and Arthur Smithies.

April 1944: The National Industrial Conference Board issued an analysis of the cost-of-living dispute made by its Division of Labor Statistics, and rejecting the Meany-Thomas effort to invalidate the B.L.S. and N.I.C.B. measures of changes in living costs. (*Conference Board Reports*, "A Critical Analysis of the Meany-Thomas Report on the Cost of Living," 1944. Prepared by Robert A. Sayre assisted by G. Clark Thompson and Mary A. Wertz.)

June 15, 1944: The Technical Committee issued its report. (*Price and the Cost of Living in Wartime, An Appraisal of the Bureau of Labor Statistics Index of the Cost of Living in 1941-44*, Pts. I, II, and III, 1944.)—*F. Taylor Ostrander, Pittsburgh. "The Mitchell Committee's Report on the Cost-of-Living Index." American Economic Review.* D. '44. p. 849-51.

WAGE ADJUSTMENTS FOR LABOR

THE SECOND ECONOMIC RIGHT [1]

The first economic right is "the right to a useful and re-munerative job in the industries, or shops, or farms, or mines of the nation."

To assure the full realization of this right to a useful and remunerative job, an adequate program must provide America with sixty million productive jobs. We must have more jobs than workers; not more workers than jobs. Only with more jobs than workers can every man be guaranteed a job with good wages and decent working conditions. This requires private enterprise working at expanded capacity. . . .

The second economic right is "the right to earn enough to provide food and clothing and recreation."

America must remain pre-eminently the land of high wages and efficient production. Every job in America must provide enough for a decent living.

During the war we have been compelled to hold down wage increases that might have provoked runaway inflation. With all the arms and war materials we were producing, there was only a limited amount of consumption goods available. Increasing wages without increasing the amount of goods available to the consumer would have been an open invitation to inflation.

However, the end of the war, even the end of the war in Europe, will change this picture. Then there will be more goods available for America to buy, and it is only good common sense to see that the workman is paid enough to buy these goods.

The gains made by labor during the war must be retained in full. After the last war, as part of the process of returning to "normalcy," the slogan "Labor must be deflated" was adopted. This must not happen again. This time we must make sure that

[1] From statement of Henry A. Wallace, Secretary of Commerce, before the Senate Commerce Committee hearing, January 25, 1945. Department of Commerce. Washington, D.C.

wage rates are not reduced when the wartime demand for labor is diverted into peacetime channels. We must make sure that the labor market is not broken by unemployment and wages slashes.

American labor should be assured that there are not going to be any wage cuts after this war. What is even more important —when the worker's hours are cut back to peacetime levels a real attempt must be made to adjust wage rates upward.

And wages should be constantly increased as the productivity of industry is increased. An expanding American economy can continue to expand only if the increased productivity is divided equitably between business and the worker. In fact—you know, and I know, that unless the worker does get his share of America's increased production in the form of increased wages and unless business gets its share in the form of increased profits— neither will prosper and all, business men, wage-earners and farmers, will lose.

But an increase in wages is not the only benefit the American worker should secure from increased productivity. He should also benefit in the form of shorter hours of work, in the form of increased leisure and opportunities for healthful recreation. Thus increased wages and shorter hours go hand-in-hand in solving the prosperity problem the American way.

There is one further aspect of the wage-earner's problem that I would like to comment on. That is his aspiration for an annual wage or guaranteed annual income from his job. It is a terribly important part of any real attempt to implement America's economic bill of rights. The size of the wage-earner's pay envelope is important—vitally important to American prosperity. But we all know that it is equally important to know how many pay envelopes he gets during a year. I would like to see him get a guaranteed minimum annual wage and I think the time has come for America to begin tackling this most difficult problem.

Now this goal cannot be attained overnight. It cannot be achieved in a manner to harm business. Nor can it be achieved with the same speed in every business.

But we can start on the job of giving labor an annual wage. We can do a lot if we all will only agree that it is a problem business and labor must solve and if we all approach the problem with a genuine desire to succeed. And government must do its part too. It must aid business in stabilizing its labor needs so that the burden of an annual wage will not be uneconomical. This, in my opinion, is the American way to bring about the annual wage, and I have confidence in the American way of doing things.

GUARANTEEING EMPLOYMENT AND PURCHASING POWER [2]

By way of introduction to this evening's subject, I want to say a word to anyone who may hold the idea that America, or his industry, or his company, or he himself personally can survive another period of chronic mass unemployment. If anyone holds this idea, I want to disabuse his mind of it, because it is an extremely unrealistic appraisal of the postwar outlook.

We are all in this war together. Both free entreprise and free labor unions are fighting for their very existence; they could not survive defeat in this war. That is why both institutions have achieved, and are continuing to achieve, miracles of war production. That is why we are both responding with our every energy to the immediate critical demands of war production. Working together industry and labor will meet these demands, as they have all previous ones. Working together we shall continue to assure the materials with which our Armed Forces shall win complete and final victory. We—labor and industry—jointly realize that our future free and prosperous existence depends upon winning the war as quickly as possible. And I hope we are agreed that winning 60 million jobs in the postwar is essential to the continued free and prosperous existence of what you gentlemen call "free enterprise," and what I call free labor unions. Yet this fact is no less true than is the accepted fact that our joint future depends upon winning the war. Let me, briefly, explain why:

[2] By Philip Murray, President, Congress of Industrial Organizations. Address before the National Industrial Conference Board, New York, January 18, 1945. *Commercial and Financial Chronicle.* 161:362+. January 25, 1945.

War does things to human beings, especially those who experience actual combat. The returning soldiers and sailors will hardly tolerate a condition of mass unemployment for long; they may well be inclined to greatly alter or abolish a system of doing business that condemns millions upon millions to idleness. This is no less true in the case of war workers who have actually experienced a state of full production and employment. Therefore, unless we can abolish mass unemployment in the postwar, it may abolish free enterprise and free labor unions.

To those who say that five to ten million unemployed would be a good thing, I say: "Wake Up!" Because once you open the sluice gates of unemployment, the deflationary flood will be uncontrollable; it will engulf your business, your industry, your country, and, yes, your world as well. How will you (1) care for the unemployed, and (2) pay an annual six billion dollar carrying charge on the national debt with mass unemployment and the accompanying low level of national income? Clearly America's future does not lie along the dark, dismal road of "a manageable level of unemployment," as mass unemployment, like a rampaging flood, cannot be controlled. It will run its course, and that course may well be the destruction of America's free institutions.

This being so, the only postwar road America can safely take is that of full production and full employment. Whether this is 60 million or 57.5 or 58.2 million I leave to the statisticians to argue. Personally I like the 60 million figure, and, judging from last November, so do a majority of the American electorate.

Sixty million jobs is admittedly a desirable postwar road. But how do we get on it?

This may startle some of my anxious and conservative business friends, but do you gentlemen realize that we now are—at this very moment—actually on the road of full employment?

"Yes, Mr. Murray," you reply, "but this is war. We are talking about peacetime, and that is a different thing."

Well, is it? I do not think that it is necessarily different. To paraphrase this evening's subject, the war economy has been built upon a program of "government guarantee of war production and profits." Let us examine the elements of this program, which consists of a series of government guarantees.

1. The government needed expanded capacity to meet war production needs. Industry said to government: "You may need more capacity for war, but we doubt that we will need it after the war." The government replied with a guarantee: the right of industry to amortize new facilities over a five-year period. More than a thousand certificates of necessity for this shortened amortization period have been issued. Hence industry was guaranteed against the loss of money in building new facilities, and war production and profits followed.

2. But the government needed still more capacity to produce for the war. Industry said to government: "We cannot finance it." Whereupon the government built over 15 billion dollars' worth of production facilities. Defense Plant Corporation holdings of plants, facilities and machine tools alone amount to $10.7 billion. These government-financed plants have guaranteed industry against the hazards of building them, and war production and profits have flowed from them.

3. Still the government needed more war production, and industry's facilities readily adaptable were converted to war orders. Industry said to government: "These war orders are increasing our costs, and what looks like profits in a war year might turn out later to be costs." The government replied with still another guarantee: the carry-back, carry-forward provisions of the Federal Tax Laws. With all of the publicity given these provisions by C.I.O., I trust you gentlemen are all familiar with them. In effect, they guarantee any corporation—for two years after the war—a level of profits that compares very favorably with the prewar 1936-39 level. And so the tax laws have also been used to provide guarantees that assure war production and profits.

I do not want to create the impression that industry demanded these guarantees as a condition of engaging in war production. What I am emphasizing is the fact that the war economy is based upon a series of guarantees to industry that have been devised to facilitate war production. Few of these guarantees end with the war; they carry over into the postwar. Coupled with a few other guarantees they can be the basis for facilitating full production and employment when peace returns.

A year ago the United Steelworkers of America proposed to the steel industry the guaranteed annual wage. We requested a guaranteed minimum weekly wage for each week during the life of a proposed two-year collective bargaining contract; the wage to be computed on the basis of a forty-hour week and straight time average hourly earnings. The purpose of the guarantee is to shake steel management out of its "prince-and-pauper" complex, provide management with a financial incentive for stabilizing operations and regularizing employment, and to assure steel-workers a minimum annual wage so that they, in turn, could most effectively raise the level of active purchasing power and consumer expenditures.

The desirability of the annual wage is conceded. The War Labor Board Steel Panel found:

Both parties (industry and labor) readily agree that regularized and steady employment would be highly desirable.

Religious leaders likewise agree, and also point out the need for the annual wage. Reverend James Myers, of the Federal Council of the Churches of Christ in America, says:

Guaranteed weekly earnings by all industries would not only inject new life into the entire national economy in normal times, but would tend to nip in the bud the first signs of the creeping paralysis of cyclical economic depression.

Father B. J. Masse, of *America* magazine says:

Human beings, unlike animals, do not naturally live from hand to mouth. They require food, shelter, clothing, education, medical care and recreation not just for a day, or a week, or a month. They need these things regularly and continuously. . . .

Every normal adult workingman whose only access to the wealth of nature is his pay envelope has a right to an annual family living wage.

I cannot improve upon these eloquent statements. It is obvious that industry should guarantee a minimum annual wage. The question is: Can industry make such a guarantee? Is it practical?

The President of U. S. Steel does not think so, and argues:

It is both impractical and illusory for the steel industry, of all durable goods industries, to attempt to grant its employees a guaranteed annual wage in the future.

I am unimpressed by these disclaimers of practicality, because it so happens that steel management among others has an unbroken record of having denounced as impractical every social and economic advancement made in the twentieth century. History reveals that industry leaders said that (1) the eight-hour day was impractical, (2) that genuine collective bargaining would not work, (3) that the 40-hour week was impractical, and (4), yes, four decades back, they said that workmen's compensation was impractical. They were wrong in all instances. On the last measure Tom Girdler, head of Republic Steel, has confessed:

In steel mills, laborers and executives commonly said: "You can't help having accidents in this kind of work." . . . Nevertheless, industry found out that it could help having accidents, a force was applied to safety work—the profit motive. . . . Legislation (Workmen's Compensation) spurred safety work into really effective performance.

By the same token that accidents have been substantially reduced, the steel industry can, and will, largely eliminate chronic unemployment when it becomes more costly to have its workers unemployed than to provide them with year-around work. The measures that steel management said were impractical in the past have since proved practical. A hard-headed newspaper, the *Philadelphia Bulletin*, said in an editorial last May:

In view of the great resources of this country as revealed in the war, a future guaranteed annual wage cannot be dismissed as utopian.

Though confined to steel, in reality the annual wage proposal is directed toward industry generally. Many years ago the senior J. P. Morgan is reported to have said:

I have always been taught in a business way to regard the iron and steel industry as an accurate barometer to general business conditions, and likewise to believe that no other power would exert as important a bearing on the general prosperity of America.

It so happens that on this point I agree with this great financier, and in proposing the annual wage the steelworkers' union afforded the steel industry the opportunity of rendering great service to America. Assuming that J. P. Morgan, Sr. agreed with the annual wage—a sizable assumption, of course—he would also agree that its adoption in steel would have a profoundly beneficial effect "on the general prosperity of America." And he would be right because the ramifications of steel run to the very heart of American industry.

Steel is the main raw material of the nation's most important industries. To stabilize steel operations, through the means of a guaranteed annual wage to steelworkers, would be reflected in the automotive industry, construction, railroad equipment, can manufacturing, shipbuilding, and other industries that go to make up the main steel consuming industries. Let's take a look at what is involved. Using the pattern of finished steel production in the last peacetime year, 1940, we find the following picture:

1. The biggest consumer of steel is the automotive industry. It takes 16 per cent. I know of no economic or legal law that requires the auto companies to purchase their steel seasonally. In fact, the sales and model-changing policies of the auto industry lend themselves to improvement toward the end that (a) steel purchases can be made on an annual basis, and (b) auto and steelworkers can be employed and paid on an annual basis.

2. The second largest outlet for steel is jobbers, dealers, and distributors. Warehouses take 15 per cent. With the experience gained during the war, and the postwar development of steady steel demand, the steel shipments to warehouses lend themselves to regularization which, in turn, can be reflected in year-around employment in steel.

3. The construction and railroad industries respectively consume 11 and 8 per cent of steel output. Both of them for many years have received a great deal of attention from Congress. Is it too much to expect the development of industry and government policies that will regularize the consumption of steel by these industries on a year-around basis? I hardly think so.

4. The container industry consumes 7 per cent of steel output, where much progress has already been made toward year-around tinplate production, and more progress is possible.

5. In 1940 steel exports were at least twice their level of the Nineteen Thirties, being 18 per cent. But in the postwar this might not be abnormal. Steel exports may well be this high for several years after the termination of hostilities.

I shall not take the time to go into the other steel outlets. These that I have mentioned account for 75 per cent of 1940 production. Each one, it can be seen, has possibilities for the development of annual programs of steel purchases. To be sure, each industry has many problems, and to get them operating on a year-around basis is not as simple or as easy as may appear from my remarks. The point—the undeniable fact—is, however, that it can be done. Given the will to accomplish the stabilization of America's basic industries on an annual wage, sales, and production basis, the difficult practical problems can be solved. I am one who believes that for each problem that the Lord has created, He has also created a solution. All we mortals have to do is find it.

Fortunately, President Roosevelt is in the process of creating a Presidential Commission on the Annual Wage in which, it is hoped, labor and industry will have representation. Here is a working mechanism, soon to be created, through which industry and labor can cooperate toward the common good of full production and full employment. The problems of the annual wage on which I have briefly touched can be fully explored by this Commission, and solutions found for them. Will leaders of industry, especially steel leaders, accept this challenge?

The guaranteed minimum annual wage is a specific, constructive proposal in which industry as well as labor can find the solution to many of their vexing problems. The "prince-and-pauper" steel industry may well hold the key to full production and employment, because, as J. P. Morgan has observed, "no other power (can) exert as important a bearing on the general prosperity of America." Embrace the idea of the annual wage and cooperate with labor to make it work, and you leaders of industry will not have to worry about "government guarantee of employment and purchasing power."

Before continuing my remarks on this specific subject, I want to discuss another important and equally specific proposal that has to do with purchasing power. That is the question of wages.

The Little Steel formula of the War Labor Board is tending to hold back the war production program. You will recall with this formula, which is more than two years old, holds wages and salaries down to a level but 15 per cent above January 1941. The formula was based upon conditions in May 1942 when living costs supposedly had risen only 15 per cent above January 1941. Wages and salaries, being tied to living costs by the formula, were frozen at this 15 per cent point. This freezing of wages and salaries has worked a great hardship upon the vast majority of American people, because the cost of living has multiplied—not twice as much as the Little Steel formula allows, but three times as much.

As a consequence, the Little Steel formula cries out for revision upon an equitable and realistic basis. The manpower needs of critical war production programs demand a prompt lifting of the formula so that our armed forces will not be lacking in needed materials. The great victories of our armed forces are not yet complete. Final victory will not come until the last shot is fired. In the meanwhile, the Little Steel formula, and the hardships and injustices it imposes, cannot be permitted to continue, except at the peril of our war needs.

To speed up final victory, war production, which is so dependent upon a realistic wage and salary policy, cannot—for any reason—be permitted to lag. The mounting cost of living, and its attendant consequences, make it imperative that the 15 per cent limit of the Little Steel formula be substantially raised. The President's Committee on the Cost of Living found that since January 1941, retail prices—which is only one element in total cost of living—show that they have risen 30 per cent, twice as much as the formula, while special studies conducted by C.I.O. show that total living costs have risen 45 per cent—three times as much as the formula, since January 1941.

We therefore seek a wage adjustment to compensate American workers for the loss they have suffered as a result of the rising cost of living—an adjustment in the Little Steel formula that will bring wages back into their proper relationship with current prices. The stabilization policy, thus restored, can—and must—be held by effective price controls, over-all democratic rationing, effective limitation of profits, and the stabilization of wages.

From the viewpoint of postwar it is equally necessary to raise wages now. This is emphasized by the maldistribution of the nation's savings. It is commonly believed that postwar prosperity will be built upon the accumulated savings of the American people. But the facts are to the contrary. The Office of Price Administration studies show that for 1942, 66 per cent of the spending units—families and single consumers—received $2,500 or less in annual income, and they have only 11.6 per cent of the total savings. The huge wartime savings, unfortunately, are not in the hands of the people who make up the vast majority of the buying public.

Many people ask, in the face of these facts, where is the money going? I do not profess to know, except some indication is afforded by a recent report on the nation's "billionaire" banks. It appears that there has been a 100 per cent increase since 1939 in the number of banks in this classification. In 1944 16 banks had total assets above one billion as compared to only eight at the close of 1939. And the combined total assets of the "billionaire" banks rose from $20.8 billion dollars in 1939 to $38.1 billion at the end of 1944, or an increase of 83 per cent.

Thus savings, which some count on as a huge reservoir of postwar purchasing power, are for the most part held by too few people to be highly effective in creating a demand for consumer goods. Even those savings being held for the purchase of goods after the war may be withheld from the market if the economic security of the holders is jeopardized; and may be spent very sparingly for bare necessities by the worker who finds himself either unemployed or his job security highly uncertain. This underlines the necessity for providing American workers with a guaranteed annual wage. Because, unless the mass of American consumers has the prospect of sustained earnings, the postwar can hardly be a period of prosperity.

Another development that makes an upward revision of wages necessary is the tremendous technological gains made during the war. These are even recognized by the National Association of Manufacturers which recently referred to the "incredibly increased productivity" of American industry during the war. The meaning in the postwar of this greatly increased man-hour output of American industry is that fewer workers will be required to produce war goods, and unless their wages are substantially raised there will not be the purchasing power to employ the displaced workers.

The steel industry provides a good example. From 1940 to 1944 steel ingot capacity rose by more than 15 per cent to a total of more than 94 million tons. Industry sources report that at least "10 per cent of the present steel capacity will be written off after the war with Japan ends as being too obsolete and too high cost to keep in operation." Assuming these industry sources are correct, this means that approximately 12 million tons of the most modern low-cost facilities will replace almost 10 million tons of the oldest and most obsolete parts of the steel industry. What this will mean in terms of increased man-hour productivity can be seen from the fact that at a modern DPC steel plant in Homestead, compared to an old unit there, . . . the new unit requires 15 per cent fewer workers and produces 26 per cent more tonnage than the old steel plant. Unless the remaining workers receive higher wages, the displaced workers can hardly be absorbed in our economy.

The inequity of the Little Steel formula is again demonstrated by the fact that it has frozen wage rates while productivity —man-hour output—has been rapidly increasing. America cannot afford to permit the basic wage rates of its workers to lag behind the rise in productivity. The Little Steel formula, therefore, must be abandoned. In its place there must be an upward revision in wages to enable them to catch up with the constantly rising productivity of American industry. Consequently, over and beyond the several other important reasons why the Little

Steel formula should be abandoned, a change in the national wage stabilization policy is made mandatory by the enormous rise in productivity.

"Free enterprise" alone is not capable of guaranteeing postwar employment and purchasing power. It was not even organized to handle the war program alone; it needed a lot of help and guarantees from government, and it needed the cooperation of labor. So too in postwar: "free enterprise," unless similarly aided, is going to doom America to chronic mass unemployment.

I, of course, am opposed to the outright guarantee by government of employment and purchasing power, because I realize the dangerous bypaths down which this would lead America. I am equally opposed to leaving the job of postwar full production and employment to "free enterprise," because I know it is not organized, and is incapable of that degree of self-organization necessary to assure full employment. Our free institutions would be just as much threatened by the inevitable economic depression that would surely follow in the wake of the failure of "free enterprise," as it would be by government assumption of a guarantee of full employment.

What is needed and sorely lacking in industry, is a different concept of the role of government and the part organized labor must play in America's economic life. Labor and industry have to work out their common problems together, and the role of government should be to assist them with such measures as will be helpful.

In the annual wage, which I have espoused this evening, we have a specific and constructive proposal to materially help in providing full production and employment in the postwar. It entails finding the solutions to accompanying practical problems. Industry and labor can work together in finding the necessary solutions, and whatever measures or guarantees are required from government we can jointly secure.

It is not alone the welfare of labor or of industry that is involved. The future free and prosperous existence of America is at stake. On behalf of labor, I ask industry to join hands with us to meet the challenge of the postwar.

SHOULD WE SCRAP THE LITTLE STEEL
FORMULA? [3]

There are four reasons why the Little Steel formula should
be stricken from the books of wartime wage regulation:

First, because the Little Steel formula is too little. Its meas-
urements bear no relation to the expansion of production and
worker productivity. Any sound and just method of compensation should relate the measure of the worker's effort, his output
and his skill to the worker's pay. All along the line our wartime
wage structure has suffered from what may be called "Little
Steel Deformities." In some areas of production these deformities have become large, they have hurt production, deterred
war output, and have served to slacken our pace toward victory.

Right now it is of crucial importance to increase war production, including strategic items in ordnance, heavy-duty trucks,
heavy tires and other fighting equipment.

What is holding back this critically needed expansion? They
say foundries are a bottleneck. They say there is a manpower
shortage in foundries. The reason foundry labor is hard to get
and to keep is that foundry wages are far too low. It is not a
manpower problem, it is a wage problem.

As General Clay has said, "the work in foundries and casting
and forging shops is a hard, dirty, back-breaking job requiring
physical endurance." Working conditions are bad. The foundry
worker's pay does not measure up to the heat, the grime and the
physical strain he has to put into his job.

But the formula keeps the pay down. Instead of adjusting
foundry wages, the government spends all kinds of money to get
Mexicans and Bahamans to fill these jobs. Is that fair to the
Mexicans and Bahamans? Is that fair to our workers? Is that
a sound wage policy? Yet that is what the Little Steel formula
does.

Second, the formula should be scrapped because it is out of
date. It is getting more and more antiquated. To say on the

[3] Statement by Boris Shishkin, Economist for the American Federation of
Labor, at Town Hall Meeting Radio Forum, November 9, 1944. *Town Meeting*.
10, no. 28:4-6. November 9, 1944

eve of 1945 that a wage policy based on January 1941 is an up-to-date and a proper method of regulating pay is to confess complete bankruptcy of the national wage policy. To claim this is to pretend that the vast increase in war output during the intervening years—the modern miracle wrought by labor and management in this war—never happened.

What the formula did was this. The War Labor Board said: January 1941 is our anchorage. We should pay out the anchor chain 15 per cent, because between January 1941 and May 1942 the living costs rose 15 per cent. But that's all. Forget the tide and don't pay out the anchor chain another inch.

Well, the tide of the cost of living went right on rising. Pulled down by the anchor the ship of wage stabilization is listing badly and is about ready to capsize. The farther the current carries us away from the anchorage the more imminent is the danger. Labor does not propose that we let go of all controls. It merely asks that we change our anchorage to the realities of today and set our whole wage stabilization on an even keel.

Third, the Little Steel formula should go because it is unfair. It is unfair not only because it cheats every worker out of the rise in the cost of living after May 1942. It is unfair also because it deprives of his just compensation the worker who is doing more and better work. And it is unfair, above all, because it favors the high paid worker against the low paid worker. That is because it is a percentage formula.

You are paid 40 cents an hour. Your cost of living adjustment is only 6 cents an hour. The other fellow is paid $1.20 an hour. His cost of living adjustment is 18 cents an hour. But the intent of the formula is to enable the workers to meet the rise in living costs. And living costs hit the low paid worker and the high paid worker as hard—if anything they hit the low paid worker harder.

And let me say that when I speak here tonight as a representative of the American Federation of Labor, pleading for the removal of the Little Steel formula, I am pleading not only on behalf of the organized workers, but the unorganized workers as well, for those white-collar workers, clerks and others whose meager pay, frozen by the formula, has borne the brunt of rising prices. It is time we put an end to this gross inequity. . . .

Fourth, the formula should be replaced because it is crippling. Its continued application will become the main obstacle to the return to full employment in our transition to peace. As overtime hours are reduced and the weekly earnings are cut, and as workers are forced to shift from higher paying war jobs to low paid jobs in trade and services, the formula will make impossible adjustments in pay which would assure them the maintenance of income sufficient to support high employment and a high standard of living. For the sake of full employment after the war, let us scrap the Little Steel formula.

MODIFICATION OF THE LITTLE STEEL FORMULA [4]

Thirty-two representatives of the American Federation of Labor argued in support of the petition and presented their views. The Panel, in accordance with the resolution of March 22, 1944, attempts in this report to summarize their arguments and statements. We have not tried to examine the evidence critically. We have assessed neither the validity of assertions of fact or the soundness of conclusions drawn. We have limited ourselves to the classification, synthesis, and restatement of the facts and arguments presented without comment of our own.

It is, of course, to be understood that no statements made herein necessarily represent the opinions of any one of the Panel members.

I. *Stabilization of wages was based on the assumption that the cost of living would be stabilized and peacetime standards preserved.* The President, on April 27, 1942, set forth a unified plan to prevent inflation which was to be the national economic policy for the duration of the war. That plan consisted of the following seven points: (1) tax heavily; (2) regulate prices of manufactured goods; (3) regulate wages and salaries; (4) regulate farm prices; (5) induce voluntary saving by urging

[4] Report of the Special Panel Summarizing the Contentions Advanced by the American Federation of Labor in Support of its Petition for the Modification of the Little Steel Formula. 24p. mim. National War Labor Board. September 8, 1944.

the purchase of war bonds; (6) ration all scarce goods; (7) discourage loose credit extension and encourage liquidation of debts.

No single one of the seven points was intended to be independent of the others. The President himself in his message to Congress of April 27, 1942, emphasized the unity of the program. He said:

There are obvious reasons for taking every step necessary to prevent this rise. I emphasize the words "every step" because no single step would be adequate by itself. Action in one direction alone would be off-set by inaction in other directions. Only an all-embracing program will suffice.

Relying on past and present experience, and leaving out masses of details which relate more to questions of methods than to the objective itself, I list for the Congress the following points which, taken together, may well be called our present national economic policy.

Again, in a radio address on September 7, 1942, in speaking on the stabilization of farm and food prices, he said:

It is obvious, however, that if the cost of food continues to go up as it is doing at present, the wage earner, particularly in the lower brackets, will have a right to an increase in his wages. That would be essential justice and a practical necessity.

Therefore I have asked Congress to pass legislation under which the President would be specifically authorized to stabilize the cost of living including the prices of all farm commodities. The purposes should be to hold farm prices at parity, or at levels of a recent date, whichever rate is higher. The purpose should also be to keep wages at a point stabilized with the cost of living. Both must be regulated at the same time; and neither can or should be regulated without the other.

At the same time that farm prices are stabilized, I will stabilize wages. This is plain justice—and plain common sense.

The National War Labor Board itself based its decision of July 16, 1942 in the Little Steel cases on the assumption that the cost of living would not be allowed to rise further and that peacetime living standards could be preserved. . . .

Because of its intent to preserve peacetime standards the American Federation of Labor gave its unqualified support to the President's stabilization program. But the over-all program has not been achieved. Wages have been effectively stabilized. But the cost of living has soared and standards of living have declined. If the nation is to fulfill its pledge to its workers and its fighting men, the former balance between wages and the cost of living must now be restored.

II. *The cost of living has not been stabilized and peacetime standards of living have declined.* Peacetime standards have not been preserved but have in fact deteriorated since January 1941, by an amount ranging from a minimum of 25 per cent to a maximum of 45 per cent. The cost-of-living index of the Bureau of Labor Statistics sets the amount of decline at 25 per cent. The Report of the Labor Members of the President's Committee on the Cost of Living indicates that the Bureau of Labor Statistics figures are inadequate and that the real dollar of wage earners has declined 43.5 per cent. This figure the labor members based on surveys conducted under their direction which indicated that between January 1941, and December 1943, food prices increased 74.2 per cent; clothing prices increased 72.2 per cent; rents increased 15 per cent; fuel, electricity and ice increased 8.6 per cent; house furnishings increased 62 per cent; and miscellaneous items increased 15.9 per cent. If other factors, such as the effect of black markets, shifts in the distribution of family expenditure due to wartime conditions, the more rapid rises in the cost of living in small communities expanded by war production, or the extra expenses incident to wartime shifts and dislocations in population, had been considered, the figure of 43.5 per cent would have had to be raised.

In this connection, the Board should give consideration to the index of the Bureau of Agricultural Economics. This index shows an increase in the price of items paid by farmers for their living necessities of 45.1 per cent. The major items purchased by the farmers are the same or similar to the items purchased by workers.

The index of the Bureau of Agricultural Economics includes basic foods, clothing, shoes, furniture, fuel and cost of operating the home, and is based on prices from nearly all those communities which are not covered by the index of the Bureau of Labor Statistics.

The rise in the cost of living indicated by these figures must be compared with the 15 per cent rise in average straight time hourly wage rates permitted by the Little Steel formula. Attempts to bring average hourly or weekly earnings into the comparison are misleading and unfair. Increased earnings figures may reflect such things as overtime, increases in the use of night shifts, transfers of employees from lower paid to higher paid industries, increased earnings from incentive payments, etc. Much of the increase in earnings is thus accompanied by increased production and could hardly be inflationary. After the war, moreover, the work week may be reduced, the night shifts and overtime may disappear, and it will then be upon wage *rates* that returning soldiers and workers in general will have to depend for their livelihood.

Evidence of the decline in peacetime standards of living is found not only in cold statistics, but in the living experience of employees, as observed by impartial investigators. Thus Senator Thomas, of Utah, Chairman of the Senate Committee on Education and Labor, and a member of a Senate Subcommittee established to investigate the conditions of white collar workers, wrote in the American Magazine:

There just can't be many whose standard of living has gone down. Not many. Well, I have before me incontrovertible testimony that shows that 20 million Americans and their dependents are living as best they can on incomes that have not risen appreciably since Pearl Harbor. While their incomes were frozen, their taxes have increased, they have bought war bonds, they have contributed to war charities, and their cost of food, clothing and shelter has gone up.

The United States Bureau of Labor Statistics says the rise in the cost of living is 23.4 per cent. Mr. Murray, President of the C.I.O. says it is 50 per cent. Our committee isn't sure as to the exact figure, but we do know that millions upon millions of good American citizens have had their income cut in effect from 25 to 50 per cent. . . .

In most areas now a white collar family cannot exist upon much less than $50.00 a week. An independent business girl needs $30 a week, and millions of these low-salaried workers and their dependents will suffer dire poverty if the cost of living continues to rise; piling up are fixed expenses incurred before the war, installment purchases, insurance payments, payments on a home, for dependents and a car needed in business. No longer can they save. They must sell their war bonds, spend the funds accumulating for education of the children, give up their life insurance and their home.

When we increase by millions the number of persons who are debt ridden, we are endangering the economy of the nation. But that is not the only danger. Upon this future class depends future growth of American education and culture.

The American Federation of Labor represents over one million workers who can be classed as white collar workers. The article of Senator Thomas indicates a national feeling of frustration on the part of millions of American workers over the government's wage policy in relation to the rise in the cost of foods and other items which make up the cost of living.

The representatives of the American Federation of Labor emphasized that wage earners expect to contribute equitably in the fight against inflation. Though ordinarily organized labor aims at a progressive improvement in the standard of living, it asks no such improvement during the war. But it does ask that the government's pledge to maintain peacetime standards be fulfilled. It does ask that the inequities resulting from success in wage stabilization and failure in price stabilization be corrected by a realistic modification of the Little Steel formula.

III. *Objections to Bureau of Labor Statistics Index.* The Bureau of Labor Statistics cost-of-living index shows that the cost of living has increased 23.4 per cent between January 1, 1941, and the present date. American workers, on the other hand, under the War Labor Board's Little Steel formula have been allowed increases in the amount of 15 per cent to offset a reported increase of 23.4 per cent in living costs. Thus even if the figures of the Bureau of Labor Statistics are accurate, the inequity of the Little Steel formula is self-evident.

However, as has already been noted, the investigations recently conducted by the labor members of the President's Committee on the Cost of Living have shown that the increase has been 43.5 per cent, or almost double the increase shown by the Bureau of Labor Statistics index. The American Federation of Labor alleges that the conflict between the two sets of figures is due primarily to the fact that the labor members have made a more realistic survey of the increase in prices.

1. *Quality deterioration not considered by the Bureau of Labor Statistics.* While the cost of living has increased, the quality of the goods purchased has deteriorated. Food and clothing, housing facilities, and transportation have deteriorated in

quality, with the result that the worker receives less in quality while paying more for the same quantity.

For example, shoes purchased in January 1941, were made out of the best available leather. Today the working man pays more money for an inferior grade shoe made of a substitute material that will not stand the wear that a less expensive shoe purchased in 1941 would stand. The shoe purchased today must be replaced more frequently and cannot be repaired as often.

According to the Office of Price Administration, the wearing quality of shoes was 30 per cent less in 1943 than it was in 1941. This means that if the price of the two pairs of shoes was the same in 1943 as it was in 1941, the shoe purchased in 1943 cost 40 per cent more than the shoes purchased on 1941.

It is no longer possible to purchase the "two-pants" suit. Not only has the cost of the suit increased, but the absence of the second pair of pants now makes it necessary to purchase a whole new suit after the one pair of pants has worn out.

In general, there has been a deterioration in the quality of clothing. It contains inferior material which cannot be laundered as often as the better clothing that could be purchased before the war. The problem of laundering is of particular importance at the present time when less laundering is being done at the home. Housewives are unable to obtain parts for the washing machine or may be too occupied with other present-day problems to be able to do the laundering themselves at home.

There has also been deterioration in food without a corresponding decrease in price. Inferior grade oranges, for example, are mixed with the better grade oranges, and all are charged for at the price of the better grade. Grade labeling has been eliminated, making it possible to increase the price of canned food items without the buying public becoming aware. The amount of vegetables contained in a bunch has decreased. Asparagus formerly sold for 39 cents per bunch and contained 60 to 64 stalks. In February and March 1943 asparagus sold for 19 cents a bunch and contained approximately five stalks. All these are examples of hidden price increases which the Bureau of Labor Statistics Index fails to record.

2. *Shifts in the relative importance of commodities and expenditures.* The Bureau of Labor Statistics Index has failed to indicate adequately the changes in the family expenditures resulting from wartime conditions. Family expenditures have shifted from goods that are no longer available to other goods.

An example of a change in the way the worker is now forced to spend his earnings is the increased expenditure for food consumed away from home. The Bureau of Labor Statistics has failed to give consideration to the fact that there has been an increase in the patronage of restaurants necessitated by such factors as rationing, lack of home-cooking facilities, and unequipped and crowded living quarters. For example, in St. Louis the number of persons patronizing restaurants has increased from 100 per cent to 150 per cent. Food prices in restaurants have been abnormally high due to the fact that hotel and restaurant owners had been warned in advance of the date of price ceilings.

3. *Grading-up, or the disappearance of low price lines.* Upgrading and the disappearance of low price lines in favor of higher priced items has brought about hidden price increases.

Many items of clothing which are listed by merchants are not actually obtainable. House dresses may be listed at $1.98 or $2.25, but house dresses cannot be purchased at that price. The result is that house dresses must be purchased at twice the price.

A statement by Mayor La Guardia of New York in a recent radio address was cited as demonstrating the fact that medium and lower priced items have disappeared. Mayor La Guardia had a work shirt priced at $1.03, but that particular shirt was no longer on the market and could not be purchased. The result of the disappearance of the lower grade lines forces the consumer to purchase a higher cost line of goods, a factor to which the Bureau of Labor Statistics has given inadequate consideration.

In many localities the cheaper lines of goods have completely disappeared and low priced goods that were formerly available in large quantities can no longer be purchased. This has borne most heavily upon workers in the lower income brackets.

4. *Criticisms of procedure followed by Bureau of Labor Statistics in preparing its index.* (a) *Illegal increases are not*

adequately reported in the index. In computing the cost-of-living index the Bureau of Labor Statistics has not included substantial increases in costs due to illegal price increases. Price violations in the corner grocery stores in both large and small cities are common. Workers are convinced that many corner grocery stores have never heard of the Office of Price Administration.

(b) *The selection of localities is not representative.* The stores investigated by the Bureau of Labor Statistics are not truly representative of the stores which are used by workers. In St. Louis, for example the Bureau of Labor Statistics investigated independent stores located in the wealthy home-owner district, where the homes ranged in value from $50,000 to $150,000. Out of thirty stores so investigated, four were definitely in the wealthy home-owner district and in no way represented the type of store used by the worker. The other twenty-six stores were not located in the sections where the working men lived, but on the outskirts of those sections. There was no investigation of the stores located in the area where the lowest paid workers live. . . .

(c) *Actual reports of the Bureau of Labor Statistics on price increases are inadequate.* Investigations conducted by the representatives of the American Federation of Labor in their particular localities disclosed that the cost of living for many items had increased in excess of the increases shown by the Bureau of Labor Statistics. . . .

Another item to which the Bureau of Labor Statistics was said to have given inadequate consideration was the matter of rents. Increases in rents in Joliet, Illinois, for example, were estimated as high as 500 per cent, due to the fact that thousands of workers were imported into a limited area. Two or more persons were crowded into small apartments and single rooms, but rents were not decreased proportionately.

It was also alleged that the Bureau of Labor Statistics has failed to report what has taken place, for example, in New York City, where three or four families were accustomed to live together in one flat and spread the amount of the rent. Today landlords refuse to agree to this arrangement, with the result that the price of rent has more than doubled. . . .

IV. *Complaints against the policies used in applying the Little Steel formula.* 1. *Unfairness of a percentage increase.* Many of the American Federation of Labor representatives objected to the Little Steel formula, among other reasons, because it called for a percentage increase. It was urged that a percentage increase is unfair to workers in the lower brackets. On the basis of an average rate of 50 cents per hour the 15 per cent limit would permit total increases only of 7½ cents; but if the limit is applied to an average rate of $1.50 per hour an increase of 22½ cents per hour is permissible. Thus of two workers employed in the same locality, one might receive an increase three times as great as the other, despite the fact that the increase in the cost of living is equally applicable to both.

That a percentage increase operates unfairly for the small wage earner was recognized five years ago by the Tobacco Workers International Union when it ceased to negotiate wage increases with any company on a percentage basis.

The 15 per cent Little Steel formula has brought but little relief to wage earners in such low paid industries as the foundry industry. It has discriminated against the low paid skilled workers in the printing industry. For instance, binding women after several years of training might on January 1, 1941, have been receiving a fixed wage of $20.00 per week. A 15 per cent increase would result in their receiving only $23.00 per week. Unskilled women in other fields, on the other hand, might not on January 1, 1941, have been receiving a fixed wage rate, with the result that unskilled women are in many instances receiving more than the skilled and have, in fact, had their wages doubled.

2. *The Little Steel formula is frequently computed on an inequitable basis.* It was argued that in many cases it was unfair and inequitable to base an increase on the rates existing on January 1, 1941, for the reason that equitable wage rates had not been established as of that date. For example, the Commercial Telegraphers Union was in January 1941, in the process of organizing the employees of the Western Union Telegraph Company. The wage rates of the Company's employees on that

date reflected their unorganized status and therefore did not constitute a normal basis upon which to apply the principle of the Little Steel formula.

The workers and craftsmen in the wallpaper industry received in 1941 an increase of 10 cents per hour. This increase of 10 cents was not a cost-of-living increase, but was granted in order to make up for wage cuts which the workers in the wallpaper industry had taken during the depression years. The War Labor Board, nevertheless, credited this 10-cent increase against the amount allowable under the Little Steel formula.

3. *The Little Steel formula fails to take into consideration the increased productivity of workers.* The Little Steel formula was called completely unrealistic because it did not take into account the increased productivity of the worker in such industries as the building maintenance industry. Because of the Selective Service Act and the exodus of workers into higher paying war industries, the manpower problem has resulted in buildings frequently being maintained by less than 60 per cent of the normal working staff. Occupancy in the buildings has, nevertheless, increased, with the result that in many cases employees are servicing twice as many units as they were formerly called upon to service. To such a group of employees the application of the Little Steel formula is particularly unjust.

Increases in wage rates which have been accompanied by increases in productivity should not be taken into account in computing the amount due under the Little Steel formula. It was stated that in the wallpaper industry figures showed that wage increases between 1941 and 1942 amounted to 13 per cent. But actually there was only a 7 per cent labor cost increase. Six per cent of the 13 per cent increase was absorbed by increased productivity and a consequent reduction in the labor cost per hundred rolls of wallpaper. No credit was given for the increased productivity of 6 per cent on the part of the workers, in spite of the fact that the profits of the industry rose from a normal of 2 per cent to a level of 6.6 per cent. This situation was said to be typical of conditions throughout American industry.

4. *The full 15 per cent cost-of-living adjustment has not been received by all groups of workers.* In addition to the arguments against the Little Steel formula itself, a number of American Federation of Labor representatives stated that under the wage policy of the Board there were many groups of workers who had been denied even the 15 per cent cost of living adjustment.

For example, the Board in order to correct intraplant inequalities and to adjust a group or groups of employees up to a commensurate level with other employees has awarded certain increases. These increases have then been offset against the amount all the workers in a plant should have been entitled to under the cost of living adjustment. Thus in a plant of one hundred employees, twenty-five might have received an increase of 10 cents per hour in order to correct intraplant inequalities and that 10-cent increase has been averaged over the total number of employees, despite the fact that 75 out of the 100 employees had received no increase at all.

Likewise, because of increases as a result of a job evaluation study to 500 workers out of 1000, the remaining 500 who have received no increases at all may find that their cost of living adjustment has been exhausted.

Many workers represented by the International Association of Machinists have been denied their full cost of living increase on the ground that a 15 per cent increase would result in wage rates above the brackets of the so-called sound and tested going rates.

Also, in printing trades the full 15 per cent has in many cases been denied because such an amount would have brought the rates above the maximum of the brackets.

5. *In determining the unit upon which the 15 per cent cost of living adjustment is based the Board has violated established union rights.* In determining wage disputes the Board has, by indirection, set aside the rights which have been guaranteed to American workers under Federal laws enacted by Congress. Section 9 of the National Labor Relations Act provides that representatives designated by the majority of the employees in the unit found appropriate for collective bargaining shall be the

exclusive representative of all the employees in the unit for the purpose of collective bargaining in respect to rates of pay, wages, hours and other conditions of employment. The Pattern-makers League, the exclusive bargaining agent for the employees in an appropriate unit in the Firestone Tire and Rubber Company, collectively bargained with the employer for the employees in the appropriate unit in accordance with the provisions of the National Labor Relations Act. A case involving wages for these particular employees came before the War Labor Board for determination. At the same time a case involving the employees in another unit represented by United Rubber Workers, C.I.O., in the Firestone plant was before the Board for decision. The latter case was decided by the Board and an award of 3 cents per hour was made. The Board then rendered, after a hearing before a hearing officer, an identical decision for 3 cents per hour in the case involving the employees who were in the pattern-makers unit. By this decision the patternmakers were not only denied a wage increase amounting to 15 per cent above the January 1941 level, but they were also denied wage rates equal to reasonable bracket rates. Even had the full 15 per cent increase been granted the rates for the patternmakers involved in the case would have still remained only one cent above the very lowest base rate in Akron.

But more important than the amount of the wage increase was the fact that the Board's decision denied to the pattern-makers the right to have their wage rates negotiated by their chosen representatives. The decision was based not on what these workers in a unit found appropriate by the National Labor Relations Board for collective bargaining were entitled to, but on the group fixed by the War Labor Board, namely, the workers in the entire industry. The Board thereby denied to these workers their statutory rights.

The result of the Board's decision was that the pattern-makers in the Akron plant of the Firestone Company received a rate of $1.39 per hour. The lowest rate in the area, other than the Firestone rate, is $1.40 per hour; the bulk of the patternmakers receive an hourly rate of $1.65; and the high rate is $1.80.

There have been similar instances, in the printing trades where craft unions of highly skilled workers have been denied the full 15 per cent cost of living adjustment because of limits placed upon the increases of employees in other bargaining units. If this policy is continued it will ultimately result in the destruction of craft unionism.

6. *Little Steel formula is inequitable because it fails to give consideration to previous training.* In applying the Little Steel formula no consideration is given to the skill required to become a proficient journeyman or journeywoman in a skilled trade such as the bookbinding industry. Workers may after two to five years in learning the trade find because of the Little Steel formula they are held to inadequate wages. For example, employers in Washington, D.C., were willing to give their binding girls an increase of 16 per cent, thus bringing their scale up to $25.00. The Regional Board in Philadelphia denied this increase which had been agreed upon and cut it to $24.50.

V. *Inequities resulting from Board's wage policies other than Little Steel Formula.* 1. *The bracket method for determining wage rates.* Besides the Little Steel formula, other principles followed by the Board in determining wage disputes and in the fixing of wage rates have brought about grossly inequitable results. Particular criticism was directed by the representatives of the American Federation of Labor against the so-called bracket method of determining wage rates.

(a) *Improper rates have been taken into account in the setting of brackets of sound and tested rates.* Rates in the St. Louis area are set in accordance with bracket rates which allegedly represent the sound and tested rates in the area, but which are wholly inadequate because of the conversion of industries in the area to war production.

Many new war industries which did not exist in January 1941, such as a small-arms plant employing 40,000 employees, a TNT plant, employing 8000 employees, the glider industry, the shipbuilding industry, a bomb manufacturer, employing in all thousands of workers, are now in operation. These new operations have revolutionized manufacturing in the area, and involve entirely new machinery, new routines of work, and new classifications. There are no truly comparable rates which represent the tested going rates for the classifications involved in these war industries. But workers in these new classifications find themselves frozen at jobs with rates set in accordance with rates paid in ten unorganized plants in St. Louis, which prior to the war were engaged in operations that bore some slight similarity to the work now being performed in the war plants. Thus the rates for the large percentage of the employees in war industries in St. Louis are bound by arbitrarily established tested and going rates.

The bracket method for determining wage rates was criticized because under this method wage rates are fixed not in accordance with what is known as the "prevailing rates" but in accordance with rates alleged to be sound and tested going rates, which include the rates of unorganized workers. The basic principle underlying the fixing of the "prevailing rates" under the relevant laws is that the public's money, the money of the workers themselves, raised through taxation, should not be used for public expenditures in such a manner as to depress rates which have been attained in private industry only after years of struggle and collective bargaining. The prevailing rate is not the average rate, because the average rate would naturally be below the rate obtained by organized labor. The prevailing rate is the standard rate paid to the greatest number of people in an industry. The prevailing rate should be followed by the War Labor Board in determining wage rates, and not the brackets of the so-called sound and tested going rates. The sound and tested going rates appear to be rates established by the Bureau of Labor Statistics at the very lowest grouping found, which is practically always an unorganized group. Therefore, under the bracket system there is nothing to offer unorganized workers in the way of trade union benefits, because under the bracket system their rates cannot be brought up to the prevailing or union rate.

In the printing industry certain of the Regional Boards have recognized the need of following the principle of the prevailing rate and have established wage rates which are consistent with what are really sound and tested going rates, that is, the rate paid to the greatest number of people. In some highly organized

cities, such as New York, Chicago, and Cincinnati, the brackets
do reflect the rates paid to the organized workers. But in the
majority of the regions the so-called sound and tested going rates
do not reflect the rates paid to organized workers. Hence a
union is at a great disadvantage because it cannot offer to unorganized workers the wage benefits already attained by organized
workers.

(b) *There should be greater flexibility in determining appropriate areas for establishing brackets.* Criticism was further
directed at the areas used by certain Regional Boards in determining the brackets of sound and tested going rates. It is
inequitable to divide the country into sections and to hold that
wage rates must be within the brackets of sound and tested
going rates in that particular section, regardless of the rates
which may be paid in an adjoining section. Brackets have been
set within fixed boundary lines. If consideration were given
to rates in existence immediately across the boundary line, it is
possible that a cluster of rates might be found that would up the
maximum of the brackets by a considerable amount.

In other cases the procedure of Regional Boards has been to
group together a great many diversified communities with consequent hardship on the workers. In the South brackets have
been set according to the size of the community. Brackets in
the larger metropolitan areas were fixed at higher figures than
the brackets in the smaller cities. The lowest brackets were in
the "C" or rural area. This system of establishing brackets has
brought about unsound results. An example was the case where
rates for one of the largest manufacturing operations in the
South and for the only copper mining, copper smelting and sul-
phuric acid chemical operation in the South were set in accordance with Class C brackets because it happened that geographi-
cally the operations were not located in the vicinity of any large
city.

The bracket system was criticized because it was set up on a
purely local basis. In the trucking industry, because the area
of competition is spreading, there should be more flexibility in
the fixing of brackets.

An example given of the unfairness of the bracket system
and the need for establishing broader labor market areas was

that of truck drivers in the metal industry in New York. The Regional Board set up a rate of 87 cents. Union rates for many drivers in the metal industry run fro $1.00 to $1.40 per hour depending on the size of the equipment and the city. The 87 cent rate was based on investigations made of about thirty plants engaging about one hundred and thirty truck drivers. The largest class of those rates used by the Regional Board in fixing the brackets received $1.10, with 90 cents being the second largest. The War Labor Board found a weighted average and by taking 10 per cent below that weighted average arrived at the 87 cent rate. The unfair result of this method is seen from the fact that there are thousands of truck drivers in the metal industry receiving wages of $1.10 and $1.25 per hour.

(c) *Regional Boards have failed to consult unions when establishing brackets and have refused to permit unions to examine data upon which brackets have been made.* Objection was taken by many A.F.L. representatives to the fact that the Regional Boards had established brackets of alleged sound and tested going rates without consultation with the unions or without permitting the unions to review and criticize the material upon which the brackets had been based. It was claimed that many of the persons who had been assigned to study brackets had no experience or knowledge of what really were the prevailing rates of wages; rather their experience had been limited to the setting of minimum decency standards in the field of women in industry and child labor.

The brackets which were set for workers in the hotel and restaurant business were not at all representative of the established wage rates predominant in the industry. The investigators who compiled the data for the New York Board had no knowledge of the restaurant industry. Rather than questioning the labor organizations which had the necessary information concerning the established rates the Regional Boards have questioned nonunion workers who were not ready or able to give the true information. The labor organizations were in a position to show the actual contracts setting forth established rates for this industry.

Other American Federation of Labor representatives argued that the information upon which the brackets of sound and tested going rates were based had been obtained from nonunion employees.

It was claimed that the Regional Boards had set brackets on the basis of information and figures alleged to be confidential. The labor organizations were therefore never afforded an opportunity to study or comment upon the information upon which the brackets were based.

(d) *The Little Steel formula has not been applied if the increase resulting from an application of the Little Steel formula results in rates above the bracket minimum.* It was argued that if there is to be a bracket system, no such system should be established until the workers have received the 15 per cent they are entitled to under the Little Steel formula. Any bracket system based on the rates of employees who have not received the 15 per cent increase would be based on unrealistic figures. In the printing industry the full 15 per cent has in many cases been denied because such an amount would have brought the rates above the maximum of the brackets.

In a large number of cases in which the International Association of Machinists is the bargaining agent, the 15 per cent formula has not been applied apparently for the reason that the full 15 per cent would have brought the rates beyond the range of sound and tested going rates. But the brackets of the sound and tested going rates were based on low figures which were not representative of the wage rates in the area.

Section G of the *Application of the Little Steel Formula,* a pamphlet released by the Board's Division of Public Information in January 1944, stated that a cost-of-living adjustment may not in the discretion of the Board be approved if it would bring the wage earnings or average straight time hourly earnings for a job classification above the maximum of the bracket of sound and tested going rates for that classification in the labor market area. Under this application of the bracket system technical engineers have been prevented from obtaining a wage scale above the average of nonorganized technical employees.

2. *The Board's wage policy has failed to give adequate consideration to substandard wages.* The Board's wage policies have not given proper consideration to the need for the elimina-

tion of substandard living conditions. According to the Bureau of Labor Statistics subsistence wage budget, a married worker with two children should receive approximately 83 cents per hour in order to maintain a decent American standard of living. But thousands of workers in such industrial areas as St. Louis, for example, are receiving wages far less than 83 cents per hour. . . .

Labor leaders in the hotel and restaurant industries have constantly told the worker that the Government would never compel these low paid wage earners to work for substandard wages. But because of the Little Steel formula and the failure to give adequate consideration to substandard wages the Government is now forcing workers to work for very low wages. More than 70 per cent of the employees in the hotel industry receive no gratituties, but derive their sole income from their wages, which in 1941 were far below $1,000 per year. The workers were hopeful that they would be able to rise out of the depressed condition of working for substandard wages, but their hopes of earning a sufficient amount to live in decency have been removed.

The Board's policy of offsetting against the 15 per cent cost of living allowance amounts given on the ground that wages were substandard has had the effect of freezing large segments of American labor at a submarginal level of existence. For example, if a man has been receiving 40 cents per hour he would be entitled to a 15 per cent cost of living adjustment, or 6 cents, but if he had been increased to 50 cents under a substandard rule he would have exhausted his cost of living increase and would under the Board's wage policy be precluded from receiving any further increase.

Charts were introduced to show the percentage of workers receiving wages below the Bureau of Labor Statistics maintenance budget of 80 cents per hour, the percentage receiving wages below $1.20 per hour, the amount established in the Heller Budget as necessary to maintain health and decency, and the percentage receiving above $1.20 per hour. Out of a total of 13,820,000 wage earners in all manufacturing industries only 15 per cent received above $1.20 per hour; 40 per cent received between

80 cents and $1.20 per hour; and 45 per cent received below 80 cents per hour.

Out of 8,600,000 wage earners in war industries 21 per cent received above $1.20 per hour; 49 per cent received between 80 cents and $1.20 per hour; and 30 per cent received 80 cents per hour or below.

Out of 5,220,000 wage earners in nonwar industries, the industries upon which returning servicemen will depend for their livelihood, only 7 per cent receive $1.20 or above; 25 per cent receive between 80 cents and $1.20; and 68 per cent receive below the 80 cent rate. . . .

3. *The Board's wage policies fail to provide means for eliminating regional and other disparities in wage rates.* The National War Labor Board fails to give recognition to the necessity for eliminating regional disparities in wage rates in order to achieve maximum production in all regions in the country. This failure has served as a detriment to improve war production in the South.

The maximum amount received by members of the Stove Mounters International Union in the South for mounting stoves is 56 cents per hour while in the North workers receive 97½ cents per hour.

The Little Steel formula has prevented the elimination of wide disparities among the various wages of the merchant seamen. The Masters, Mates and Pilots Union, American Federation of Labor, had many diversified contracts with shipping companies. Collective bargaining to remedy this situation and to bring about stabilized wage rates in the industry was interrupted because of the Little Steel formula. As a result of the Little Steel formula it is possible for seamen on two ships in a convoy, leaving the same port and going to the same port, to receive differences in basic take-home wages of between $400.00 and $500.00. . . .

4. *Inconsistency in wage decisions of the Regional Boards.* The spokesman for the International Brotherhood of Pulp, Paper and Sulphite Workers stated that much of the criticism against the Board's wage policy has been due to the fact that the Regional Boards have taken inconsistent positions in the handling

of wage applications. For example, an agreement providing for an increase of 5 cents per hour was negotiated with a company on the Pacific coast. A joint application was presented to the appropriate Regional Board, but before the application was passed upon by the Regional Board, the company, without contacting the union, submitted an application to the Missouri Board requesting approval of a cost-of-living bonus of 5 cents for the employees in all of the company's plants. Approval was given. The Regional Board in the State of Washington is now and has been for several months withholding a decision in the case first presented to it because of the action of the Missouri Board.

Decisions of the Regional Boards in the handling of cases involving the printing trades were cited as examples of inconsistencies in Regional Board action. . . .

Some of the Regional Boards have ignored the bracket system as it has been promulgated by other Regional Boards. Some have permitted increases up to the prevailing rates, the rate paid to the most number of people in the particular locality, while in other localities the Regional Boards have held wages down to the low nonunion rates.

VI. *Effect of Board's wage policies on health and morale of workers.* The failure of the wage stabilization program to take into account the increased rise in the cost of living has brought about conditions which threaten the health and morale of American workers.

The rank and file worker is rapidly losing confidence in the institutions of the government because of the application of the Little Steel formula. There is a growing desire on the part of the workers to take positive action themselves because they are reaching the conclusion that they cannot obtain redress through the normal channels. . . .

VII. *The wage policies of the War Labor Board are a hindrance to war production.* The wage policies of the War Labor Board have resulted in wage freezing. This has been accompanied by job freezing and the combination of the two serves to destroy the traditional incentive of the American worker at a time when there is urgent need for greater production. Workers cannot be expected to put forward their best efforts when their

families are in want and while profits are soaring and prices are
rising.

WHAT ISN'T GUARANTEED [5]

The demand for a guaranteed annual wage is officially before
us. The C.I.O. has officially endorsed it, and the President has
"shown interest" in it. Almost everyone will grant—at least
publicly—that workers are entitled to the security of a regular
income and that the loss of wages due to causes beyond their
control is not just. It is against this injustice that the demand
for an annual wage is aimed.

It is against this inhuman aspect of the wage system, which
provides sustenance for its workers only when it has work for
them, that people are led to demand the wage. They remember
that even the slave was fed, clothed and given shelter on the
days and for the seasons when his labor was not needed.

But is the problem so easy? That is, can state capitalism
really provide security for American workers by means of the
guaranteed annual wage? Before too many people get too far
out on the limb on this issue we want to present the following
problems which must be considered in any discussion of plans to
realize this demand.

1. An annual wage plan which calls for the worker to owe
time to an employer is more than an annual wage. It is a device
for escaping the payment of overtime pay. As such, it is not a
stimulus to production, but for less planning, since it does not
penalize the lengthened work week or work day.

For example, many of the plans now being praised call for a
weekly wage. For this, the worker may be given days or a few
weeks off, at times when his work is not needed. But he owes
time, and so may be called upon for overtime work when work
is available.

For this overtime work he receives no time-and-a-half pay.
Many workers may still prefer this security, but this approach
may result in a serious cut in the yearly take-home pay.

[5] By William Becker, Labor Secretary of the Socialist Party and Labor Editor
of the *Call*. *Call*. 12:3. April 2, 1945.

2. What is much more important, however, is that the success of any plan for a guaranteed annual wage, even when it solves the problem of overtime pay, depends on available employment.

A guaranteed wage, at a low level of employment, simply means that a part of the working force, has a regular income while the rest of the working force, is completely out.

If the steel industry or the auto industry should agree to guarantee the annual pay of their working force, they could do this at a level of production much lower than their present wartime levels. But then there would be no demand for the labor of those not included in this original working force by these planned industries. The workers not included in the plan would be more permanently excluded from employment than before.

It is this problem which makes so significant the fact that Walter Reuther has come to speak of "Full employment and the guaranteed annual wage" as one demand. They cannot be separated without creating a permanent outcast class.

The fact is that full employment and regular production and employment, are dependent upon the general health of the economy.

If there is a high level of production—of goods ordinary consumers want to buy—and workers are paid enough then there will be comparatively constant production and employment at high levels.

The guaranteed annual wage in itself is not the creator of a healthy economy. It is possible only in a high wage, full production economy. Such economies, under capitalism, have been wartime economies.

3. The manner in which the guaranteed wage is paid, and by whom it is paid, is another problem. If it is paid by industry, and so results in long range planning, and more concern for the working force, it will be conducive to more efficient production.

It can in such a case, cause prices to drop, since industry, if it has to produce regularly, may as well set prices at which it can sell all of its production. (That is, if it starts with a high level of production as its base, rather than the curtailed levels which have been typical of the controlled-price industries.)

But if the wage is guaranteed by the government, the entire system of high prices, curtailed production, unused plant capacity and unplanned production will continue, with the government bearing the costs by means of deficit financing, with no greater production of wealth to off-set it.

This is no answer at all. Any such tendencies by the President's latest investigating committee must be repudiated by labor.

EXCERPTS

A joint resolution directing the National War Labor Board, in passing on requests for wage increases, to consider any rate below 65 cents an hour as "substandard," was offered in the Senate this week by Senator Claude Pepper, Robert M. LaFollette and Olin D. Johnston.

The proposed rate, Pepper said, is the rock-bottom minimum for subsistence. That fact, he recalled, was demonstrated by a Senate commitee which last summer investigated the plight of low-wage workers.

Organized labor is supporting the Pepper-LaFollette-Johnston proposal.

Under the Wage-Hour Act, the legal minimum is 40 cents an hour. In many cases the War Labor Board has granted a minimum of 50 cents an hour, and has now boosted the "floor" to 55 cents.—*American Federation of Labor Weekly News Service. Mr. 27, '45.*

The American Federation of Labor members have called attention to the fact that even though a kind of "take-home pay" be considered as the basis of *wage rate* regulation, the fact cannot be avoided that reconversion pay envelopes will be flattened. Long hours, night shifts, steady production and incentive plans will disappear. Administered prices will continue to be characteristic of our economy. Deflation and disaster can be the only consequences.

Faced with the problem, the public members admit the accuracy of what the future will mean for wage earners and propose continued government regulation of collective bargaining. The organized labor movement in this country has cherished its freedom and prospered because of it. As a consequence, the proposals made by the public members of the Board that there be more government in collective bargaining are not only objectionable but an indication of a dangerous trend of thinking.

Submission to government regulation of wages and interference with the rights of American workers during a war fought to defend the freedom has been necessary. But even a suggestion that free collective bargaining shall be supplanted in large measure by government regulation during the undefined reconversion period is a timely warning that the organized workers of America can ill afford to overlook. The eventual outcome of this kind of thinking is government dominated and controlled unionism. We cannot subscribe to this "solution" of the problem which will be inescapable if the rigid control of wages represented by the Little Steel formula is continued—*George Meany and others. Statement of American Federation of Labor Members of the National War Labor Board on the Report filed by the Public Members. F. 23, '45. mim. p. 4-5.*

The Federation proposes: (1) That 60 days after V-E day, managements and unions return to collective bargaining, and that the minimum wage be raised for workers in industries where collective bargaining is not established. (2) That management and workers cooperate in every way with the Price Administrator.

Acceptance of this proposal would restore to managements and unions their rightful freedom and responsibility. It would mean voluntary responsibility to adjust wage increases so that they would not break price ceilings, and voluntary responsibility on the part of workers to avoid inflationary spending. As citizens of a free democracy, we have proved our responsibility throughout the war. It is high time that freedom of collective bargaining be restored.

We know that the dangers of autocratic control will not cease with the war's end. The menace of a totalitarian state here looms in the economic field. Workers' buying power at present wage rates is not large enough to carry American industry over the reconversion period into full production and full employment. And widespread unemployment would lead to government controls over industry. Figures given by A. F. of L. Board members show that, at present wage rates, workers' buying power will fall $13 billion short of the amount needed in postwar to support full employment, and a wage increase of 15¢ per hour will be required to eliminate this shortage. Return to collective bargaining will make possible progressive wage increases to restore workers' buying power without increasing prices. Free enterprise cannot exist without a high national income and high workers' buying power to create a market for its products. Labor must be ready to enter the conversion and postwar periods with a wage rate that will assure purchasing power. And those wage rates must be established in advance so that industry can go forward with assurance.

It is time to end the mistaken idea that wage increases lead to price increases. Wage increases can be paid out of savings from the worker's enormous increase in production per man-hour. In 1944, the War Labor Board granted wage increases in 150,523 voluntary cases. In only 1 per cent of these cases did companies even say they would ask for price increases, and the price increases actually granted involved much less than 1 per cent. Wage increases agreed on by unions and employers in collective bargaining, with regard for price ceilings, do not cause inflation. —*Labor's Monthly Survey (American Federation of Labor). Mr. '45. p. 3-4.*

Unable, for reasons beyond their control, to deliver the goods, unions will try to compensate by promising more—in the form of bigger demands. The most immediate question will be that of wages, threatened by the dislocations of reconversion. Labor will strike out for a speedy lifting of the wage-stabilization regulations. The War Labor Board hasn't exactly had smooth going during wartime. Its final days, until the threat of inflation is over, will be rough indeed. Wage stabilization will go by the board when pay rolls begin to plummet and jobs disappear. Unions, with redoubled ferocity, will attempt to hold something approximating the wartime levels. The struggle against a drop will be a bitter one. As the hours of work diminish, both A.F.L. and C.I.O. leaders will concentrate their energies on raising the hourly rate of pay so that the weekly take-home total bears some resemblance to what it was during the war. Adjustments to a lower standard of earning will not come without resistance from labor.

That labor's wage demands will be rejected by industry is equally assured. With profits falling, production going into a slump, and markets uncertain, industry will not yield. In the economic environment of the first transition years there is no possibility that the unions will meet with more than slight success. The retreat will be on—though neither willing nor strategic.

In the reconversion period the unions will fight for dismissal pay or for some sort of holiday pay to bridge the time it takes to retool. Pressure will be brought to bear on industry, and, failing that, the heat will be applied to government; but no expansion of government spending is likely. Here and there employers with sufficient reserves will work out some arrangements, but by and large the attitude will be, "Look to your unemployment insurance." Benefits, however, will not be increased in time to meet the first wave of reconversion joblessness. All in all, the unions will do poorly on the money questions.—*Leo M. Cherne, Executive Secretary, Research Institute of America. From his book "The Rest of Your Life." Doubleday, Doran and Company, Inc., Garden City, N.Y. '44. p. 167.*

I am sometimes bewildered by wage stabilization and wonder if I can discuss it properly. The bewilderment to which I particularly refer is a recent decision of a regional War Labor Board. You have all heard about sound and tested going rates and know that wage stabilization regulations provide for approving wage increases up to the minimum of the sound and tested going rates, except in rare and unusual cases. In the case I have in mind, a wage increase to a large group of employees was approved up to the maximum of the sound and tested going rates for the area, and with respect to some jobs, the increase approved was above the sound and tested going rates, according to available information. The effect of this decision was to make the wage rates of the workers who received the approval higher than the majority of workers on similar jobs in their area. Now this is confusing because it is hard to understand why the War Labor Board went beyond its established policy.

I do not tell you about this decision in a way critical of the War Labor Board because I have gotten along very well with the War Labor Board. It may be, if all the facts were known, that the War Labor Board had a good and sufficient reason for the decision. The War Labor Board has a certain amount of discretion in rare and unusual cases according to the particular circumstances. The point I am trying to make is that decisions are often made by the War Labor Board that appear to be liberal in the light of the stabilization regulations and some employers may learn of these decisions and feel that the whole wage stabilization policy has been liberalized. This may lull the employer into believing that he may make similar adjustments without War Labor Board approval. However, the employer must not, under any circumstances, do so. Regardless of how meritorious a wage adjustment may be and regardless of whether it is in line with approved cases, if the adjustment requires prior approval of the War Labor Board it is a violation of the regulations if made without prior approval.—*Willis L. Russell, Tax Accountant, National Cash Register Company, Dayton, Ohio. Controller. Ja. '45. p. 19.*

Because of wage freezing through the Little Steel formula, hourly wage rates in the United States are at a level so low as to cause alarm. Wages have been held down while prices of living necessities have soared. We know that hours will be reduced to 40 per week after the war to create full employment, and that weekly pay envelopes will contain only the straight time hourly wage rate paid for 40 hours.

At today's prices and today's straight time hourly wage rates paid for a 40-hour week, only 8 per cent of all American workers employed by private industry will have enough income to support a family of four in health and efficiency (according to the Heller Committee Budget), and 60 per cent will be below even the Labor Department's Maintenance Budget, which provides a bare subsistence living level for a family of four.

Today's low wages are of the greatest significance for two reasons:

1. They mean that after the war more millions of workers and their families will be condemned to live in poverty unless wage rates are raised, for we cannot expect that today's high living costs will decline in the postwar period. In fact, living costs are more likely to rise after the war.

2. These low wages also mean that consumer buying power will fall far short of the amount necessary to maintain full production and full employment in the United States.

Your Executive Council cannot impress too strongly on the convention the following facts: Full production and full employment make possible a high level of wages. Increased costs of government and payments on our war debt will require large revenues from taxes. If production and national income are at high levels a relatively low tax rate will bring in the necessary funds. However, if industry operates at low levels, using only part of its capacity, high wages will become a burden which many companies cannot pay, and the necessary taxes on corporations and individuals will also be burdensome at low levels of production. Such burdens tend to discourage the business initiative on which employment depends.

At today's wage rates there is a shortage of workers' buying power. This shortage is so serious that it will undermine the very basis of our future prosperity, threatening to plunge the country into a disastrous business depression.

To correct this shortage, substantial wage increases for all union members must be secured. But our task will not be ended there. Millions of low paid, unorganized workers must also have their wages raised. Full production and full employment will not be possible unless they too receive very substantially higher wages. To secure the necessary wage increases throughout industry we recommend the following program:

1. That all unions affiliated with the American Federation of Labor make a concerted drive for wage increases for all workers.

2. That the necessary legislative action be taken to raise substantially the wage floor provided in the Fair Labor Standards Act.

3. That a concerted drive under Federation leadership be carried out during the coming year to assist international unions in organizing workers in their jurisdictions in the low paid industries and in raising their pay; and where there are no international unions having jurisdiction that the workers be organized in federal labor unions and the necessary wage increases secured.—*From Executive Council Report at the Sixty-Fourth Annual Convention of the American Federation of Labor, New Orleans, November* 1944. *American Federation of Labor Weekly News Service.* N. 21, '44.

John L. Lewis, in negotiating for a new contract for his miners, is taking a leaf from the book of experience of wartime labor relations. He now is attempting to apply some very practical lessons learned through administration of various wartime labor laws. . . .

These are some of the things the miners are demanding:

A $60,000,000 royalty. Mr. Petrillo thought up the royalty idea in 1943, and later induced record and transcription companies to pay a royalty on records into the unemployment fund of his A.F.L. musicians' union. The War Labor Board did not pass directly on this phase of the contract, but government stabilizers did nothing to prevent the royalty payments. Now Mr. Lewis demands a 10-cent-a-ton royalty on all soft coal mined, the money to be used to maintain the physical welfare of the miners.

Mr. Lewis insists that there is nothing inflationary about this demand, nothing that runs counter to stabilization policy. He would use the royalty funds to provide the miners with medical and surgical care, hospitalization, insurance, rehabilitation and economic protection. Based on the present production goal of 620,000,000 tons of soft coal a year, the fund would run in the neighborhood of $60,000,000 annually.

Mr. Lewis, John O'Leary, the miners' vice president, and other union negotiators doubtless know that they cannot expect government approval of royalties of this size, but apparently hopes to use the idea as a bargaining weapon to win other concessions.

Shift differentials. In this demand, a policy inaugurated by W.L.B. in the steel wage dispute is coming home to roost. The miners are asking 10 cents more an hour for working the second shift and 15 cents more for the third shift. W.L.B. granted differentials of 4 cents and 6 cents an hour to C.I.O. steelworkers for similar shifts.

Vacation pay. The miners are asking vacation payments of $100 instead of the $50 now received. W.L.B. raised the amount two years ago from $20 to $50.

Equipment. Companies are asked to provide certain articles of equipment now paid for by the miners. These include tools, explosives, hats, caps, etc. Just recently, W.L.B. directed packing-house companies to pay for certain types of work clothes worn by employes.

Overtime pay. While there are ample W.L.B. precedents for awarding overtime payments beyond a regular work day and week, W.L.B. will examine the miners' latest overtime demands closely in search of hidden wage increases that could be construed to violate the Little Steel formula.

The miners' new overtime demands, if granted, would net them the biggest single increase of any of their requests. It is proposed to return to the seven-hour day in the mines, with time and one half to be paid for additional productive and underground travel time beyond seven hours a day and 35 hours a week. The miners now are paid for 45 minutes of travel time a day and work a nine-hour day, including a 15-minute lunch period for which they are not paid. At present, overtime for the miners begins after 40 hours each week.

Those are the principal methods by which the union proposes to boost miners' earnings and still stay within the stabilization rules. As estimated by Charles O'Neill, a spokesman for the operators, Mr. Lewis's demands amount to a daily increase per worker of $3.30 a day. This estimate includes the royalty income that would be paid into the union treasury and not directly to the miners.—*Reprinted from the United States News, an independent weekly magazine published at Washington. Mr. 9, '45. p. 34, 36.*

Recently, one of the largest and most important corporations in the nation presented a document to the National War Labor Board, arguing against the union's request for a wage increase. This company states, in reply to the union's claim that the need for postwar prosperity makes a wage increase an absolute necessity, that the union "overlooks the economic law, that as total weekly income decreases, demand falls off, prices decline, and the relative standard of living is maintained."

Here, stated briefly and clearly, is a philosophy which, unfortunately, is advocated by too many corporation executives. Here is a point of view which does not merely oppose wage increases; it menaces the future of our people and our democracy.

Instead of planning for a future of rising demand, increasing consumption of goods, more production, full employment, high wages, and fair prices—in short, a better life for the people—this philosophy looks backwards. It is reconciled to falling demand, lowered consumption of goods, slack production, widespread unemployment, low wages, and prices brought down, not by intelligent economic progress, but by depression and poverty. In short, we can go back to all the miseries which blacken our memory of the '30s.

Labor is unwilling to accept this philosophy of despair. The American people on November 7, 1944 demonstrated their unwillingness to accept a dismal future. Our boys and girls returning from the armed forces will not accept joblessness and poverty.

There can be no question that the prophets who cannot see an America in which high wages and prosperity can flourish, will be rejected by the American people and their government.

What, then, stands in the way of immediate action to grant the C.I.O. wage demand?

At every hand in the devious corridors of Washington's government offices, one can see a desperate last-minute effort to forestall the coming wage increase. Certain individuals have created a new fantasy, a fairy tale not fit for telling to grown ups. Yet, I must discuss it, because it has received widespread attention in the press and may influence to some degree a portion of the government's policy.

I refer to the thought that while wage increases are necessary and justified, nevertheless, they should be delayed until V-E Day. Then they will come! Or so the story goes.

This problem of labor's purchasing power is too serious to be subjugated to the idle theorizing of men who understand so little about reality.

It is difficult to believe that we are being asked to believe that now, when labor's bargaining position is strong and when labor's cooperation is an absolute requirement, pressures are so great against our modest wage program as to forestall its effectiveness, but later, when unemployment threatens the land, when hours are being cut, when service men are being demobilized, and when orders for goods are being cancelled, that the atmosphere will be conducive to wage increases.

What will prevent management from spurning labor's wage demands? Who in government will have the courage to invoke justice then, if it turns out that now, when labor's case is strongest, common fair play is not forth-coming?

I hesitate to believe that the V-E Day fantasy can receive serious attention among the responsible officials of our Federal Government.

All roads converge to the same point—the justice of the C.I.O. wage demand. I cannot help but believe that sober judgment will prevail—*Philip Murray, President, Congress of Industrial Organizations. Progressive. Ja. 1, '45. p. 5.*

OTHER ASPECTS OF THE WAGE PROBLEM

IS CONTROLLED INFLATION POSSIBLE? [1]

Before considering the question of how well—or poorly—more "controlled inflation" is likely to "work" during the transitional postwar period, it is pertinent to examine briefly the various reasons which, in combination, have made it possible to manage inflation with such relative success during the war period to date. During the five war and early postwar years 1916-1920 the cost of living (official index for wage earners) went up about 92 per cent. Although the proportion of national productive effort diverted to war this time has been far greater, during the five years since 1939 the living cost increase has been only 25 per cent or less than 28 per cent as great as in 1916-1920.

The reasons for this difference include: (1) We entered this war with relatively much greater "slack" in employment and industrial capacity than existed in either 1914 or the spring of 1917 when we became a belligerent in World War I; (2) due to the great growth of the consumer durable goods industries after the First World War—especially the motor and accessory industry, electrical equipment and radio—we had a larger relative capacity in the segments of industry readily convertible to war production; (3) more advanced techniques and "know how" in plant construction permitted a relatively faster increment in new industrial facilities; (4) we entered this war with relatively larger inventories of consumer goods to draw on; (5) largely as a result of experience gained in the First World War, the over-all government planning and control—including reasonably prompt adoption of rationing of scarce consumer goods, higher taxes, emphasis on war-bond savings, price ceilings, etc.—

[1] By John C. Cresswill, Economic Writer. *Magazine of Wall Street.* 75:288-94. December 23, 1944.

were much more effective than last time; (6) from the start the general public, as well as the government, was much more "inflation conscious" than last time, this awareness of the problem contributing to greater voluntary moderation in consumer spending and consequently greater savings.

Now for the future, it should be obvious that the controls—especially rationing, price ceilings and wage-salary stabilization—cannot be safely terminated until a sharp reduction in war production and increase in civilian production bring the current supply of consumer goods into adequately effective balance with the current consumer demand. Just when that might be is unpredictable.

At present—and all the portents suggest that this will be even more true after defeat of Germany—the weakest link in the chain of controls is wage stabilization. The labor unions continue to nibble away at this "line." At irregular but periodic intervals it has been "bent," the latest example having been the recent "fringe" pay increases granted steel workers by the War Labor Board, estimated to amount to an average of about 7 cents an hour. Other unions are now busy cooking up "fringe issues" such as higher pay for night work, "substandard" pay, elimination of job rate inequalities, etc.

However, despite making small concessions in a generally stubborn and time-consuming rear-guard defense of the "line," the Administration shows every sign of being adamant in its determination not to terminate wage-salary stabilization at least until after defeat of Germany. But by now it is virtually a foregone conclusion that wage stabilization will then go out the window and that the government will support and sponsor higher hourly wage rates under the New Deal "puchasing power" theory of prosperity. This will not be called "controlled inflation." It will sound better to call it "anti-deflation."

Whatever it is called, if industry enters the transitional period of reduced volume with materially higher hourly wage rates than now prevail, there must inevitably be either a substantial upward adjustment of O.P.A. price ceilings or a sharp squeeze of business profits. The tentative evidence seems to promise a combination of both. At least as to general principles,

O.P.A. policy for meeting the situation it knows is coming is already indicated. Its idea is that higher wage costs should be absorbed partly by higher prices, partly out of business profits, partly out of future increases in the efficiency of production. It will strive to limit the price increases as closely as possible. For purposes of business planning—which requires something more than loose generalities—the thing remains an enigma.

It is undeniable that for national prosperity we need a high level of consumer income. But inflation, controlled or not, can not be a satisfactory or effective method of getting it, and the "purchasing power" theory, of which we have heard so much over the past New Deal decade, makes sense only within reasonable—that is, workable—limits. Carried to excess, it must defeat its professed national purpose; and under the program to which the Administration appears leaning there is exactly that potential danger.

Private wages and salaries can only be paid out of the revenues obtained from production and sale of goods and services. If excessive labor costs impinged chronically on profits, there would be less business expansion and less labor employed. If excessive labor costs forced higher prices of goods, actual purchasing power of the public as a whole would be proportionately reduced. The true road to economic progress is the hard road, the road on which enduring advances can never be made as rapidly as many demand; the road of ever increasing producing efficiency, with the fruits attained thereby equitably divided among workers, owners and consumers. These are the most elemental economic realities—yet some people in Washington and in the labor unions seem to need to be reminded of them.

As it operated before the war—and since—the "purchasing power" theory brought very uneven gains among employed persons—large gains to a minority of the most powerfully organized factory workers, smaller gains to others, no gains at all to a large group with incomes either fixed or relatively inelastic for immutable economic reasons. To cite how much the incomes of most all groups have increased since the depression year 1932 is to confuse the issue. Compare any average or "normal" year of the mid-1920's with 1937 or 1939—or 1944—and these are some of the significant changes: (1) a large net increment in purchasing power of a minority of organized factory workers; (2) a slackened rate of long-term price reductions growing out of technological progress; (3) reduced purchasing power for much of the "white collar" middle class, which is numerically the largest group of all; (4) a substantially reduced rate of return on productive capital investment, both in terms of operating margin and net income; and (5) chronic unemployment, until temporarily ended by the war activity.

Bearing typically on point No. 2, it may be noted that the long trend of price reductions on automobiles, previously made possible by notable progress in technical efficiency, terminated when the unions "took over." There were further large gains in automobile output per man-hour over the nine years 1932-1941. There *had* to be to meet repeated increases in wages and maintain adequate profits. But for the first time in the industry's history, prices to consumers were no longer reduced.

While it varies from year to year, long experience—not materially altered by any changes of recent years—suggests that the long-term rate of technical progress in the manufacturing industries, as measured by output per man-hour, is around 3 per cent a year. Obviously, then, this figure sets a proportionate limit on continuing wage increases if they are to be economically supportable.

But even that is not the whole story. Factory workers normally make up less than one fourth of the gainfully occupied population. If they got the entire benefit, in the form of higher wages, of an increment of 3 per cent a year in output per man-hour, then capital would be deprived of the inducement to make productive investments and consumers would be deprived of the purchasing power increment which gains in manufacturing efficiency formerly made possible. . . .

[Let us compare] average hourly earnings in 25 manufacturing industries with average output per man-hour, both put on an index basis 1939 = 100, for all years 1929 through 1943. In the depression years 1929-1932, though not exactly prospering, employers, of course, had the best of this equation. From

1929 through 1933, hourly earnings declined almost 30 per cent while output per man-hour increased nearly 10 per cent.

In the single year 1934 (New Deal and N.R.A.) hourly wages made the remarkable jump of 18 per cent—a figure not subsequently equalled even in the war years—but still did not overtake the index of output per man-hour. By 1937 the position was reversed, with the hourly wage index 5 points above the index of output per man-hour. The spread increased further to 7 points, in favor of wages, in the depression year 1938. It has, of course, tended to widen sharply in recent war years. By 1942 it was 16 index points higher for hourly wages than for per man-hour output, and for 1943 it was 22 index points higher. As compared with 1929, the 1943 index of output per man-hour was 57 per cent greater, the index of hourly wages about 70 per cent higher. As compared with the prewar year 1939, the end of 1943 found the latter index 40 per cent higher, against an increase of only 18 per cent in output per man-hour.

In the ten years 1929-1939 average output per man-hour increased at an average annual rate of about 3.26 per cent. In the four years 1940-43, reflecting both exceptionally rapid innovation in production techniques and the commendable wartime speedup of effort by the average worker, the annual rate of gain was about 4.5 per cent, but average annual rate of increase in hourly earnings was about 10 per cent or more than twice as great.

On the figures cited here it appears that average wage rates in manufacturing have "discounted" future increases in producing efficiency by nearly five years if we assume continuance of gain in output per man-hour at the high wartime average rate of 4.5 per cent a year; by over six and a half years if we assume future gain in efficiency approximating the average of 1929-1939.

It is open to serious question, therefore, whether a further rise in hourly wage rates after defeat of Germany would have the stimulating economic effects which its proponents promise. Other things being equal, it would discourage venture investment, encourage investment aimed at saving as much labor as possible in existing plants, limit employment opportunities. But other things are not equal. With continuing war against Japan, the government will still be a huge buyer of the output of industry, and taxes will remain high. For both reasons the major part of the cost of economically excessive wages will continue to be absorbed by the United States Treasury, and not until we have a full peace economy would the deflationary effects of our over-high wage costs visibly come home to roost again.

For a period of perhaps one to two years after victory in Europe, demand for consumer goods probably will remain out of balance with supply. The problem will not be lack of consumer purchasing power but deficient supply of goods. Otherwise, why is the Administration warning that the defense against inflation must be maintained until supply can be reasonably balanced with demand? But if this is correct the idea of further raising wages to stimulate purchasing power is inconsistent and paradoxical. If the economic prospect after V-E Day is so deflationary that we must plan to increase wage rates as an alleged offset, why do we need to continue price ceilings? On the other hand, if the continuing danger of inflation is so great that we must keep price ceilings, why must wage stabilization be abandoned as an anti-deflation measure? We will let somebody in Washington answer these questions, for the writer can offer no answers that make sense. Although there is room for difference of opinion as to whether the greatest pressure after V-E day will be inflationary or deflationary, it would seem undeniable that it can not be both.

Some of the advocates of "controlled inflation" contend that we must have a higher price level in order to create the dollar volume of national income necessary if the vast Federal debt is to be tolerable and supportable. But higher prices of themselves can raise the real income only of producers of primary commodities. Prosperity is not really measured in money but in the things money will buy. Today there are fantastic quantities of money circulating in Greece and China—but no prosperity; on the contrary, dire poverty. The ideal price level is neither high nor low but one in which there are the fewest inequalities and the least unbalance; and at which the maximum volume of goods and services will move into consumption.

The fact that "controlled inflation" has not got out of hand during the war does not prove that control can be indefinitely successful, for our people have more or less cheerfully accepted control measures in wartime which never would be long tolerated in a political democracy after peace is attained. What we will need in peace is high production and employment. To put the emphasis on arbitrary wage-raising and "controlled" price inflation is to put the cart before the horse.

PROBLEMS OF WAGE AND PRICE STABILITY [2]

Wage questions are difficult to deal with because feelings are easily aroused, opinions are strongly held, and the facts are many-sided and susceptible of varying interpretation. In no field of debate are the limitations of statistical evidence, or perhaps more accurately the human tendency to select and arrange statistics primarily for the purpose of proving a case, more apparent; and the result is to spread confusion and obscure principles. The arguments of the unions are largely based on considerations of equity, that is, on representations that workers in general are at a disadvantage relative to other groups, or relative to some past period. These considerations are important. However, it is probably correct to say that public opinion—aware of the increases of 87 per cent in average weekly wages per factory worker, and of 59 per cent in average hourly wages, since September 1939—does not find convincing the comparisons usually offered to show workers at a disadvantage. Thus the American Federation of Labor, in its November *Monthly Survey,* compares workers' hourly wage rates (average hourly earnings adjusted to eliminate effect of shifts from lower-paid to higher-paid jobs), up 6 per cent from October 1942 to August 1943, with farm prices, up 13 per cent, and corporation profits, up 13 per cent.

All such comparisons involve choice of a base period; the farmers, if they desire to show that the inequities are on their side, can select a base period which would yield different results. In many respects the things compared are not comparable.

[2] *National City Bank of New York.* p. 136-7. December 1943.

Rates of wages and corporate earnings are unlike things. One is a rate, the other an aggregate. Since corporation earnings can drop to nothing, or less than nothing, the percentage range in their fluctuations is necessarily greater. Comparisons of percentage changes in the two things are therefore meaningless. Moreover, it is hard to determine what real corporate earnings are, since it is uncertain what future costs and losses, properly chargeable against the receipts of this period, will be. Dividends received by stockholders in general are down, not up. Wages paid, on the other hand, are money in the pocket. It would be more logical to compare the total wage payments, up 19 per cent since October 1942, with corporation earnings, up 13 per cent, which gives a different result.

Average hourly earnings received by manufacturing workers have risen more than the cost of living in any representative period that may be selected since the war started. Since October 2, 1942, through September 15, 1943, this average as reported by the Bureau of Labor Statistics, had advanced 11.3 per cent, compared with the cost of living increase of 5.2 per cent. The unions maintain, however, that the average hourly earning is not the material consideration. They point out that it is raised by premiums for overtime, by differentials for night shifts, by upgrading of workers within plants, by shifts from low wage to high wage industries, and by greater productivity of workers on incentive payment plans. Hence the statement that the B.L.S. figures are not representative of basic straight-time wage rates, which is accompanied by the claim that basic rates, controlled by War Labor Board decisions, have not kept pace with the cost of living. This is the argument for breaking the Little Steel formula.

Representations that there are differences between basic rates and average hourly earnings are manifestly correct. The question is as to the significance of the differences. Clearly it is hourly earnings which constitute the money cost of labor to the manufacturer. The premium that the manufacturer pays for overtime is an extra cost, and so is the night shift differential. A simple calculation shows that time and a half for eight hours in a forty-eight hour week adds 8 1/3 per cent to the labor cost of each unit of output during the week. This is enough to prevent overtime work in certain industries, and so to cut the national production.

To be sure, if other costs can be reduced by overtime and night work to offset the increased labor cost, the total cost per unit of product may not be raised and frequently is cut; this justifies the night shift differential, in particular. As to upgrading, or promotion, it does not raise the cost of labor if it is genuinely based on increases in skill and productivity, but it is common testimony that under conditions now prevailing much upgrading is fictitious, or at least much more rapid than formerly.

However the responsibilty may be distributed, such rough indexes as are available suggest that although production per worker has increased immensely during the war, the production per dollar of factory payroll has declined and the labor cost per unit of product has increased. According to the Federal Reserve Board's index, production in the manufacturing industries as of September 1943, was 145 per cent greater than the 1939 average. The rise in factory employment, according to the Reserve Board's index based on B.L.S. figures, was 70 per cent. The increase in factory payrolls was 228 per cent. From these figures can be derived indexes of production per employee, up 44 per cent; production per dollar of payroll, down 25 per cent; and wages per unit of output, up 34 per cent.

If increases in basic wage rates should now spread generally through the industries a further rise in the labor cost per unit of production would have to be expected. Additional pressure to lift prices would be generated. If the industries should absorb the higher wages without raising prices, their taxable income would be reduced and much of the cost of the wage increase would therefore fall on the Treasury. The increase in taxes received from the increased workers' income could not compensate, since workers are taxed at lower rates. Also, the "take home" pay would be increased further, widening the inflationary gap between incomes at the disposal of individuals and the value of consumers' goods and services produced.

Finally, the public interest is concerned not only with inflationary dangers during the war but the situation that will exist after the war. The practical reason for the unions' emphasis on the basic straight time rate as the measure of the price of labor is to be found in the fact that the basic rate, established by collective bargaining, will last as long as the bargaining agreement lasts, while overtime premiums, shift differentials, abnormal upgrading, and shifts into higher-paying plants may disappear, in varying degree. Labor leaders foresee a drop in weekly wages after the war. They seek to prepare against it by obtaining further increases in basic straight time rates, in addition to those it has already obtained under the Little Steel formula.

The question is, can the industries stand such an increase in costs in the postwar situation, and still be able to set prices that will sell their goods and enable them to give employment? Will farmers, nonmanufacturing labor, white collar workers, pensioners and other people who are not in the labor force, be able to pay for the products of such high-wage labor? Will foreigners be able to buy American goods?

The misfortune of inflation is not only that it gets the economic situation up on stilts, but that it creates distortions in cost, price and wage relationships. These distortions may not seem important during the war, for the government is the great customer of the industries and government purchases keep trade going. For the postwar period, however, they present sobering questions.

WAGE AND PROFIT DIFFERENTIALS [3]

Our thinking about wages has become so charged with emotion as to dim the prospects of a solution that will do justice to the legitimate claims of labor, of capital and of the consumers. The attitude of the typical businessman is as confused as that of the typical wage earner. Fortunately his selfish interests lead him toward the correct wage policy. He strives to pay a wage as low as is consistent with obtaining the quantity and quality of labor required for his operations. This simple

[3] By John V. Van Sickle, Chairman, Department of Economics, Vanderbilt University. *Trusts and Estates*. 79:411-15. November 1944.

rule, modified by collective bargaining to prevent wages which exploit labor, will make for maximum employment and maximum real wages for wage earners as a whole, if the total economy can be kept reasonably competitive. But businessmen cannot expect labor to use its bargaining power in accordance with this wage principle if the owners of capital invested in high profit enterprises block entry of capital from less profitable lines. The price of flexibility in the labor market is flexibility in the capital market.

Most spokesmen for labor hold that wages should be (1) as high as the income (or even reserves) of an industry will permit, and (2) equal for similar effort *throughout the entire labor market.*

But if one of these propositions is correct the other must be incorrect. If wages are to vary with the varying profitability of industries, the wages of workers of equal skill cannot be equal. Which proposition is correct? Clearly it is the second. It is not the function of wages to equalize profits. Rather it is the function of larger than average profits to induce shifts of capital investment and consequently labor from low profit enterprises.

In this way, equalization of profits comes about with a minimum of transitional unemployment and in a manner most beneficial to all concerned, determined by the free verdict of consumers. This shifting, essential in a dynamic economy, calls for a slight modification of labor's second proposition: Wages for similar work should be substantially equal throughout an entire labor market area, a little but not much higher in high profit enterprises, and a little but not much lower in low profit enterprises.

Labor's present strategy is to hold wage levels in unprofitable lines and bring about the wage differential by forcing up wages in the profitable lines.

The wages of railroad employes were pretty well maintained throughout the interwar period despite the fact that the railroads were overstaffed and in need of venture capital to meet the challenge of new methods of transportation. A more moderate wage policy might well have enabled the railroads—and equipment companies—to hold some of the million men laid off during the period, and to secure greatly needed equity capital. During the early 1920's the wages of full-fashioned hosiery workers in Philadelphia rose to fantastic heights, to the great prejudice of that city as a hosiery center once the bottle-neck on the production of new machinery could be broken. Rigid wage rates of coal miners in this country and in England provide another example of bad wage policy.

It is bad policy because it increases the magnitude of un-employment by forcing resources out of unprofitable lines more rapidly than would otherwise be necessary, while retarding their absorption into more profitable lines, to the extent it reduces those profits. When this new risk is added to those caused by the double taxation of business earnings through the corporation tax and the high progressive rates of the personal income tax we have a sufficient explanation of the so-called "investors' strike," of which critics of the capitalist system made so much during the depression of the '30's.

Instead of removing these obstructions, however, social plan-ners declared that our economy was "mature" and could no longer absorb the available savings. These, they claimed, should be acquired by the government (through borrowing and heavier taxation of corporations and large incomes) and invested in public works, thereby maintaining full employment and provid-ing useful things which private enterprise could not be expected to undertake. This prescription, of course, increases the volume of idle funds and necessitates an ever expanding public works program. In time this expanding program must invade fields entirely suited to private enterprise. This further weakens the spirit of private enterprise and its ability to utilize savings. The end result can only be socialism.

How large is a labor market? Is it as broad as the United States? There is considerable evidence that American labor would so define the area. This proposition underlies the de-mand for the abolition of geographical differentials which the United Steelworkers of America recently made on the basic iron and steel industries. The union in its brief asserted that the trend has been in this direction and that the government has promoted it by such means as the Fair Labor Standards Act and the Walsh-Healy Act. This negative argument rests on the arbitrary assumption that the trend must be good simply because it is a trend.

The second argument is positive. It affirms that the trend is socially and economically sound because (a) the cost of living is substantially equal throughout the United States; (b) industries in low wage areas can afford to pay the national wage, because labor productivity is the same and only by equalizing wages will inter-area competition be placed on a fair plane; and (c) the maintenance of differentials will perpetuate lower standards of living in the low wage areas and, in so far as the South is concerned (which is the broadest area of low wages) will freeze "its status as an economic province of northern industry and capital."

Acceptance of this principle of equality would necessitate similar concessions in every other industry where geographical differences in wage rates are found—and they are found in practically every industry. In almost every instance, however, the Southern branches of the industry would be the ones most seriously affected.

Before a decision is reached on "fiat" equalization, the following conditions should be recognized:

1. The productivity of labor and capital throughout the country will be at a maximum when the effectiveness of labor and capital is everywhere the same. An individual could not then improve his position by moving from one place to another, or by shifting his investments from one place to another or from one industry to another, in the absence of some dynamic change. Equal pay for similar work would prevail and would represent economic justice. This may be called the *optimum pattern,* or geographic balance.

2. The optimum pattern can not exist if there are pronounced differences in the supply of labor in different parts of the country, relative to the supply of capital, natural resources, and managerial know-how. The economic value of ordinary labor will be low where it is in relative abundance and high where it is relatively scarce, and the contrary will be true for capital.

3. To realize the optimum pattern, both capital and labor would have to move from areas in which it is in relative abundance into those areas in which it is relatively scarce.

4. Capital "moves" in the form of goods and services supplied on credit and, in a private enterprise society, primarily in response to differentials in profits and interest. The suppliers of the capital can realize on their investments only if the lending area is willing to receive goods and services in sufficient value to service and amortize the investments.

5. In the United States at the present time marked geographical differences in the supply of labor relative to the supply of capital, natural resources and know-how necessarily result in marked geographical differences in rewards for similar work. Hence "fiat" equalization of *all* earned incomes would require large and continuing "fiat" movements of capital into the low income areas (through federal grants-in-aid or federally financed public works) or large and publicly assisted outmovements of labor from these areas, if massive unemployment were to be avoided. A free enterprise system could not function with the disequilibria created by premature "fiat" equalization. It must rely heavily upon the pecuniary inducements provided by differentials in wages, interest and profits to bring about the two-way movements of labor and capital required to realize progress.

6. "Fiat" movements of capital adequate to equalize all incomes in low income areas could not protect standards in high income areas, since the capital would have to come exclusively from the people in the high income areas, and would hence reduce their real incomes.

7. If "fiat" equalization were applied to selected categories of income only—say to employees of industries whose products entered into competition between areas—employment in those industries would decline to the point where the last worker employed in each industry would be just worth the imposed wage. Those displaced would be forced back into the unprotected industries where their competition would reduce wages, or they would be forced to move to the high wage areas where their competition would also reduce wages. If access to all these fields were blocked they would have to depend upon private

charity, public relief or public works. None of these solutions represents either effective production or social justice.

8. "Fiat" equalization within any large and diversified economy would result in a higher level of money prices and money costs than would otherwise prevail. But real wages would be lower. "Fiat" equalization within a single country will not promote harmonious relations with its neighbors. The high general price level would expose the whole economy to such severe competition from countries operating under a more flexible system as to require the erection of many and complicated barriers, such as high tariffs, quotas, exchange controls and a managed currency, to protect domestic employment, and subsidies to develop the exports necessary to pay for essential imports.

So we see that the labor market area within which wage rates for similar work should be substantially equal is fairly small, because within it there must be a really substantial mobility of labor. In Sweden, for example, where nation-wide bargaining with strong organization on both sides has long prevailed, all the contracts that I have seen recognize some half-dozen wage districts, between which significant wage differentials are provided. If that is true for little Sweden with its unusually homogeneous and highly educated population, it would appear that even a single American state is usually too large to constitute a workable labor market area.

If the above analysis is correct the results of imposing the C.I.O.'s wage theory upon the American economy at this stage in its development will be just the opposite of what the union predicts. Instead of a wider diffusion of industry into smaller communities, wage equalization will make of the Northeast an industrial counterpart of England, while the people of the rest of the country will live in relative poverty, and under conditions that tend to perpetuate the large family pattern. The resulting pressure will defeat every effort to check the processes of soil erosion which already threatens the very existence of rural life, and nowhere more so than in the South.

Wage, profit and interest differentials are all needed to bring about this transformation. It is going on. For several generations now Northern capital and know-how have been going south to provide the means. Industry has been growing steadily here and, for at least two decades, at a somewhat faster rate than elsewhere. Meantime, thanks to these industries, the South is beginning to move goods and services into other parts of the country. It is becoming a factor in inter-regional industrial competition instead of just the furnisher of raw and semi-processed products. These exports are enabling the South to service the investments of the past and to demonstrate the credit worthiness necessary to secure the additional extra-regional capital still urgently needed.

Standards of living are still very low because of the downward pressure exerted by the region's high birth rate. Capital movements in and population movements out are still needed on a considerable scale. But in the past too much reliance was placed on migration. It carried with it too much of the human topsoil of potential local leadership, while the migrants have not always found it easy to adjust to nonfarm work or large city life.

Further industrialization will pay big dividends and not only to those who actually invest their capital in the South. The industrialized areas will find an expanding market there, not merely for the machinery and tools needed, but also for the better grades of consumer goods that the people will buy as their incomes rise. Much of the expanding production within the South will be consumed locally but a part will have to find outlets elsewhere in order that the South may attract needed capital. The established industrial areas must therefore expect and be prepared for increasing competition if the process of equalization is to continue. Some lines of production may pass entirely to the South. Meantime, however, other enterprises will be expanding precisely because of the expanding purchasing power in the South, generated and sustained by the more effective use of Southern natural and human resources.

These expanding fields can absorb the displaced labor and capital, if the wage rates in the contracting fields are allowed to fall slightly while those in the expanding fields rise only enough to recruit the necessary labor force. The wage decline in the contracting fields will postpone the time when the existing equipment will have to be scrapped or shifted physically to more effective locations, and this will enable the industries to provide for the older workers who would find it difficult to learn new skills or to move to new centers. A slight rise of wages in the expanding fields, on the other hand, will not prevent the rise in profits that is necessary to attract new capital. Unemployment compensation, the public employment service and a vocational retraining program, with modest stipends during the retraining period, can further contribute to making the transition relatively painless.

If change is allowed to proceed along some such lines as these we may confidently look forward to the realization of the goal which represents labor's aspirations. It is a generous and proper goal and an attainable one, but it cannot be reached over night. Drastic fiat narrowing of wage differentials will carry this country away from rather than toward the twin goals of high employment and regional equality. The present structure of enterprise would be perpetuated, with our big cities growing bigger and our rural areas more rural.

Enormous sums would have to be spent by public authorities to make the huge metropolitan centers fit places in which to live and bring up children. Enormous sums would also have to be transferred to the rural areas to provide health and educational services in order to assure a supply of vigorous and healthy recruits for the urban industries. Money wages might be prevented from falling, but not real wages.

Meanwhile the whole price level would be such that American industry could not possibly compete with any economy that operated on more rational lines. Prohibitive tariffs and all the other restrictive measures devised during the 1930's for insulating the nations one from another would have to be thrown into the defense of the program. Our entire international trade policy would be emasculated and relations with other nations, as well as the rehabilitation program, jeopardized.

If the American government supports labor's thesis and declares that it is contrary to public policy for the labor in high wage areas to have to compete with American labor in low wage areas, there is small hope that it will take any other view when it comes to international competition. If it is an intolerable injustice to expose an unskilled steelworker in Pittsburgh to the competition of an unskilled steelworker in Birmingham, despite the fact that the latter is now able to live as well and earn close to twice as much as the majority of the rural school teachers in Alabama, then it will be still more intolerable to ask the Pittsburgh worker to compete with the Polish miner in Upper Silesia.

Governments are going to play a far larger role in the postwar world than that assigned to them a generation ago. If they use their power to make their economic systems rigid on the capital side, through excessive patent and tariff protection and cartel privileges, and on the labor side, through inflexible wage-fixing, with ever expanding public works as the mechanism for providing employment for the capital and labor legislated into idleness by their policies, there can be but one outcome—national socialism at home and growing tension in the international sphere which will mark the beginnings of the Third World War.

WAR PROFITS, PAYROLLS, TAXES AND DIVIDENDS [4]

Charges that business in this country is making exorbitant profits have again become prominent in recent weeks, chiefly no doubt because of statements made by labor leaders in connection with applications for wage increases and for the breaking of the Little Steel formula. In wartime especially, it is hardly possible to argue for wage increases without arguing that the industries can pay the increases without raising prices, which requires claiming that profits are unreasonably high. Such claims are part of the news of the proceedings, and are disseminated in the press and through other channels, usually without much accompanying analysis. Misconceptions, confusion and unwitting misrepresentations follow.

[4] National City Bank of New York. p. 52-6. May 1944.

For another reason also the subject is one of continuous discussion. War production and price rises have created a great rise in the money income of the country, while at the same time the war requires sacrifies by the people as a whole. Inevitably various groups and occupations dispute as to the share which each is obtaining of the increased income, and as to the extent to which each is making the necessary sacrifices. Much of this debate is uninformed, and much is animated by partisanship or prejudice. Those who are not familiar with the facts lack the means to judge critically what they read or hear, and misinterpretations which gain general acceptance are hard to catch up with.

One of the common errors with respect to business profits is to assume that exceptional instances are typical. Where profit is put above cooperation in the war effort, where salary-boosting is inordinate, or where extravagance is on an offensive scale, criticism is deserved; and the same applies to excessive demands or extravagances by any group of the population. The facts are, however, that a means of dealing with cases of exceptional profits is in operation through the Renegotiation Act, in addition to the drastic excess profits tax. Sound opinions as to business earnings can be reached only through study of over-all or typical experience, rather than of the exceptions.

Corporate reports for 1943 are now available from most of the leading war producers, and from many of them facts can be ascertained not only as to earnings and profit margins, but also as to the distribution of gross income among labor, capital and the other factors in production.

We publish herewith an analysis of the figures of 50 large manufacturing companies, whose reports give payroll figures and whose 1943 sales in most cases exceeded $50 millions each and were principally of war materials. These companies are not "selected" in any sense except that they are large war producers; all available reports which give the desired detail are included. Certain composite figures for the group are shown, while total income and expense figures are given in greater detail.

50 LEADING MANUFACTURERS OF WAR MATERIALS
(In Millions of Dollars)

Income Account	Year 1940	Year 1941	Year 1942	Year 1943	% Change 1940-43
Net sales and other revenues	$8,292	$12,182	$15,212	$20,567	+148
Cost of goods and services purchased from others, depreciation, interest and other expenses and reserves	4,201	5,919	7,459	10,497	+150
Balance of gross income	4,091	6,263	7,753	10,070	+146
Distributed as follows:					
Wages and salaries	2,699	3,886	5,379	7,333	+172
State, local, social security, foreign and misc. fed. taxes	282	386	422	455	+ 61
Income and excess profits taxes	364	1,165	1,325	1,642	+351
Total taxes	646	1,551	1,747	2,097	+225
Dividends paid	494	533	406	419	— 15
Income retained	252	293	221	221	— 12
Total net income ...	746	826	627	640	— 14
Percentage distribution of above "Balance of gross income"					
Wages and salaries	66.0	62.0	69.4	72.8	
Taxes	15.8	24.8	22.5	20.8	
Net income	18.2	13.2	8.1	6.4	
Total net income ...	100.0	100.0	100.0	100.0	

These companies, a large number of whose plants have been awarded the Army-Navy "E" for excellence in production, include the following:

Alleghany Ludlum Steel Corp.
Allied Chemical & Dye Corp.
Allis-Chalmers Mfg. Co. .
American Brake Shoe Co.
Am. Radiator & Std. San. Corp.
American Rolling Mill Co.
American Viscose Corp.
American Woolen Co.

Armstrong Cork Co.
Baldwin Locomotive Works
Bethlehem Steel Corp.
Blaw-Knox Co.
Botany Worsted Mills
Bridgeport Brass Co.
Burlington Mills Corp.
Caterpillar Tractor Co.

Container Corp. of Amer.
Crucible Steel Co. of Amer.
Dresser Manufacturing Co.
Douglas Aircraft Co.
Eastman Kodak Co.
Fruehauf Trailer Co.
General Electric Co.
General Motors Corp.
Goodyear Tire & Rubber Co.
Inland Steel Co.
International Harvester Co.
Johns-Manville Corp.
Jones & Laughlin Steel Corp.
Lukens Steel Co.
Glenn L. Martin Co.
National Gypsum Co.
National Steel Corp.

National Supply Co.
Packard Motor Car Co.
Pepperell Manufacturing Co.
Pittsburgh Steel Co.
Pullman, Inc.
Radio Corporation of Amer.
Republic Steel Corp.
Sun Oil Co.
Thompson Products, Inc.
United States Rubber Co.
United States Steel Corp.
Western Electric Company
Westinghouse Air Brake Co.
Westinghouse Electric & Mfg. Co.
Wheeling Steel Corp.
Willys-Overland Motors, Inc.
Youngstown Sheet & Tube Co.

As indicated by the list of companies, the group includes representative producers in the steel, machinery, electrical equipment, automotive, aircraft, chemical, rubber, textile and other lines which are the backbone of the country's new war industries, and which have been largely responsible for the tremendous expansion of output achieved during 1942-43. These 50 companies account for a sizable part of total war production.

PAYROLLS, TAXES AND DIVIDENDS PAID BY 50 LARGE
MANUFACTURERS OF WAR MATERIALS
(In Millions of Dollars

	1940	1941	1942	1943
Payrolls	2699	3886	5379	7333
Income Taxes	364	1165	1325	1642
Other Taxes	282	386	422	455
Dividends	494	533	406	419

It will be seen from the table that aggregate sales of the 50 companies expanded from $8,292 millions in 1940 to $20,567 millions in 1943, or 148 per cent. After deduction of the cost of goods and services purchased, depreciation, interest and other expenses and reserves, the balance of gross income increased from $4,091 millions to $10,070 millions and was distributed as follows:

1. Wages and salaries increased from $2,699 millions to $7,333 millions, or 172 per cent.

2. Total taxes—federal, state and local—increased from $646 millions to $2,097 millions, or 225 per cent.

3. Total dividends—preferred and common—decreased from $494 millions to $419 millions, or 15 per cent.

4. Retained net income decreased from $252 millions to $221 millions, or 12 per cent.

In some cases 1943 published figures may overstate real earnings, in that net income as reported is subject to renegotiation of government contracts.

The total average number of employees of these companies, partly estimated, increased from approximately 1,514,000 in 1940 to 2,711,000 in 1943, or 79 per cent. Average annual compensation increased, as a result of higher basic wage rates and overtime, from approximately $1,800 to $2,700, or 50 per cent. The combination of these increases in numbers and in compensation resulted in the increase in total payrolls of 172 per cent.

In contrast with this expansion in payments to labor, the dividend payments to approximately 2,002,000 registered shareholders were, as stated, 15 per cent lower in 1943 than in 1940. Total net income, after taxes but before dividends, was 14 per cent below 1940.

After deduction from gross income of all expenses and charges except labor and taxes, the distribution of the remaining balance was as follows: wages and salaries 72.8 per cent in 1943 compared with 66.0 per cent in 1940; taxes 20.8 per cent compared with 15.8; and net income (which is the "wage" accruing to the shareholders for supplying plants, tools, and working capital for carrying on production), 6.4 per cent compared with 18.2. Payrolls in 1940 were $3\frac{1}{2}$ times net income; in 1943 they were 11 times net income.

Carrying the earnings comparison to years prior to 1940—not shown in the table—net income of these companies in 1943 was less than in 1937, substantially greater than in the depression year 1938, and larger than in 1939. It was 24 per cent larger than the 1936-39 average (years of partial depression).

Another significant point brought out by the figures is the decline in profit margins. Despite the increase in volume of business during the war, the average margin of net profit after

taxes per dollar of sales, for the 50 companies, has narrowed as
follows:

1939	8.0c
1940	9.0c
1941	6.8c
1942	4.1c
1943	3.1c

These figures demonstrate the fact, not always understood,
that war production has been carried on at substantially smaller
profit margins than the normal peacetime business of these companies. As compared with World War I, the Treasury statistics
on income show that all manufacturing corporations carried 10
per cent of their gross through to net after taxes in 1917, and
5.5 per cent in 1918.

Published financial statements of corporations—from which
the foregoing figures are taken—are sometimes criticized on the
ground that net income is shown *after* deduction of reserves
for contingencies, reconversion of plants or other postwar purposes, and that this causes an understatement of real earnings
during the war. It has been charged that corporations are preparing a "postwar orgy" for shareholders. The need for reserves
of this sort, however, is undeniable, and the treatment of reserves
as proper charges against income is standard accounting practice.
The various common types of wartime reserves have been the
subject of extensive study during the past year by such organizations as the Treasury Department, Securities and Exchange Commission, and American Institute of Accountants.

All of these studies accept postwar reserves in principle: the
only question is one of size. While it is hardly to be expected
that forecasts exact to the last dollar can be made of the numerous extraordinary expenses and losses that large war products
manufacturers will face at the end of the war, resulting from
conversion to war work and therefore proper charges against
war earnings, anyone who claims that reserves are excessive is
setting his own opinion against the experience and judgment of
the companies' own executives and accountants. The prices at
which shares of such companies are selling indicate that if an
"orgy" is being prepared for them, stockholders are unaware of
it. There is no saving of taxes through setting aside contingency

reserves of excessive size, inasmuch as such reserves are not legal deductions for tax purposes, but become so only when the anticipated expenses or losses are actually incurred.

In the balance sheets of the 50 large war material manufacturers in our study, the combined total of all reserves—including reserves allocated to specific purposes, general or unallocated reserves, and reserves not definitely described, and including routine operating reserves as well as special wartime reserves—increased from $435 millions at the end of 1940 to $892 millions at the end of 1943.

The latter figure is a large dollar amount. However, it represents but 6 per cent of the total assets of these companies, which during the same period had expanded from $9,868 millions to $13,960 millions in meeting the unprecedented demands for production of war materials. In view of the problems and uncertainties which these companies face in the postwar period, the real danger is that the reserves may prove to be less than adequate, rather than excessive.

With respect to the large war producers, the foregoing figures are conclusive, and if they had as much currency as the unsupported charges that war producers are "having a field day," etc., the charges would soon be disposed of. Many current misrepresentations, however, relate to the earnings of corporations as a whole rather than to war producers specifically.

In the last issue of this Letter appeared a table giving the net income after taxes of all active corporations in the United States as reported by the Treasury, including Treasury estimates for 1942 and 1943. The 1943 estimate is $8,550 millions, which is an increase of 84 per cent over the 1940 figure, and of 157 per cent over the 1936-39 annual average. Statements of labor leaders refer to these increases as if they were conclusive evidence of profiteering.

The first point to consider about these figures is that they represent income in the statutory sense; i.e., they disregard all charges for contingencies or similar reserves which are not allowable deductions in computing taxes. Estimates used by the Department of Commerce and published in the *Survey of Current Business,* which are often quoted, are on the Treasury basis rather than the customary accounting basis.

The second point is that percentage increases signify little when applied to earnings without consideration of conditions in the base period, changes in volume, capital employed and similar factors. The active corporations in the United States, numbering about 469,000, include a vast number which in the prewar period were operating either at a loss or close to it. An "increase" in profits of companies which had been operating at a loss is not computable in percentage terms, and reasonable gains made by those which had been barely breaking even become astronomical when expressed as percentages.

It is natural and beneficial in all respects that "poor" companies or industries should show large earnings increases when the country requires a greatly increased output of their products or services. The point to be made here is that their showing inflates the figure of average percentage gain and makes that figure unrepresentative of the efficient, going concerns which were earning reasonable profits before the war. Few such concerns have had increases corresponding to the averages above given; few could have had, in view of the excess profits taxes and the renegotiation statute.

Comparisons of percentage increases in wage rates with percentage increases in business earnings—which of course show the former at a disadvantage—are frequently made, in support of assertions that labor is receiving an inequitable share of the increase in national income. But this comparison is logically unsound, for the things compared are unlike. One is a rate, the other an aggregate. One has a firm and relatively stable base, the base of the other is unstable. Corporation earnings are good in busy times, but shrink rapidly or turn into losses in poor times, while wage rates hold or decline relatively little even during depression. The rigidity of wage rates, which represent the cost of labor, may in fact be a major cause of the drying up of corporate income.

There is little excuse for misrepresentation as to the distribution of national income, for the facts are easy of access. The U.S. Department of Commerce compiles the figures and analyzes them in many ways. The following table shows the distribution of income for 1943, 1940 and the prewar years, giving separately the compensation of employes and of the other factors in production. It will be seen that employes received 71.1 per cent of the total as against 68 per cent in the prewar years, and that agriculture likewise increased its percentage, while the share of business (combining corporate and non-corporate) decreased.

DISTRIBUTION OF NATIONAL INCOME

	Percentage of Total		
	1936-39	1940	1943
Total National Income	100.0	100.0	100.0
Total compensation of employees *	68.0	67.4	71.1
Net income of incorporated business	5.0	7.5	6.0
Dividends	6.0	5.2	2.7
Corporate savings	—1.0	2.3	3.3
Net income of agriculture	6.5	5.7	8.3
Net income of other proprietors	9.7	9.8	7.9
Interest, rents, and royalties	10.8	9.6	6.7

* Includes salaries, wages, employers' social security and pension fund contributions.

A familiar statement, given circulation recently by C.I.O. President Philip Murray in a Senate hearing, is that in World War I the war profits "created 23,000 millionaires." Along with this Mr. Murray pointed out that total dollar profits in this war are larger than in the last, and said, "It is difficult to prognosticate the number of millionaires this war is going to create." The implication is that "it happened before and it is happening again."

Space does not permit discussion of the claim that the last war created 23,000 millionaires, except to say that it is based upon questionable assumptions and interpretations of income statistics. The question of present importance is not whether the history is correct but whether the implication that "it is happening again" has any foundation. People who are impressed should recall that at the present level of individual income taxes (disregarding the unforgiven part of 1942 taxes) even a man with an income of a million dollars a year, if he spends nothing at all on personal living and pays out nothing except his federal income taxes, would require about ten years to accumulate a million dollars. How little substance there is in Mr. Murray's suggestion may be judged from this fact.

On January 6th a minority of the Senate Committee on Finance submitted a report on the revenue bill of 1943 in the course of which the "23,000 war millionaires" of World War I were referred to. But this same report said: "The renegotiation statute has provided an effective means of limiting war profiteering. Under it war contractors have been allowed liberal profits on their war business but *inordinate profits have been eliminated.*" (Italics ours.)

Vice President Wallace in an address before the Political Action Committee of the C.I.O. in New York on January 15 made the following statement:

. . . Some claim that the corporations have been growing rich out of the war. This may be true in some cases but, even though Congress has not carried out in full the recommendations of the President and the Secretary of the Treasury, the facts are that in this war we have done a much better job in [re]covering back into the Treasury excess profits than we did in World War I. The corporations during the past two years made gross profits two and a half times as great as in the two years of World War I but they paid taxes nearly five times as great. Taxes in World War II have been used twice as effectively to recover excess profits as in World War I.

It may be added that in comparing gross profits with those of World War I the reader should allow for the over-all growth in economic activity and the tremendous increase in the plant, tools and capital employed compared with 25 years ago.

It should be said in conclusion that comparisons of earnings with the *past,* and arguments erected upon them, not only prove little but confuse the issue. Whether profits are too high or too low is to be determined, not by reference to past relationships or arbitrary standards, but by their effect upon the growth of business and employment. The fundamental question is whether a strong and healthy economy, able to meet the needs of the *future,* is being maintained.

At the outbreak of the war business had gone through a long depression, during which the net worth of all active corporations declined by $25 billions. . . . At the end of 1943 some $10 billions of this loss had been recovered. But business capital is still much below pre-depression levels.

The wartime earnings of the corporations are being devoted chiefly to replenishment of capital rather than distributed to shareholders, as shown by the table on the distribution of national income and the other evidence as to dividends previously given. Earnings are being plowed back for the purpose of accumulating the financial resources necessary for the future, and for retiring debt and strengthening capital structures. Reserves for postwar expenses, losses and contingencies are being set up.

If the country is to prosper after the war it will want a higher level of production and employment than ever before, and business needs to build up its capital resources accordingly. It can do so only if profits are high enough to induce enterprise and investment and to supply savings needed for investment. Incomparably the most important principle to be observed in the discussion is that prosperity depends upon strength and health in business enterprise.

WHAT CHANGE IN PRESENT WAGE POLICY WILL BEST SERVE NATIONAL INTEREST [5]

The National Association of Manufacturers has nearly 12,000 members, 71 per cent of which employ fewer than 500 people. I appear at your invitation, which stated that the purpose of this hearing was to determine whether or not the National War Labor Board is to recommend to the President "a change in the present wage stabilization policy, and if so, when and how any change should take effect."

I assume that by "a change in the present wage stabilization policy," you mean breaking the Little Steel formula.

You also requested that I advise you "of industrial views as to what change, if any, in the present wage policy will best serve the national interest."

I'm glad you asked our opinion as to the effect on the national interest because if this were simply a wage dispute between management and labor, the National Association of Manufacturers would not be justified in appearing. In no sense of

[5] Statement by Robert M. Gaylord, President National Association of Manufacturers, before the National War Labor Board, October 2, 1944. *N.A.M. News.* Section 2. p. 1-3. October 7, 1944.

the word do I represent Association members in any phase of collective bargaining. Our members do not make wage agreements among themselves, nor are wage rates a matter of association policy.

You have asked two questions: (1) Should there be a change? (2) If a change is decided upon, when should it be made?

The second question is the easiest. All decisions involving labor grievances or the public interest at large should be made promptly.

It is unfortunate that a decision on this issue has been postponed until this time when circumstances make it a political football.

Now let's consider whether there "should" be a change in the Little Steel formula!

There apparently was no need to change it last April when the Stabilization Act was extended by Congress. Your chairman then assured Congress that the Board could "hold the control of wages, if Mr. Bowles can hold prices down."

There has been no change since then, according to President Roosevelt who said on June 30th of this year—"for a whole year the cost of living had been held without change"!

No matter whose special cost of living study you use it will show no increase in the cost of living since the President spoke.

In spite of these facts the argument is still made that wages can be increased simply because business can afford to pay higher wages.

Let's look into this:

Businesses fall generally into two groups: those whose profits before taxes are high enough so that they could absorb increased wages without charging higher prices to their customers; and those whose profits are so low that they could pay higher wages and continue to operate only by adding the increased wages to their selling prices.

So far as the first group is concerned, any higher wages they may have to pay will come primarily out of the United States Treasury. So long as excess profits taxes are set at 95 per cent the Treasury, not the employer, will then take the loss of virtually all reduction in business profits resulting from higher wages.

I need not remind you here, that the Treasury must get its funds, in last analysis, by taxes on the American people. The public—not the managers or owners of business—will have to pay any wage increases that are granted.

In the case of companies which do not have enough gross profits to absorb the increase—and numerically these are far more important—prices will have to be raised by enough to cover the increased wages. I say prices will have to be increased. What I mean is that either prices will have to be increased or else these companies will go out of business and their workers will join the unemployed.

You know just as well as I do that the money to pay this increased wage has to come from some place. And the only place it can come from is the public. In some instances it will be taken directly from the public through increased prices; in other instances it will be from more taxes upon the public at large to offset the lower taxes received from business.

If a general wage increase should be authorized it will not come out of the pockets of industry. It will come out of the people's pockets.

What you should be mainly concerned about is whether it is fair, and sound and just to grant an increase which the whole public will have to pay.

"But, with higher wages the people will be able to pay more," someone says.

Not if 25 per cent of the workers get the raise and 100 per cent of the workers have to pay the bill.

Will the national interest be served by increasing the pay of only 25 per cent of the workers?

It is true the cost of living has advanced since the war started. It is true that taxes have been increased. But 100 per cent of the American people—not just the 25 per cent employed in industry—pay the butcher, the baker and the tax collector. Shall our more prosperous workers have a still greater advantage?

In the national interest why not call in the people who will really feel the effect of your decision?

1. Call before you Mr. Morgenthau, Secretary of the United States Treasury to learn how much federal revenue will be lost

through the heavy reduction in corporation taxes resulting from a general wage increase.

2. Call before you representatives of the farmers to learn how they will be able to pay the higher wages of industrial workers in the form of higher taxes, higher prices, or both.

3. Call before you representative educators to learn what has already happened to the real income of school teachers.

4. Call before you local and state officials to determine whether city firemen, policemen, sanitation department employees, and all the other thousands of men and women who are engaged in public service can afford those wage increases for 25 per cent of our workers.

5. Call before you representatives of all our white collar groups, and people living on old-age and retirement pensions, and ask them whether it is fair to them to scrap this anti-inflation formula.

6. Finally, but foremost in the public's best interest, call some of the families of our fighting men and women whose fixed government incomes have already failed to keep pace with inflation.

I know you've been deluged with quotations from every Washington official who could possibly be concerned with stabilization, but I do not believe that the President's "hold the line" order of April 23, 1943 can be emphasized too strongly, and I urge you not to lose sight of it in making your recommendations.

At that time the President said in part: (and I quote)

To hold the line we cannot tolerate further increases in prices affecting the cost of living or further increase in general wage or salary rates, except where clearly necessary to correct substandard living conditions.

The only way to hold the line is to stop trying to find justification for not holding it here or not holding it there.

No one straw may break a camel's back, but there is always a last straw. We cannot afford to take further chances in relaxing the line. We already have taken *too many*.

It is impossible to escape the clarity of these words. The only way to hold the line is to hold it and not attempt justification for not holding it.

There are many in industry and elsewhere who believe this hearing is called for the primary purpose of finding the very justification that the President warned against. They see nothing in the economic picture that changes the meaning of his words or requires any change in policy.

I'm not here arguing against all wage increases. American manufacturers pay high wages—the highest in the world. They believe in high wages. They want them pust as high as production will permit. We know that only through production can wages be increased and at the same time prices kept at the level people can afford to pay.

We believe, too, that where real inequities exist they can and should be adjusted—just as price increases should be permitted in specific cases of inequity. However, that is totally different from either a general wage increase or a general price increase. Neither one is in the public interest.

In conclusion, let me urge you not to base your decision on the financial records of a selected group of big companies who have been doing a great volume of war business.

Nearly three quarters of all the men in the manufacturing industry work in shops employing fewer than 500 men. These small businesses are the backbone of the nation. I ask that they be given your earnest consideration in making your recommendation.

I ask that you be fair to those who fight as well as those who work for victory by avoiding special privileges to a few or raising the cost of living for all.

LITTLE STEEL FORMULA CONSIDERED IN RELATION TO THE RECONVERSION PERIOD [6]

Labor has urged . . . that general wage rate increases should be made now as an offset against a threatened deflation in the reconversion period.

[6] From Report to the President by the Public Members of the National War Labor Board on the Relationship of Wages to the Cost of Living, and the Changes Which Have Occurred under the Economic Stabilization Policy. William H. Davis, Chairman. p. 19-22. mim. The Board. Washington, D.C. February 23, 1945.

In this . . . argument for a change in the Little Steel formula representatives of labor speak of the need to protect the workers against loss of earnings as a matter of justice to them and they also say that general wage increases now will benefit the whole economy by helping to sustain full production and full employment after V-E day through the maintenance of consumer purchasing power. And they urge that wage rate increases are not likely to be made at a time when workers are being laid off because of cutbacks, when overtime is giving way to unemployment and work-spreading, and when the ranks of labor are being augmented by returning servicemen. We have no doubt that the workers' apprehension about the future contributes to unrest and job shifting now, and will do so more acutely as the prospect of cutbacks in war production comes closer. Our experience of last summer is sufficient evidence of this.

We believe, however, that to change the Little Steel formula now, because of the risk of future wage losses, would subject all our citizens, and particularly wage earners and the lower salaried employees, to other and still greater risks. The change proposed would fairly rapidly bring about a new round of general wage increases throughout American industry. The resulting pressure upon prices would, in our judgment, be so formidable as to jeopardize the whole wartime stabilization program.

The present situation is very different from that confronting the Board when the Little Steel formula was adopted. At that time the formula was intended to be, and it was in fact, a procedure to terminate a then substantially completed cycle of general wage increases and to avoid starting another one. Considerations of equity as well as the demands of stabilization and wartime production led to the allowance of an appropriate wage adjustment to those groups of workers whose wages had lagged behind increases given to the large majority of workers to compensate for the increase in the cost of living. Now the proposal is to lift the general level of wages as a safeguard against the loss of earnings and employment and the loss of purchasing power that might come with reconversion. But we have no assurance that such a round of general wage increases could be made effective without bringing on a corresponding increase in the general level of prices and so defeating its own purpose. The wage earner's real wage, and real purchasing power, is not measured in dollars but in dollars divided by prices of the things the wage earner has to buy. An improved standard of living for all our people can come only with a rising volume of civilian goods and services. It hardly needs to be repeated that if general wage increases were followed by general price increases the working people of the country would be the eventual losers in the renewed race between prices and wages.

Restraints on wage increases have been imposed by the necessities of wartime stabilization in the interests of all our people. They should be ended as soon as resumption of the flow of consumer goods and services from converted factories and facilities, or the immediate prospect of such resumption, removes the danger of inflationary price increases. They may be ended as a part of a broad economic plan developed by the government. The War Labor Board meanwhile must be alert to changing levels of war production and civilian production and to their effect upon the continued necessity of wage restraints. The time has not yet come, in our judgment, when general wage increases can be freely resumed without danger of an inflation which would be disastrous to the war effort and to the economic security of all segments of our population.

As to the maintenance of purchasing power in the period of reconversion, the wage rate increases proposed for that purpose are really put forward as a first step toward the higher level of national economy and of real wages that we are looking forward to in the postwar period. As we go forward to a time of full conversion to peacetime economy after the war, the goal is a level of production, distribution and consumption high enough to absorb into peacetime production all the enormous capacity for production we have demonstrated in war. This means a level of civilian demand and purchasing power high enough to substantially replace all the present wartime demands of the government. Any such level of civilian consumption means a very great increase in our standards of living. As we move out of the wastage of total war back to peacetime and the promise of the future, we will no longer be thinking or speaking about "maintaining prewar wage standards." The cost of living adjustment of the Little Steel formula will have to give way to wage and price adjustments which definitely raise the general level of real wages. Planning for prosperity, however, is by no means solely, or even primarily, a matter of increasing wages but must necessarily call for a comprehensive program on all economic fronts. If action is taken now on wages alone and if price increases were to follow we would have to face the same problems in the reconversion period but at a higher level and with more inequities between various labor groups and among the other segments of society.

For the reasons stated in this section, the public members of the War Labor Board do not recommend a present change in the Little Steel formula as necessary to eliminate any over-all inequity in the wartime stabilization program. Nor can we now recommend such a change, taken as a single step on one sector of the economic front, toward solution of the problems of reconversion.

The urgency attached to the requests for a change in the Little Steel formula, and the resulting concentration of energy, not only by labor and industry, but by the Board, on the consideration of that subject, have obscured the importance of other phases of the wage stabilization policy which also need to be examined in the light of what may be ahead of us. There are, apart from the Little Steel formula, certain important adjustments which are permissible under the wage stabilization policy. The most significant of those are adjustments made (1) to correct intraplant wage rate inequities, (2) to correct interplant inequities within the limitations of the "bracket" system, and (3) to correct substandards of living. In each of these fields the administration of the stabilization rules has a direct relationship to the reconversion period, and raises questions of policy and procedure which need much more attention, on the part of industry and labor as well as of the government, than they have yet received.

Furthermore, the Stabilization Act calls for stabilizing wage rates against a deflationary downward movement as well as against an inflationary upward movement. Presumably this statutory principle, and the Board's responsibility for carrying it out, will remain in effect during the reconversion period and until the production of civilian goods has so far progressed as to render stabilization controls unnecessary. The Board is therefore required to look ahead and to consider appropriate rules and procedures for stabilizing wages against deflation in the reconversion period.

LABOR UNIONS AND WAGE RIGIDITIES [7]

What effect will union wage policies have upon the creation or the maintenance of rigid wages in the postwar period? A leaf out of Britain's book of postwar experience in the 'twenties may throw some light on the answer to this question, while a reference to present union policies in this country may shed additional light.

Following the 100 per cent increase in trade union membership in Great Britain between 1914 and 1920, British labor entered the period following World War I conscious and jealous of its power and position. The unions sought to maintain the high rates of wages which prevailed before the break of the postwar boom in 1920. The basic, heavy industries such as coal mining, iron and steel, shipbuilding and textiles were well organized and the unions refused to allow wage rates to drop even in the face of rapidly increasing unemployment. Many British markets had disappeared during the war years, and flexible costs and flexible wages would have been necessary to regain them in a period of falling prices, but the trade unions stood adamant in their demands.

The Italian and Scandinavian markets for British "coals" which had been most important in the prewar period, were now in, or passing into, other hands. "Reparations in kind" sent German coal to the Italian railways. The Scandinavian countries were still willing to use British coal, if they could get it, although they had expanded water power to take the place of coal during the war period. But they could not afford to pay the prices Britain demanded in the face of new competition. Poland as

[7] From "Rigid Wages, Unionization and Reconversion Problems," by Frederick E. Lee, Professor of Economics, University of Illinois. *Commercial and Financial Chronicle*. 161:414-15. January 25, 1945.

a new entity had come into the family of nations. She had to have exports to build up her internal economy and to strike a balance in her international accounts. Her coal miners were not held back by the short hours and high, rigid wages which English miners demanded. They worked a twelve-hour day for a wage about half that demanded by British unions, with the result that they took over the coal market in the Baltic countries.

Then in 1925 Britain returned to the gold standard at the prewar parity with the dollar. Hawtrey, famed British economist, says that the social costs of this return to financial integrity on the part of the United Kingdom was a million unemployed persons. Prices had to be forced down to force the exchange rate up. Had wages, which were a substantial portion of costs in the heavy industries, been flexible so that they could have been adjusted downward to meet the new price situation, the problem might have solved itself. The unions, however, in the deflationary phase of the business cycle held out for rigid and high wages, with the result that industry in general suffered. It was not until after the disastrous coal stoppage and the unsuccessful general strike, both in 1926, that the trade unions began to see the errors of their ways and to take steps to correct them.

By 1927 they had lost half of their membership and millions of their own members were unemployed. I attended the 60th "Diamond Jubilee" Congress of the British Trade Union movement in September 1928, in the depressed South Wales mining area at Swansea, Wales, by which time the delegates were a sobered lot. They faced frankly the question of the causes or reasons for the decline in membership and power of the unions. Had this movement, they asked, which for over one hundred years had upheld the principles of collective bargaining and aimed at the betterment of working class living conditions reached and passed its peak of influence and lost its hold on the work-people of Britain? Perhaps the best answer to these questions was given by "Lord Jim" Thomas, a trade union and Labour Party leader, given that name by reason of his portfolio of "Lord Privy Seal" in the first MacDonald Labour Government. He had been one of the leaders in the general strike of

1926. "When we had the power, at least in numbers," he said, "we lacked the sense to use that power . . . we did not know how to use our power wisely." He then went on to say that now, with waning power, at least in numerical strength, he hoped that judgement and wisdom in cooperation with employers would take the place of their former arbitrary and unreasonable stand. Some of the evils of fourteen years of depression between 1921 and 1934 might have been avoided or mitigated if they had had a less rigid wage policy. . . .

Capital, in the form of savings or capital goods will seek to enter an expanding industry only if the value of the marginal products produced by such expansion is equal to or above the cost of such capital. Or, put in another way, business men or enterprises will not seek to employ new capital in the expansion of their industry unless they are confident that the capital goods to be obtained with the savings used will increase the total product of their business by an amount sufficient to cover the necessary interest payment. If capital gets a return of less than its marginal productivity, i.e., the money value of its marginal product, it will, through the principle of opportunity or alternative costs and returns, flow into other industries where its return or reward will be adequate to cover the risks involved.

Professor Slichter points out that the marginal efficiency of capital depends, among other things, upon the control or management over costs. Speaking further of the growth of unionization during the war and postwar periods, he adds: "In the face of large and powerful labor organizations, will American business possess sufficient control over costs to maintain a high marginal efficiency of capital? Or will unions keep investment opportunity limited by promptly converting any increases in demand for labor into higher wages? . . . In other words, will unions prevent any expansion of demand from producing more employment by causing it to produce higher wages?" After discussing these questions from different angles he stated his conclusion. "For the time being, however, one must conclude that the spread of unionization tends to reduce the marginal return of capital." This might go so far as to limit materially the capacity of the economy to expand in the postwar period but he hardly thinks so.

One of the most elementary principles of wage theory which the beginning student of economics is taught is that net wages in the long run cannot be higher than the marginal productivity of labor. The business man employing labor may not know just what the marginal product of such labor is, but if he pays, or is forced to pay, a wage higher than the marginal productivity of labor, he will soon encounter financial difficulties and will find himself forced out of business. If he pays less he will soon lose most of his workers to other enterprisers who are willing to pay labor its rightful share, based upon the money value of its marginal product. But when union demands and union wage policies force a higher payment to labor, at the expense of the other agents of production, the marginal efficiency of the other agents of production is thereby reduced. They will then seek employment other than in the industries in which such condition exists.

EXCERPTS

The reason why wage controls will go first is an economic one; not tied in with New Deal labor policies. In fact, the existence of the present wage ceiling is a tribute to political forthrightness, loose as their administration has seemed at times. Never before in American history have workers been told they could have no general wage increases even when their employers were willing to grant them. The fact that wage controls were imposed on so complete a scale, and brought about practical wage stabilization, was one of the major economic facts of 1943 and 1944.

The actual reason is that once the shortage of labor is overcome there will be no point to wage ceilings. The present pressure to prevent increases, for the sake of stabilization, will turn into a pressure to prevent reductions for the sake of mass purchasing power. For in studying what will happen to wages and prices we come back once again to the one transcendent theme that underlies every move in postwar planning: the necessity for maintaining mass purchasing power and high employment if we are to avoid another disastrous war-to-depression cycle. Collective bargaining will, in effect, take over the regulating function when wage stabilization is dropped.—*John R. Beal, member Washington Bureau of Time. Commerce Magazine. Ja. '45. p. 13-14.*

The difficulties in the way [of an annual wage] are formidable. How can we change the purely seasonal need for a great deal of farm labor? How can the steel industry, for example, possibly guarantee all-year-round employment for the same number of men year after year, when the orders that it gets enable it to operate at practically 100 per cent of capacity in wartime, while the orders that it gets in a severe depression, as in 1932, enable it to operate at only 20 per cent of capacity?

Are the seasonal or cyclical variations in employment in certain industries primarily the fault of the employers in those industries? Are they not primarily the "fault"—if that is the word for it—of the customers of those industries? Can a solution of all this be worked out by voluntary agreement? Or must it necessarily be done by more government coercion and regimentation of business? If only seasonal employment can be provided in certain industries, is it fair to pay workers in those industries just as much annually for working only part of the year as workers in other industries receive for working without let-up the whole year round? Is not the solution, in many of these cases, rather to find supplementary work of another kind for the displaced workers in the off-season of the first industry?

These are only a few of the questions raised by the problem, but they indicate its complex and formidable nature. It is a problem that has engaged the attention of economists for many years. Employers have also been concerned about it; for even from the most narrowly selfish point of view, every employer loses when he cannot work his plant and equipment at full capacity the whole year through, and when he has to offer higher wages than otherwise to compensate for the irregular type of work that he provides.—*Editorial. New York Times. Mr. 22, '45. p. 22.*

The manner in which subsidies may be used to prevent a wage-price spiral was effectively illustrated in December 1942.

In Canada, general wage increases are not permitted unless they represent bonuses to compensate for rises in the cost of living index. These bonuses are determined every three months, and, in general, the bonus is equivalent to 25 cents weekly for each point change in the index. Rising food prices caused increases in the cost of living index and it began to look as though a bonus would be necessary unless action was taken before the January 1, 1943, index number was reported.

Early in December, therefore, reductions in the retail prices of five products included in the cost of living index were ordered: tea 10 cents a pound, milk two cents a quart, oranges seven to ten cents a dozen, coffee four cents a pound, and butter two cents a pound. The cost of each product, except milk to the retailer was reduced enough to make possible the price reduction ordered. Milk distributors continue to pay the same price, but each month are reimbursed by their local banks to the extent of two cents per quart sold. Distributors were reimbursed for reductions in the value of stocks of coffee, tea, and butter. Unlike the other subsidies for inventory losses and to alleviate the squeeze, these subsidies were uniform to all distributors and were not made dependent upon their profit status. Largely as a result of this program, which is estimated to cost about $40 million annually, the cost of living index on January 1 was 1.7 points lower than on December 1, and no cost of living bonus, therefore, had to be paid.

The Minister of Finance has estimated that total subsidies in the fiscal year 1942-1943 aggregated about $80 million, or about 2 per cent of the $4 billion war budget. During the current fiscal year, it seems likely that the total will be substantially greater due to the program inaugurated in December and the likelihood that there will be increasing pressure on the ceiling, with the consequent need for greater subsidies to prevent a significant break through. Largely due to the subsidies paid on more than half of the 45 products included in the food index, it is now only about 128 (August 1939 = 100), as compared with 124 in October 1941. During the same period the cost of living index has recorded only a minor increase to 116, from 114.6

While the stability of the cost of living indexes in Canada and Great Britain was due to many measures, it seems clear that subsidies have played a significant role.

The criticisms in this country against the use of subsidies have been based on the peacetime experience and include the following: they promote inefficiency, destroy initiative, delay the correction of fundamental maladjustments in supply and demand, are subject to political abuse, they represent concealed price rises, and are difficult to abandon once they are adopted. This writer does not dispute these criticisms. However, safeguards similar to those noted above in Canada can be established to prevent the abuse of subsidies. Unfortunately the subsidies we have paid to date have not met all these tests, since they have involved the payment of uniform amounts per unit to each recipient regardless of his profit position. Unless such standards were established and *adhered to,* it appears true that a subsidy program would become an open invitation to every pressure group to get its share, with consequent aggravation of the inflationary situation. But subsidies *per se,* if the experience of England and Canada counts for anything, are far less inflationary than rising prices.—*Jules Backman, New York University. Barron's: National Business and Financial Weekly. My.* 10. '43. *p.* 16.

BIBLIOGRAPHY

An asterisk (*) preceding a reference indicates that the article or a part of it has been reprinted in this book.

BIBLIOGRAPHIES

International Labour Office. Wage regulation and wage policy; articles published in the International Labour Review up to and including December 1944. 6p. mim. The Office. 3480 University St. Montreal, Can. ['45.]

Johnsen, Julia E. comp. Wage stabilization and inflation. (Reference Shelf. Vol. 16, no. 4) p. 177-87. H.W. Wilson Co. New York. My. '43.

Summers, Robert E. comp. Wages and prices. (Reference Shelf. Vol. 15, no. 6) p. 207-19. H.W. Wilson Co. New York. Ap. '42.

Willigan, Walter L. and O'Connor, J. J. Social order, wages and prices. *In their* Social order. p. 132-6. Longmans, Green & Co. New York. '41.

BOOKS, PAMPHLETS AND DOCUMENTS

Bergson, Abram. Structure of Soviet wages. 255p. (Harvard Economic Studies. Vol. 76) Harvard University Press. Cambridge, Mass. '44.

Brody, Maurice S. Wage rates and living costs in a war economy. (Studies in Business Administration. Vol. 13, no. 3) 38p. University of Chicago Press. Chicago. '43.

Chamber of Commerce of the United States. Economic policy: means and ends; report of the Committee on Economic Policy. (Post-war Readjustments Bulletin no. 12) 21p. The Chamber. Washington, D.C. N. '44.

Chamber of Commerce of the United States. Department of Manufacture. Cost of living and the earnings of industrial workers; tabulation. 4p. The Chamber. Washington, D.C. N. 24, '43.

Cherne, Leo M. Organized for retreat. *In his* Rest of your life. p. 159-78. Doubleday, Doran & Co. Garden City, N.Y. '44.

*Clark, John M. Demobilization of wartime economic controls. (Committee for Economic Development Research Study) 219p. McGraw-Hill Book Co. New York. '44.

*Daniel, Edward G. Federal finance, prices and public welfare. (Bureau of Business Research Pamphlet) 47p. School of Business Administration. University of Oregon. Eugene. My. '44.

Davis, William H. and others. Wage policy. (American Forum of the Air. Vol. 6, no. 15) 15p. Ransdell, Inc. Washington, D.C. Ap. 11, '44.

Dunlop, John T. Wage determination under trade unions. 431p. Macmillan Co. New York. '44.

Feldman, Herman. Stabilizing jobs and wages through better business management. 334p. Harper & Bros. New York. '40.

Flanders, Allan. Wage policy in war-time. 24p. International Publishing Co. 12 Great Castle St. London. Distributed by the Universal Distributors. 38 Union Square. New York. n.d.

Haake, Alfred P.; Burns, R. K.; and Krueger, M. Should labor strike in wartime? (Reviewing Stand. Vol. 2, no. 9) 12p. Radio Department. Northwestern University. Evanston, Ill. D. 26, '43.

Haake, Alfred P. and Mitchell, Broadus. What is labor's part in postwar adjustments? (Wake Up, America! no. 259) 10p. American Economic Foundation. 295 Madison Ave. New York. '45.

Howenstine, E. Jay, Jr. Economics of demobilization. 336p. Public Affairs Press. Washington, D.C. '44.

Johnsen, Julia E. comp. Federal price control policy. (Reference Shelf. Vol. 15, no. 9) 113p. H.W. Wilson Co. New York. Ag. '42.
Bibliography, p.99-113.

Johnsen, Julia E. comp. Wage stabilization and inflation. (Reference Shelf. Vol. 16, no. 4) 187p. H.W. Wilson Co. New York. My. '43.

Johnson, D. Gale and Brownlee, O. H. Food subsidies and inflation control. (Pamphlet no. 10) 53p. Collegiate Press. Ames, Iowa. '44.

Katona, George. War without inflation; the psychological approach to problems of war economy. 213p. Columbia University Press. New York. '42.
Problem of wage stabilization. p.119.23.

King, W. L. Mackenzie. Battle against inflation. 11p. Wartime Information Board. Ottawa. D. 4, '43.

League of Nations. Delegation on Economic Depressions. Economic stability in the post-war world; the conditions of prosperity after the transitions from war to peace; report. (Official no. C.1.M.1.1945. II.A) 319p. The League. Geneva. Distributed by International Documents Service, Columbia University Press. New York. Mr. '45.

McCabe, David A. and Lester, Richard A. Labor and social organization. (Economics and Social Institutions. Vol. 6) 374p. Little, Brown & Co. Boston. '38.

McCabe, David A.; Shishkin, B. B.; and Walsh, J. R. Labor's views on American economic policies. 38p. Economic and Business Foundation. New Wilmington, Pa. Ap. 29, '43.

McGregor, Alexander G. Right wages and abundance. 316p. E. P. Dutton & Co. New York. '38.

Mayer, Joseph. Postwar national income, its probable magnitude. (Pamphlet no. 55) 34p. Brookings Institution. Washington, D.C. '44.

Meany, George and Thomas, R. J. Cost of living; recommended report for the Presidential Committee on the Cost of Living, submitted January 25, 1944. (CIO Publication no. 101) 104p. Congress of Industrial Organizations. 718 Jackson Pl. N.W. Washington, D.C. '44.

Millis, Harry A. and Montgomery, Royal E. Organized labor. 930p. McGraw-Hill Book Co. New York. '45.

Morley, Frank V. and others. Collective bargaining and wage policies. 35p. Economic and Business Foundation. New Wilmington, Pa. Mr. 16, '44.

Moulton, Harold G. and Schlotterbeck, Karl. Collapse or boom at the end of the war. (Pamphlet no. 47) 40p. Brookings Institution. Washington, D.C. '42.

Murray, Philip. Your wages and the war. 15p. International Union, United Automobile, Aircraft and Agricultural Implement Workers of America. 411 W. Milwaukee St. Detroit. n.d.

Murray, Philip and Thomas, R. J. Living costs in World War II, 1941-44. (Publication no. 107) 161+76p. Congress of Industrial Organizations. 718 Jackson Pl. Washington, D.C. Je. '44.

National Association of Manufacturers. Effect of the war on income, wages, and living costs. 30p. The Association. 14 W. 49th St. New York. '44.

*National Conference of Social Work. Proceedings. 1944: 59-66. Stable economy for the postwar world. D. D. Humphrey.

National Industrial Conference Board. Critical analysis of the Meany-Thomas report on the cost of living. Robert A. Sayre and others. 36p. The Board. 247 Park Ave. New York. '44.

National Industrial Conference Board. Wage and salary stabilization. (Management Research memo. no. 13) 27p. The Board. 247 Park Ave. New York. '43.

National War Labor Board. Comments of American Federation of Labor members of the National War Labor Board on the public members, report to the President on the relationship of wages to the cost of living and the changes which have occurred under the economic stabilization policy. 12p. mim. The Board. Washington, D.C. Mr. 2, '43.

National War Labor Board. Report of the President's Committee on the Cost of Living. v.p. mim. The Board. Washington, D.C. F. 23, '45.

Includes report by the public members of the Board; separate statements by the industry members, the C.I.O. members, the American Federation of Labor members; and appendixes as follows: Analysis of the problem. F. P. Graham; History of the proceedings which gave rise to this report; history of the stabilization program. L. K. Garrison; Wage stabilization policy of the National War Labor Board. G. W. Taylor; Trend of wage standards under the national economic stabilization program. G. W. Taylor; Prices and purchasing power. L. K. Garrison.

*National War Labor Board. Report of the special panel summarizing the contentions advanced by the American Federation of Labor in support of its petition for the modification of the Little Steel formula. 21p. mim. The Board. Washington, D.C. S. 8, '44.

National War Labor Board. Report of the steel panel; in re: United States Steel Corporation, et al, and the United Steelworkers of America, CIO. Case III-6230-D. 3 pts. 285, 69, 94p. mim. The Board. Washington, D.C. S. '44.
Part 1 signed by all six members of the panel; part 2 by the two industry members, and part 3 by the two labor members.

National War Labor Board. Report of the Technical Committee appointed by the Chairman of the President's Committee on the Cost of Living. Wesley C. Mitchell and others. v.p. mim. The Board. Washington, D.C. Je. 15, '44.

National War Labor Board. Division of Public Information. National wage stabilization code and its practical application. 8p. The Board. Washington, D.C. Jl. '44.

National War Labor Board. Division of Public Information. National War Labor Board wage stabilization general orders and interpretations under Executive order 9250, Executive order 9328, and the regulations of the Director of Economic Stabilization. 88p. The Board. Washington, D.C. N. '44.

Noyes, Charles E. Wages and the standard of living. In his Economic freedom. p. 194-210. Harper & Bros. New York. '43.

Riegel, John W. Wage stabilization and adjustment policies of the National War Labor Board. In University of Michigan. Bureau of Industrial Relations. (Bulletin no. 14) p. 95-136. University of Michigan Press. Ann Arbor. '43.

Roth, Almon E. and others. Toward a national labor policy. (Personnel series no. 72) 40p. American Management Assn. 330 W. 42d St. New York. '43.

Schmidt, Emerson P. Inflation and the post-war. (Post-war Readjustments Bulletin no. 10) 22p. Chamber of Commerce of the United States. Washington, D.C. '44.

Seward, Ralph T. and others. Wage stabilization and adjustment. (Personnel series no. 61) 28p. American Management Association. 330 W. 42d St. New York. '42.

Shachtman, Max. For a cost-plus wage. 25p. Workers Party. 114 W. 14th St. New York. O. '43.

Slichter, Sumner H. Union policies and industrial management. (Pub. no. 85) 597p. Brookings Institution. Washington, D.C. '41

Sufrin, Sidney C. Labor policy and the business cycle. 52p. American Council on Public Affairs. 2153 Florida Ave. Washington, D.C. '43.

Summers, Robert E. comp. Wages and prices. (Reference Shelf. Vol. 15, no. 6) 219p. H. W. Wilson Co. New York. Ap. '42.

Taylor, George W. and others. National wage labor policies and problems. (Personnel series no. 70) 63p. American Management Assn. 330 W. 42d St. New York. '43.

United States. Bureau of Labor Statistics. Changes in cost of living in large cities in United States, 1913-41. (Bulletin no. 699) 112p. The Bureau. Washington, D.C. '41.

United States. Bureau of Labor Statistics. Cost of living index of the Bureau of Labor Statistics. 60p. The Bureau. Washington, D.C. F. 25, '44.

United States. House. Committee on Interstate and Foreign Commerce. Railway pay of nonoperating employees; hearings, December 13, 16, 17, 1943 on S.J.Res. 91 and H.J.Res. 187. 176p. 78th Congress. 1st sess. '44.

United States. Senate. Committee on Education and Labor. Substandard wages; hearings before a subcommittee, November 17-18, 1944, pursuant to S. Con. Res. 48. Pt. 1. 432p. 78th Cong. 2d sess. Supt. of Docs. Washington, D.C. '44.

University of Illinois. Office of High School Visitor. Fight against inflation. 24p. processed. The University. Urbana. Mr. '43.

*Wallace, Henry A. Charter for postwar prosperity; text of prepared statement before the Senate Commerce Committee January 25, 1945. 4p. The Author. Department of Commerce. Washington, D.C. Same. New York Times. p.12. Ja. 26, '45.

Walsh, J. Raymond and Haynes, Eldridge. Would wage incentives help us solve the manpower crisis? (Wake Up, America! no. 252) 12p. American Economic Foundation. 295 Madison Ave. New York 17. '45.

War labor reports; wage and salary stabilization. Vol. 16. 816p. Bureau of National Affairs. Washington, D.C. '44.

Wartime wage control and dispute settlement. 600p. Bureau of National Affairs. 2201 M. St. N.W. Washington, D.C. '45.

Watts, Vervon O. So we want free enterprise? (Economic Sentinel. Vol. 2, no. 1) 165p. Los Angeles Chamber of Commerce. 1151 S. Broadway. Los Angeles. '44.

Whitney, A. F. Wartime wages and railroad labor. 228p. Brotherhood of Railroad Trainmen. 1370 Ontario St. Cleveland, O. '44.

Willigan, Walter L. and O'Connor, J. J. Social order, wages and prices. In their Social order. p. 98-139. Longmans, Green & Co. New York. '41.

PERIODICALS

Academy of Political Science. Proceedings. 20:23-34. My. '42. Price and wage control in Canada. A. F. W. Plumptre.

Academy of Political Science. Proceedings. 20:79-86. My. '42. Labor's view of wage policies from now on. J. B. Carey.

Academy of Political Science. Proceedings. 20:336-51. Ja. '44. Inflation and wages. S. H. Slichter.

Same abridged. Commercial and Financial Chronicle. 158:2002. N. 18, '43.

Academy of Political Science. Proceedings. 20:417-30. Ja. '44. Postwar control of industrial production and prices. J. W. Scoville.

*Academy of Political and Social Science. Proceedings. 21:64-88. My. '44. Problems of wage policy after the war. Sumner H. Slichter.

Advanced Management. 9:64-7. Ja. '44. What the War Labor Board will approve in wage incentives. T. W. Kheel.

Advanced Management. 10:23-30. Ja. '45. Wartime lessons in wage administration. C. C. Balderston.

American Economic Review. 32:sup. 290-306. Mr. '42. Wage policies of trade unions. J. T. Dunlop.

American Economic Review. 33:sup. 27-38. Mr. '43. Government function in a stabilized national economy. A. A. Berle, Jr.

American Economic Review. 33:sup. 218-37. Mr. '43. Effects of the war on wages and hours. R. A. Lester.

American Economic Review. 33:892-7. D. '43. Wage policies and wage trends in the war boom; latter half of 1941. G. F. Bloom.

American Economic Review. 34:98-110. Mr. '44. War Labor Board; an experiment in wage stabilization. J. C. Record.

American Economic Review. 34:111-16. Mr. '44. Note on cyclical wage rigidity. Joseph Shister.

*American Economic Review. 34:sup. 181-92. Mr. '44. Wage regulation in postwar America. G. W. Taylor.

American Economic Review. 34:561-7. S. '44. British white paper on employment policy. M. F. W. Joseph.

American Economic Review. 34:572-7. S. '44. War Labor Board: an experiment in wage stabilization; reply with rejoinder. Milton Derber.

American Economic Review. 34:849-56. D. '44. Mitchell Committee's report on the cost-of-living index: comments.

American Federation of Labor Weekly News Service. 35:1. Ja. 23, '45. Labor's war and post-war programs outlined. William Green.
Prepared for the Washington Star and the North American Newspaper Alliance.

American Federation of Labor Weekly News Service. 35:1. Ap. 3, '45. Labor-management charter adopted to encourage post-war recovery; with text of charter.

American Federation of Labor Weekly News Service. 35:1. F. 25, '45. Final word on wage freeze now up to FDR, AFL insists.

American Federationist. 48:28-9. My. '41. Should wages be frozen?

American Federationist. 48:8. N. '41. Wage freezing is opposed.

American Federationist. 48:18-19. N. '41. Control inflation.

American Federationist. 49:16-17. Je. '42. Wage increases.

American Federationist. 49:3-5+. Ag. '42. Wages and inflation. Boris Shishkin.

American Federationist. 49:18. Ag. '42. Keep collective bargaining.

American Federationist. 50:2-6. Ap. '43. Inflation crisis. Boris Shishkin.

American Federationist. 50:4-7. O. '43. Incentive wage schemes.

American Federationist. 50:16-17. O. '43. Incentive pay.

American Federationist. 50:22-3. O '43. Five years of the wage-hour law. L. M. Walling.

American Federationist. 51:5-6. Mr. '44. Economic squeeze; wages frozen and living costs rising. George Meany.

American Federationist. 51:20-2. Ap. '44. WLB's wage bracket system. G. T. Brown.

American Federationist. 51:4-7. Jl. '44. Labor must have a real cost-of-living index. George Meany.

American Federationist. 51:3-6+. O. '44. Next depression. Boris Shishkin.

American Federationist. 51:9-10. O. '44. Wage freeze must go.

American Federationist. 51:16. O. '44. Strange omission. George Meany.

American Federationist. 51:6-7. D. '44. Wage freeze is assailed by A.F. of L. delegates.

American Federationist. 51:24-5. D. '44. Wage policy.

American Federationist. 52:21-2. Ja. '45. Caught in the nutcracker; public employees squeezed as living costs zoom. Joseph Mire.

American Federationist. 52:4-5. F. '45. Our war and postwar programs. William Green.

American Federationist. 52:3-4+. Mr. '45. America's wage policy. William Green.

American Magazine. 135:39+. Je. '43. You still can get a raise. W. H. Davis.

American Magazine. 139:20-1+. Ja. '45. Labor faces a crisis; ed. by B. Smith. W. M. Leiserson.

American Political Science Review. 38:1124-36. D. '44. Federal government's role in the postwar economy. J. G. Patton.

American Statistical Association. Journal. 38:271-86. S. '43. Observations on the cost of living index of the Bureau of Labor Statistics; with discussion by A. J. Wickens and F. M. Williams. Lazare Teper.

American Statistical Association. Journal. 38:387-405; 39:57-95. D. '43-Mr. '44. Appraisal of the U.S. Bureau of Labor Statistics cost of living index. F. C. Mills and others.

American Statistical Association. Journal. 38:425-37. D. '43. Statistics for wage stabilization; Occupational wage rate project. R. J. Myers and H. Ober.

Antioch Review. 1:441-51. D. '41. How England controls inflation. Ernest Dale.

Antioch Review. 4:21-46. Mr. '44. C.E.D.—what is it and why. R. A. Brady.

Antioch Review. 4:126-44. Mr. '44. Serious blunder on the right; plans for a nice, new depression. J. D. Kingsley.

Antioch Review. 4:449-64. S. '44. Problems of the peace: boom and bust? Lewis Corey.

Atlantic Monthly. 173:37-41. F. '44. Labor crisis. S. H. Slichter.

Barron's. 23:16. My. 10, '43. Case for subsidies in price control; choice lies between them and a rising wage-price spiral. Jules Backman.

Barron's. 24:3. D. 11, '44. Will V-E day bring big drop in incomes? Jules Backman.

Barron's. 25:3. Ja. 29, '45. Full employment program based on economic fallacies. J. W. Scoville.

Business Week. p. 15-16. Ja. 29, '44. Stabilization fight brews.

Business Week. p. 106. Je. 17, '44. Severance drive; campaign for dismissal pay clause in contracts.

Business Week. p. 107. Ag. 5, '44. Split on bonus; overtime award for loading and unloading cargo in port at night.

Business Week. p. 106. S. 9, '44. Money no factor; WLB insists on full retroactivity of wage increase to rubber workers.

Business Week. p. 107. S. 9, '44. Strikers penalized; brewery drivers lose six weeks' overtime for walking out during negotiations.

Business Week. p. 98+. S. 16, '44. Union bonanza; U.O.W.P. wins award of long-sought back wages for insurance agents.

Business Week. p. 102+. S. 16, '44. Pay for dressing; labor board ruling allowing bakery workers wage adjustment.

Business Week. p. 96+. S. 23, '44. Wage line falters; panel report paves way for easing Little Steel formula.

Business Week. p. 16-17. S. 30, '44. Hitting the line; attack on wage controls shifts from Little Steel formula to floor under purcasing power.

Business Week. p. 123. O. 7, '44. Portal to portal; pay for time required to change clothes opens possibilities for extension of idea.

Business Week. p. 105. O. 14, '44. Break for loggers; workers may get pay for travel time.

Business Week. p. 98+. N. 11, '44. Wages or salary? despite chilly reception in NWLB and industry, C.I.O. is pushing guaranteed annual wage for hourly workers.

Business Week. p. 103-4. N. 11, '44. Wages on farms; Agriculture Dept. wants to retain wartime increases.

Business Week. p. 116. N. 25, '44. Index sustained; final report of cost-of-living committee.

Business Week. p. 102+. D. 9, '44. Portal pay extended.

Business Week. p. 78+. D. 16, '44. Bracket battle; adjustment of pay rates on industry-wide basis.

Business Week. p. 15-16. D. 23, '44. Setting postwar wage cost.

Business Week. p. 108+. D. 23, '44. Controls for Miami; NWLB strikes at black market in common labor.

Business Week. p. 100-2. Ja. 6, '45. To ease a pinch.

Business Week. p. 108. Ja. 27, '45. Monthly pay won.

Business Week. p. 15-16. Mr. 3, '45. Little Steel formula sticks.

Business Week. p. 120. Mr. 10, '45. Future of the wage-price squeeze.

Business Week. p. 21-2+. Mr. 17, '45. Legacy to Davis; difficult fringe problem.

Business Week. p. 93. Mr. 17, '45. Wage cuts denied; policy on pay rates of concerns converting to civilian production.

Business Week. p. 96+. Mr. 17, '45. Pay springboard; NWLB orders wiping out regional differential in war plane plant, and textile wage directive.

*Call. 12:3. Ap. 2, '45. What isn't guaranteed. William Becker.

Christian Century. 61:1318-19. N. 15, '44. Labor seeks an annual wage. Kermit Eby.

Christian Science Monitor Weekly Magazine Section. p. 3. Ag. 26, '44. Should wages be increased? L. G. Reynolds.

Christian Science Monitor Weekly Magazine Section. p. 6. D. 9, '44. Is there security in an annual wage? L. G. Reynolds.

Columbia Law Review. 42:1320-32. N. '42. Union security and wage policies of the National War Labor Board.

Commerce. 40:12-14+. D. '43. Wages and inflation. S. H. Slichter.

Commerce Magazine. 41:21-2. N. '44. Wages based on productivity key to high employment. T. S. McEwan.

Commerce Magazine. 41:13-14+. Ja. '45. Government's wage-price policy after V-E day. J. R. Beal.

Commercial and Financial Chronicle. 159:1914+. My. 11, '44. Post-war wage policies. R. D. Gray.

Commercial and Financial Chronicle. 159:1918+. My. 11, '44. Post-war wage problem. C. J. Haggerty.

Commercial and Financial Chronicle. 160:1035+. S. 7, '44. Revise Little Steel formula. Philip Murray.

*Commercial and Financial Chronicle. 161:362+. Ja. 25, '45. Guaranteeing employment and purchasing power. Philip Murray.

*Commercial and Financial Chronicle. 161:363+. Ja. 25, '45. Rigid wages, unionization and reconversion problems. F. E. Lee.

Common Sense. 12:427-31. D. '43. Business plans for business; CED: free enterprise in a controlled economy. Daniel Bell.

Commonweal. 37:460. F. 26, '43. Break it up, break it up! Reuther suggests a wage commission representing management, labor and government.

Commonweal. 39:344-6. Ja. 21, '44. Mood of the workers. Francis Downing.

Commonweal. 40:604. O. 13, '44. Moving the anti-inflation line.

*Commonweal. 41:54-8. N. 3, '44. Problem of our American society. M. C. Kyne and others.

Communist. 22:443-51. My. '43. On wage stabilization; with reply by Gilbert Green. William and Pauline Young.

Communist. 23:140-7. F. '44. Teheran and the wage policy issue. Roy Hudson.

Conference Board Economic Record. 5:337-44. N. '43. What's wrong with cost of living indexes? G. C. Thompson and M. A. Wertz.

Conference Board Management Record. 5:415-17. O. '43. Wage and salary stabilization; rare and unusual cases; wage incentives. E. S. Horning.

Congressional Record. 89:6776-81. Je. 29, '43. War production cost. A. J. Engel.

Congressional Record. 91:(daily) A1824-5. Ap. 10, '45. Must 10,-000,000 Americans stay poor? a 65-cent minimum wage. Cláude Pepper.

Controller. 12:6-11. Ja. '44. Salary stabilization under the Treasury Department. J. G. Powers.

Controller. 12:12-14. Ja. '44. Wage and salary stabilization. M. K. Ellison.

Controller. 12:202-4. My. '44. Wages in war-time and after. L. G. Reynolds.

*Controller. 13:16-18. Ja. '45. Compliance with wage stabilization. Robert Littler.

Controller. 13:19-20+. Ja. '45. Decisions and regulations of wage and salary stabilization. W. L. Russell.

Current History. n.s. 4:377-81. Ag. '43. Taxes and wages on the up and up? D. G. Redmond.

Economic Journal. 53:321-42. D. '43. Full employment and security of livelihood; a wage subsidy plan. R. F. Harrod.
    Reply. R. G. Hawtrey. Economic Journal. 54:417-22. D. '44.

Economist (London). 146:687. My. 20, '44. American wage rates.

Economist (London). 147:371-3. S. 16, '44. Labour and wealth.
    Same with title. Profits the best friend of wages not their worst enemy. Industrial Canada. 45:96+. N. '44.

Editorial Research Reports. 2, no. 2:19-32. Jl. 20, '40. Labor in wartime. C. E. Noyes.

Editorial Research Reports. 2, no. 8:135-50. S. 2, '44. Revision of the Little Steel formula. F. P. Huddle.

Editorial Research Reports. 2, no. 15:263-74. O. 27, '44. Wage security. F. P. Huddle.

*Federal Reserve Bulletin. 30:1156-62. D. '44. Postwar price problem, inflation or deflation. M. S. Eccles.
    Same abridged. Commercial and Financial Chronicle. 160:2241+. N. 23, '44; also separate. 7p. The Author. Board of Governors of the Federal Reserve System. Washington, D.C.

Forbes. 55:14-15; 16-17+. Mr. 1, 15, '45. Employers answer: is 48 hours pay for 40 hours of work feasible?

*Fortune. 27:79-81+. My. '43. Wages: squaring the vicious circle.

Fortune. 28:138-40+. S. '43. More pay, more production; Murrat Corp. of America proves it at the Ecorse plant.

Fortune. 30:162-5+. O. '44. Economics of a free society; declaration of American economic policy. W. S. Benton.
Also separate. 8p. Committee for Economic Development. 285 Madison Ave. New York 17, N.Y.

Free World. 5:323-6. Ap. '43. Government and private enterprise. T. Swann Harding.

Free World. 8:68-71. Jl. '44. When our boys come home . . . peace must mean security. Philip Murray.

George Washington Law Review. 11:399-427. Je. '43. Wartime wage control. E. J. Sheffield.

Harvard Business Review. 21:5-42. Autumn '42. Postwar boom or collapse. S. H. Slichter.

Industrial Canada. 45:98-9. N. '44. Popular economic fallacy; that the cost of living is a sound basis for wage settlements. Ernest Benn.

International Labour Review. 44:669-71. D. '41. Wartime stabilization of wages in Canada.

International Labour Review. 45:125-41. F. '42. Consumer spending, inflation and the wage earner in the United States. Otto Nathan and Milton Fried.

International Labour Review. 45:664-5. Je. '42. Measures to stabilize the cost of living in the United States.

International Labour Review. 46:525-67. N. '42. Industrial relations and the determination of conditions of employment in wartime. I. Bessling.

International Labour Review. 48:522-4. O. '43. Adjustment of wages; National War Labor Board rulings.

International Labour Review. 49:102-3. Ja. '44. Regulation of wages and hours of work in the United States; review of the first five years operation of the Fair Labor Standards act.

International Labour Review. 49:246-9. F. '44. United States wage policy; recent decisions of the National War Labor Board.

International Labour Review. 50:234-7. Ag. '44. Wage developments in the United States.

Journal of Accountancy. 77:125-41. F. '44. Wage stabilization regulations and procedures. D. C. Anchin.

Journal of Accountancy. 78:311-27. O. '44. Common wage stabilization violations, their avoidance and correction. D. C. Anchin.

Journal of Political Economy. 51:1-11. F. '43. Toward a national wartime labor policy: the wage issue. E. B. McNatt.

Labor Relations Reporter. 11:169-70+. O. 12, '42. Wage bargaining in a stabilization era.

Labor Relations Reporter. 13:298-9. N. 15, '43. Reconsideration of wage control policy.

Labors Monthly Survey. 4:1-8. N. '43. Stabilization: have all groups made equal sacrifice?

Labors Monthly Survey. 5:1-8. O. '44. What wage policy?

Labour Gazette (Ottawa). 43:1597-601. D. '43. New policy of wage control.

Labour Gazette (Ottawa). 43:1602-12. D. '43. Revision of wartime wages control order.

Labour Gazette (Ottawa). 44:452-5. Ap. '44. Amendments to the wartime wages control order, 1943.

Labour Monthly (London). 26:179-81. Je. '44. Wages and prices. John Austin.

Law and Contemporary Problems. 10, no. 4:613-32. Spring '44. Problems of war contract termination affecting labor. Boris Shishkin.

Magazine of Wall Street. 73:227-9. D. 11, '43. New crisis in wage-price control; how other countries are holding the line. V. L. Horoth.

Magazine of Wall Street. 74:343-5+. Jl. 8, '44. Where wage cost differentials will importantly affect post-war investment values. P. T. Sheldrick.

Magazine of Wall Street. 75:11-13+. O. 14, '44. What higher wage trends will mean: conflict between needs for post-war buying power and inflationary threats. Lawrence Stern.

*Magazine of Wall Street. 75:288-9+. D. 23, '44. Is controlled inflation possible? J. C. Cresswill.

Modern Industry. 7:145-6+. Mr '44. Legal ways to boost wages and salaries.

Monthly Labor Review. 55:917-24. N. '42. Stabilization of cost of living by wage and price control.

Monthly Labor Review. 56:1090-2. Je. '43. Stabilization of wages and prices.

Monthly Labor Review. 57:133-44. Jl. '43. Pay differentials for night work under union agreements.

Monthly Labor Review. 57:250-4. Ag '43. Wage and price stabilization in New Zealand.

Monthly Labor Review. 57:885-94. N. '43. Cost-of-living adjustment of state and municipal wages. E. M. Snyder.

Monthly Labor Review. 57:994-1002. N. '43. Findings of investigating committee [of the American Statistical Association] on cost-of-living index of Bureau of Labor Statistics.

Monthly Labor Review. 58:400. F. '44. Wage subsidies in Australia.

Monthly Labor Review. 58:995-6. My. '44. Wage policy of National War Labor Board.

Monthly Labor Review. 59:81-3. Jl. '44. Report of President's Committee on portal-to-portal travel time in bituminous coal-mining.

Monthly Labor Review. 59:234-7. Ag. '44. Wage developments in the United States.

Monthly Labor Review. 59:237-50. Ag. '44. Intercity variations in wage levels. L. M. Solomon.
Summary with title. How wages vary. Business Week. p.94+. S. 16, '44.

Monthly Labor Review. 59:364-73. Ag. '44. Executive order 9240 in relation to wage stabilization. I. R. Feinberg and A. H. Dadian.

Monthly Labor Review. 59:1049-53. N. '44. Wartime changes in wages and salaries and per capita income in the various states.

Monthly Labor Review. 59:1062-9. N. '44. Determination of wage rates for mechanical and laboring positions in the federal service. F. L. Christman.

Monthly Labor Review. 60:41-3. Ja. '45. Basic steel decision of National War Labor Board.

Monthly Labor Review. 60:47-57. Ja. '45. Dismissal-pay provisions in union agreements, December 1944. Abraham Weiss.

*Monthly Labor Review. 60:168-74. Ja. '45. Report of President's Committee on Cost of Living; summary.
Also separate. Serial No. R. 1718. 7p. United States Bureau of Labor Statistics. Washington, D.C.

N.A.C.A. Bulletin. 24:809-25. Mr. 15, '43. Wage and salary stabilization. J. W. Havighurst.

N.A.M. Law Digest. 7:33-56. Mr. '45. National War Labor Board, policies and decisions 1942-1945.
References, p.54-6.

*N.A.M. News. Sec. 2:1-3. O. 7, '44. Statement before National War Labor Board October 2, 1944. R. M. Gaylord.

Nation. 156:437-8. Mr. 27, '43. Wages and prices.

Nation. 158:32. Ja. 8, '44. Wages and living costs.

Nation. 159:635-6. N. 25, '44. 65-cent minimum. I. F. Stone.

National Auditgram. 21:19+. F. '45. Salary and wage stabilization— W.L.B. and Treasury Department. R. T. Bigelow.

*National City Bank of New York. p. 135-7. D. '43. Problems of wage and price stability.

*National City Bank of New York. p. 52-6. My. '44. War profits.

National Municipal Review. 31:249-53. My. '42. Canada regulates wages, prices.

Nation's Business. 33:27+. Ja. '45. What wage guarantees involve; annual wage. Volta Torrey.

New Republic. 109:677-8. N. 15, '43. Labor's case for higher wages. Helen Fuller.

New Republic. 110:39-40. Ja. 10, '44. For flexible wages.

New Republic. 110:489-94. Ap. 10, '44. Wages and the cost of living; with reply by A. F. Hinrichs and editorial comment. H. J. Ruttenberg.

New Republic. 111:359-60. S. 25, '44. Will wages be thawed?

New Republic. 112:316-17. Mr. 5, '45. Little Steel formula again.

New Republic. 112:355-7. Mr. 12, '45. War over wages. Helen Fuller.

New Republic. 112:472-3. Ap. 9, '45. Controls after victory. Helen Fuller.

New York Times. p. 14-15. S. 15, '44. Text of War Labor Board panels' report on steel wage formula to the National War Labor Board.

New York Times. p. 49. N. 26, '44. Text of the Labor Board decision making some concessions to steel union on pay.

New York Times. p. 10. F. 24, '45. Hold the wage-price line; editorial.

New York Times. p. 22. Mr. 22, '45. Annual wages.

New York Times. p. 16. Mr. 29, '45. Proposed management-labor code; text.

New York Times. p. 1+. Ap. 8, '45. Four stabilizers ask firm control beyond end of war.

New York Times. p. 34. Ap. 8, '45. Inflation report to Roosevelt; text of letter from heads of the Office of Economic Stabilization, the Office of Price Administration, the War Food Administration, and the War Labor Board.

New York Times. p. 18. Ap. 9, '45. Price control: war and peace.

New York Times Magazine. p. 12+. Ap. 8, '45. Guaranteed annual wage for labor? yes. Philip Murray.

New York Times Magazine. p. 16+. Ap. 15, '45. Guaranteed annual wage for labor? no. B. F. Fairless.

Newsweek. 21:56+. F. 8, '43. Little Steel formula swaying in labor's storm for raises.

Newsweek. 21:55-6+. F. 22, '43. Specter of inflation looms up behind 48-hour week order.

Newsweek. 21:39. Ap. 5, '43. Notes on the wage situation. E. K. Lindley.

Newsweek. 22:37-8. N. 1, '43. Wage-price-tax snarls point to growing inflation menace.

Newsweek. 22:60+. N. 15, '43. Administration grasps for time as labor takes wage warpath.

Newsweek. 23:75-6. Ap. 3, '44. Assaulting Little Steel.

Newsweek. 23:66+. My. 8, '44. How Hormel does it; guaranteed annual wage.

Newsweek. 24:66+. S. 25, '44. Unions ask higher hourly wages in attack on Little Steel formula.

Newsweek. 24:68+. N. 27, '44. Unions demand wage boosts, assail cost-of-living figures.

Newsweek. 24:76+. D. 4, '44. Denting Little Steel.

Newsweek. 24:79. D. 4, '44. What kind of an America do we want? Ralph Robey.

Newsweek. 25:66. Ja. 15, '45. What is being planned for you. Ralph Robey.

Newsweek. 25:68+. Mr. 5, '45. Vinson-WLB deadlock provoking new labor fight on pay ceiling.

Oxford Institute. Bulletin of Statistics (England). 4:269-74. O. 10, '42. Problem of price and wage control. J. Steindl.

Oxford Institute. Bulletin of Statistics (England). 5:157-62. Jl. 17, '43. Wage structure and wage policy in the United States. J. Steindl.

Personnel. 21:146-51. N. '44. Guaranteed annual wage. Ernest Dale.

*Personnel. 21:224-8. Ja. '45. What about increasing wage rates? F. H. Kirkpatrick and N. E. Oberman.

Planning (PEP). no. 220:3-17. Ap. 14, '44. Wages and the cost of living index.

Political Affairs. 24:311-17. Ap. '45. Labor's victory wage policies. Roy Hudson.

Political Science Quarterly. 57:564-97. D. '42. Wage determinations: the evidence before the Wage and Hour Division. E. B. Mittelman.

Progressive. 9:5. Ja. 1, '45. Challenge to Mr. Roosevelt. Philip Murray.

Public Personnel Review. 4:73-80. Ap. '42. Some aspects of pay stabilization. Ismar Baruch.

Quarterly Journal of Economics. 57:522-42. Ag. '43. Theory of union wage rigidity. J. Shister.

Quarterly Journal of Economics. 57:543-64. Ag. '43. British prices and wage rates: 1939-1941. Buford Brandis.

Quarterly Journal of Economics. 58:196-228. F. '44. Wages and profits in the paper industry, 1929-1939. F. R. Maclaurin.

Rotarian. 62:17+. My. '43. Toward a mixed economy. Stuart Chase.

Rotarian. 62:72. Ja. '44. Little Steel, what next? Earnings of industrial workers have increased more rapidly than living costs.

Rotarian. 64:28-30. Ap. '44. They stay, if you pay; Hormel Company guarantees its employees an annual wage. K. K. Krueger.

Rotarian. 66:28-30. Mr. '45. Should the guaranteed minimum annual-wage policy be adopted? H. J. Ruttenberg; M. S. Rukeyser.

Scholastic. 42:6-8. F. 22, '43. Anti-inflation under attack; demands of farm and labor groups may cause sharp advances in cost of living.

Science and Society. 7, no.1:80-7. Winter '43. National War Labor Board: an achievement in tri-partite administration. Jesse Friedin.

Senior Scholastic. 45:9. N. 27, '44. Will our economic balloon burst? C. J. Hill.

Senior Scholastic. 45:6-7. D. 11, '44. Little Steel's last stand.

Social Research. 10:301-11. S. '43. Self-liquidating wages; how increased consumption may be financed by private enterprise. Hans Apel.

Social Research. 11:305-11. S. '44. Coming peace crisis. Alvin S. Johnson.

Social Research. 11:363-6. S. '44. Why normalcy failed. E. J. Howenstine, Jr.

Social Research. 11:491-505. N. '44. Trade union plans for postwar reconstruction in the United States. Julie Meyer.

Sociology and Social Research. 29:96-104. N. '44. Labor under review, July, 1943-June, 1944. M. J. Vincent.

*South Atlantic Quarterly. 43:111-30. Ap. '44. OPA, price control, and inflation. J. J. Spengler.

Southern Economic Journal. 9:24-32. Jl. '42. General wage ceiling. J. J. O'Leary.

Southern Economic Journal. 10:235-8. Ja. '44. Note on wages and labor costs [on the basis of data for 1919-1941]. R. A. Lester.

Southwestern Social Science Quarterly. 23:372-80. Mr. '43. Can economic planning prevent a post-war depression? T. L. Morrison.

Southwestern Social Science Quarterly. 25:134-44. S. '44. Planned war: confused peace. T. Swann Harding.

Steel. 115:43-4. S. 25, '44. Postwar period most dangerous for inflation; modification of Little Steel formula would force price advances.

Steel. 115:96-7. O. 9, '44. Avoid inflation, industry urges; War Labor Board hears final pleas of management and unions on Little Steel formula.

Steel. 115:79-81+. D. 4, '44. Will WLB ruling bring higher prices? with text of wage ruling.

Survey Graphic. 32:493-7. D. '43. Trouble on the railroads; story of the wage dispute. Beulah Amidon.

Survey Graphic. 33:422+. O. '44. Pay by the year is labor's goal. R. W. Riis.
    Same abridged. Reader's Digest. 45:11-14. N. '44.

Survey Graphic. 33:449-51+. N. '44. Should wages go up? Beulah Amidon.

Survey Midmonthly. 81:35-7. F. '45. Where all that money goes. Cornelia Dunphy.

Survey of Current Business. 24:17-20. S. '44. Components of wartime wage changes. E. C. Bratt and C. H. Danhof.

Time. 41:79. Ap. 12, '43. Formula smashed?

Time. 43:85-8+. My. 8, '44. 48 weeks a year; demand for a guaranteed annual wage.

Town Meeting (Bulletin of America's Town Meeting of the Air) 9, no.7:3-23. Je. 17, '43. Should federal economic controls be relaxed with victory? Dan Casement, Thurman Arnold, and others.

Town Meeting (Bulletin of America's Town Meeting of the Air) 9, no.27:3-23. N. 4, '43. Is the Little Steel formula a sound basic wage policy? L. M. Cherne and Donald Richberg.

Town Meeting (Bulletin of America's Town Meeting of the Air) 10, no.24:3-21. O. 12, '44. Should industry attempt to guarantee labor a minimum annual wage? H. L. Nunn and others.

*Town Meeting (Bulletin of America's Town Meeting of the Air) 10, no.28:3-24. N. 9, '44. Should we scrap the Little Steel formula? R. Frankensteen, *Boris Shishkin, George Batt and Jules Backman.
Statement by Boris Shishkin also published in American Federation of Labor Weekly News Service. 34:1. N. 14, '44.

Trusts and Estates. 77:513-14. D. '43. Wage rise route to uncontrolled inflation.

*Trusts and Estates. 79:411-15. N. '44. Wage and profit differentials; effects of wage equalization on prices and on investments. J. V. Van Sickle.

Trusts and Estates. 79:505. D. '44. Indirect wage increase policy.

Trusts and Estates. 80:60-1. Ja. '45. Inflation still the threat.

United States News. 15:45-6+. O. 29, '43. Threats to wage controls; stabilization program tested by demands of rail and mine workers.

United States News. 15:53-4. N. 12, '43. New pressure on pay ceilings; concern of union leaders over ability to keep no-strike pledge.

United States News. 15:53-6. N. 19, '43. Efforts to hold lid on wages; WLB warning that pay raise for miners can't be used as precedent.

United States News. 15:50+. N. 26, '43. Showdown on wage controls; future of Little Steel formula at stake in demands of rail workers.

United States News. 15:53-4. D. 10, '43. Behind rail wage dispute; why Congress shows desire to grant demands of the workers.

United States News. 16:57-8. Mr. 3, '44. If steel wage rise is granted; tax loss to treasury, profit cut if industry raises pay generally.

United States News. 17:19-21. S. 1, '44. Pay vs. living costs: coming cut in income; how workers' wages after overtime ends will compare with 1939.

United States News. 17:40+. S. 22, '44. Renewed drive for pay rise; offset to deflation as argument for scrapping of Little Steel formula.

United States News. 17:14-15. S. 29, '44. Pay raises ahead? outlook for workers.

United States News. 17:13-14. O. 6, '44. Wage-price climb? super New Deal in making.

United States News. 17:38. O. 6, '44. New argument for pay raises; higher wages sought by unions as a way to prevent inflation.

United States News. 17:40+. O. 13, '44. Holding lid on wage increases.

United States News. 17:47+. O. 20, '44. New hurdles for wage raises: effect of WLB's steel decision.

United States News. 17:40+. N. 10, '44. Keeping the freeze on wages; prospective retention of Little Steel formula until victory in Europe.

United States News. 17:38+. D. 8, '44. Shift in unions' wage goals; emphasis on extra pay for night work, vacations and discharges.

United States News. 18:38+. Ja. 19, '45. Shaping postwar labor policy; higher wage rates and new mediation agency among FDR's goals.

United States News. 18:22-3. F. 9, '45. Higher prices ahead: fears of runaway boom.

United States News. 18:40+. Mr. 2, '45. Growing strain on pay ceiling.

United States News. 18:34+. Mr. 9, '45. John L. Lewis's new strategy: behind demand for royalties.

United States News. 18:24. Mr. 16, '45. More pay for Congressmen? taxes, high living costs imposing economic strain on legislators.

United States News. 18:38+. Mr. 16, '45. How new wage rule works; ceilings on extra pay for vacations, night jobs and reclassification.

United States News. 18:36+. Mr. 30, '45. Hurdles for annual-pay plans.

United States News. 18:50. Ap. 6, '45. Annual pay plan: press appraisal of effect on U.S.

United States News. 18:13. Ap. 13, '45. Coming rise in wage rates; prospective easing of controls to help maintain earning levels.

University of Chicago Round Table. No. 341:1-28. O. 1, '44. Is the inflation danger passed? J. K. Galbraith and others.

Virginia Quarterly Review. 20:481-95. S. '44. Labor and the administration. George Soule.

Vital Speeches of the Day. 9:455-7. My. 15, '43. Horns of labor's dilemma. George Meany.

Vital Speeches of the Day. 9:661-4. Ag. 15, '43. Wages and the cost of living; struggle between pressure groups. P. M. Brown.

Vital Speeches of the Day. 10:401-8. Ap. 15, '44. What of free enterprise? the trend of our post-war economy. W. G. Carleton.

Vocational Trends. 8:12-13. F. '45. Wages—up or down?

Wage and Hour Reporter. 5:869-70+. N. 9, '42. Pillars of WLB wage, salary policy; War Labor Board states stabilization policy, outlines procedure to be followed in reviewing wage, salary adjustments.

Wage and Hour Reporter. 6:606-9. Je. 28, '43. Outline of WLB wage policies.

Wage and Hour Reporter. 6:1097-8. N. 15, '43. Developing drive on Little Steel formula.

Wage and Hour Reporter. 7:349-50. Ap. 10, '44. Pros and cons of wage policies.

Wage and Hour Reporter. 7:901-3. S. 18, '44. Little Steel formula: what WLB panels find.

Wage and Hour Reporter. 7:909-10. S. 18, '44. Report on success of wage curbs.

Wage and Hour Reporter. 8:193-5. F. 26, '45. Future of wage stabilization: War Labor Board reports to President on problems.

SOME ORGANIZATIONS CONTRIBUTING MATERIAL OF INTEREST

American Federation of Labor. A.F. of L. Building. Washington 1, D.C.

American Management Association. 330 W. 42d St. New York 18, N.Y.

Brookings Institution. 722 Jackson Pl. N.W. Washington 6, D.C.

Brotherhood of Railroad Trainmen. 1370 Ontario St. Cleveland 13, Ohio.

Bureau of National Affairs, Inc. 2201 M. St. N.W. Washington 7, D.C.

Chamber of Commerce of the United States of America. Chamber of Commerce of the U.S. Building. Washington 6, D.C.

Committee for Economic Development. 285 Madison Ave. New York 17, N.Y.

Congress of Industrial Organizations. 718 Jackson Pl. N.W. Washington 6, D.C.

National Association of Manufacturers. 14 W. 49th St. New York 20, N.Y.

National Industrial Conference Board, Inc. 247 Park Ave. New York 17, N.Y.

United States. Bureau of Labor Statistics. Washington 25, D.C.

United States. National War Labor Board. Washington, D.C.

6184

SPEECH AND DEBATING

Anthology of Public Speeches. Mabel Platz, comp. 895p. 1940. $3.75.

Selections from speeches representing all cultures from Pericles and Cicero to Chiang Kai-shek and Neville Chamberlain.

Competitive Debate: Rules and Strategy. By George McCoy Musgrave. 128p. 1945. $1.25.

Debate Coaching. By Carroll P. Lahman. (Handbook Series. Ser IV, Vol. 1) 2d rev. ed. 428p. 1936. $2.40.

A manual for teachers and coaches. Especially helpful to the inexperienced coach.

Discussion Methods: Explained and Illustrated. By J. V. Garland and C. F. Phillips (Reference Shelf. Vol. XII, No. 2) 2d ed. rev. 378p. 1940. $1.25.

High School Forensics: An Integrated Program. By Arnold E. Melzer. 153p. 1940. 90c.

How to Debate: A Textbook for Beginners. By H. B. Summers and F. L. Whan. 336p. 1940. $1.25.

Modern Group Discussion: Public and Private. By Lyman and Ellen Judson. (Reference Shelf. Vol. XI, No. 6) 1937. 90c.

Oral Interpretation of Literature in American Colleges and Universities. By Mary Margaret Robb. 242p. 1941. $2.75.

Representative American Speeches. By A. Craig Baird, comp. Published annually in The Reference Shelf. Seven volumes now available from 1937-1938 to 1943-1944 inclusive. Price $1.25 a volume, except that for 1939-1940 which is $1.50.

Each volume contains representative speeches by eminent men and women on public occasions during the year. Each speech is prefaced by a short sketch of the speaker and the occasion.

Selected Readings in Rhetoric and Public Speaking. By Lester Thonssen. comp. 324p. 1942. $3.